Flannery O'Connor,
Walker Percy,
and the
Aesthetic of Revelation

Flannery O'Connor,
Walker Percy,
and the
Aesthetic of Revelation

John D. Sykes, Jr.

University of Missouri Press
Columbia and London

Library of Congress Cataloging-in-Publication Data

Sykes, John, 1952–
Flannery O'Connor, Walker Percy, and the aesthetics of revelation /
John D. Sykes, Jr.
p.   cm.
Summary: "Examining the writings of Flannery O'Connor and Walker Percy
against the background of the Southern Renaissance from which they emerged,
Sykes explores how the writers shared a distinctly Christian notion of art that
led them to see fiction as revelatory but adopted different theological
emphases and rhetorical strategies"—Provided by publisher.
Includes bibliographical references and index.
ISBN 978-0-8262-1757-8 (alk. paper)
1. O'Connor, Flannery—Criticism and interpretation.   2. Percy, Walker,
1916–1990—Criticism and interpretation.   3. Revelation in literature.
4. American literature—Southern States—History and criticism.
5. Christianity and literature—United States—History—20th century.   I. Title.
PS3565.C57Z88 2007
813′.54—dc22

2007016711

Designer: Stephanie Foley
Typesetter: The Composing Room of Michigan, Inc.
Printer and binder: Thomson-Shore, Inc.
Typeface: Bembo

For Ralph Wood
mentor, friend, fellow pilgrim

Contents

ɕㄶ

Acknowledgments   ix

Abbreviations   xiii

Introduction   1

1. O'Connor and New Criticism   9

2. Romantic Symbol and the Catholic Revival   26

3. O'Connor and the Body:
   Incarnation, Redemptive Suffering, and Evil   39

4. O'Connor on Divine Self-Disclosure:
   Eucharist as Revelation   70

5. Helen Keller and the Message in the Bottle:
   Percy on Language   86

6. Percy's Novelistic Quest for Faith   111

7. Surviving Apocalypse through Hope and Love   136

8. Southern Strangers and the Sacramental Community 153

Bibliography   173

Index   181

Acknowledgments

ℒℴℂ

W hen does a book begin? I trace the genesis of this one to a Jan Term course on Flannery O'Connor and Walker Percy that I took at Wake Forest University in 1973. One of the two instructors was Tom Gossett, whose name is known to O'Connor enthusiasts from the letters Flannery wrote to him and his scholar-wife, Louise, after the three had struck up a friendship while the Gossetts lived and taught in Georgia. Through the good offices of Professor Gossett, our class was treated to a reception in the historic Cline-O'Connor house in Milledgeville hosted by Mrs. Regina O'Connor, Flannery's vigorous and gracious mother. Equally memorable was an excursion to Andalusia, the family farm where Flannery wrote most of her stories and where descendants of her peafowl still ruled the roost. Accompanying us on the visit was Sarah Gordon, a young faculty member at Georgia College and State University, who was assuming growing responsibility for O'Connor's literary legacy. But most significant for the future of this book was the presence of the junior member of the Wake Forest teaching team.

Ralph Wood, a Texan only a couple of years away from graduate school at the University of Chicago, had given me my first dose of O'Connor in a previous course and was now introducing me to Walker Percy, whose work Ralph was just getting to know himself. No doubt Ralph grew tired of my frequent taps on his office door in Wingate Hall, but he never let on. He unfailingly welcomed me, shaggy and callow though I was. Those visits marked the beginning of conversation about these two authors that continues to this day. The novelist Pat Conroy calls the cartoonist Doug Marlette his conversational caffeine. For thirty-five years, I have relied upon Ralph Cecil Wood to rouse me from my dogmatic slumbers. In gratitude, I dedicate this book to him.

Even a modest volume such as this one comes into the world owing countless debts that the author cannot hope to repay. However, good faith requires me to mention a few more of my creditors. Long before I heard the names of Flannery O'Connor or Walker Percy I was awakened to the joys of intellectual life through friendship with two other Baptist preachers' kids: John Steely and Raymond Owens. Although they are no longer as handsome as they appear in the seventh-grade yearbook, they are still well armed for any and all battles of wit. At Wake Forest, Pat Johansen and the late Warren Carr and Charles Lewis and Marcus Hester nurtured me in literary and theological and philosophical matters related to the issues of this book. Former fellow students Pam Graham Gurney, Jeff Kinlaw, and Jim McCoy have been constant in their supply of insights, quips, and quotes. From graduate school days at the University of Chicago and the University of Virginia I am particularly obliged to the late Nathan A. Scott Jr. and to Julian Hartt, Dan Via, and Doug Day. Clark Brittain and Butch Kersey amongst my fellow religion and literature aspirants fueled my enthusiasm for these writers and did more than their share to keep me more or less sane. My colleagues at Wingate University have been kind and supportive, reminding me frequently of the nuanced Art of Being Southern (and Christian), and the administration granted the semester's sabbatical leave that allowed me to complete the first draft of this manuscript. My own students have inevitably made their marks on me—most memorably Kevin Winchester, Craig Renfroe, and Jennifer Haney from summer collaborative research projects originally sponsored by Wingate University through the Jesse Ball DuPont Fund.

No doubt my most influential teachers have been the members of my family, by means of whom I have learned what little I know of love, grace, and fidelity. Because of this book, my wife, Becky, and our sons, Daniel and Owen, have always known where to find me when they couldn't see me (in my office in Burris Hall), and I hope they have known that whatever I have been thinking about, they have never been further away than the periphery of my mind. Even though I didn't take it, I especially appreciate Owen's original advice to write a short book since nobody was making me write a long one.

Finally, I want to thank those who have helped to birth this book. Gary Kass at the University of Missouri Press showed a keen appreciation for what I wanted to do and nudged me toward a better book than I started with. It has been very much to my benefit to have as copyeditor Gloria Thomas Beckfield, who knows the difference between a May and a Greenleaf. And through the many trials and tribulations of writing and rewriting, I have always been able to count on the practical sympathy of Pam Merrill and Mary Coon, righteous secretaries of the sort without whom any academic enterprise would crumble into chaos.

January 2, 2007
Wingate University

Abbreviations

ഗ

Flannery O'Connor

CW   *Flannery O'Connor: Collected Works.* Ed. Sally Fitzgerald. New York: Library of America, 1988.

HB   *The Habit of Being.* Ed. Sally Fitzgerald. New York: Farrar, Straus and Giroux, 1979.

MM   *Mystery and Manners.* Ed. Sally Fitzgerald and Robert Fitzgerald. New York: Farrar, Straus and Giroux, 1969.

Walker Percy

CWP   *Conversations with Walker Percy.* Ed. Lewis A. Lawson and Victor A. Kramer. Jackson: University Press of Mississippi, 1985.

L   *Lancelot.* New York: Farrar, Straus and Giroux, 1977.

LC   *Lost in the Cosmos: The Last Self-Help Book.* New York: Farrar, Straus and Giroux, 1983.

LG   *The Last Gentleman.* New York: Farrar, Straus and Giroux, 1966.

LR   *Love in the Ruins: The Adventures of a Bad Catholic at a Time Near the End of the World.* New York: Farrar, Straus and Giroux, 1971.

MB   *The Message in the Bottle.* New York: Farrar, Straus and Giroux, 1975.

MG   *The Moviegoer.* New York: Knopf, 1961.

SC   *The Second Coming.* New York: Farrar, Straus and Giroux, 1980.

SSL   *Signposts in a Strange Land.* Ed. Patrick Samway. New York: Farrar, Straus and Giroux, 1991.

Flannery O'Connor,
Walker Percy,
and the
Aesthetic of Revelation

Introduction

ℒℴ℺

Twenty-five years ago, Lewis Simpson suggested in *The Brazen Face of History* that the work of Flannery O'Connor and Walker Percy represented a new direction for literature from the American South. According to Simpson, with the advent of these two Roman Catholic writers, the "aesthetic of memory" that had characterized fiction of the modern South had been challenged by an alternative "aesthetic of revelation." The present book represents an attempt to specify the nature of that new aesthetic, which has implications not only for the fiction of a particular region, but also for the entire modernist project. From the perspective of literary history, O'Connor and Percy take up a new subject matter and act on a different understanding of the artist's role.

As Richard H. King in *A Southern Renaissance* joined Simpson in pointing out, the principal subject of the previous generation of great southern writers had been historical consciousness. Although the turn to memory as a way to appropriate the past for human subjectivity and so overcome the alienation of mechanical temporality was far from unique to the South, the application of modernist techniques to the history of this particular, defeated, would-be nation was new. The genius of such writers as Faulkner, Welty, Warren, and Tate was to seize upon literary art as a way to overcome the loss of traditional, communal structures of meaning. Thus, in the pleasure of recovering for human subjectivity a history with no inherent meaning, there is a kind of victory, although a temporary one—a common savoring of one memory's madeleine by authors and readers in a moment of recognition. However, while the aesthetic of memory can serve the vital moral purpose of breaking through sentimental myth and the false values it engenders (including racist ones), its resources for supplying a positive alternative to the tragically flawed cultural edifice of the past are severely limited. Or so it seemed to O'Connor and Percy, for whom history remained irredeemable so long as it lacked a transcendent dimension.

For the previous generation of white southern writers, the question had been, how do we escape the past? For the next generation, the question became, what do we do with our freedom? And for O'Connor and Percy, the answer had to be a religious one. This is so for at least two reasons. First, with the waning of the myth of the Lost Cause, now debunked, the South was losing its spiritual moorings and was in desperate need of some new means of social cohesion. And second, the flatness and thinness of modern life—a condition shared with the rest of the country and indeed the entire Western world—was simply intolerable. Percy in particular would highlight the spiritual poverty of a South that had acknowledged the untenability of slavery and forsaken its obsession with the idealized antebellum order only to turn its attention to building suburbs, playing golf, and watching TV. In Richard King's terms, the past had already been "recollected" as the result of such work as Faulkner's; Percy's problem was what to do with the present, which had now been rendered thin and weightless, in part because the past seemed to be of no consequence. Faulkner's Quentin Compson and Gail Hightower fail to escape a past that is oppressively present, foreclosing the future, while O'Connor's General Flintrock Sash, though a Confederate veteran, is a mere mascot—a kind of tourist token of a South that has become a Hollywood fantasy, and Percy's "last gentleman" wanders distractedly through a prosperous South where the past has ceased to signify.

The characters of O'Connor and Percy are waiting (whether they know it or not) for God to break into a world that is otherwise petty and feckless. Even a Christ who "thown everything off balance," as the Misfit says, is a relief after the vapid squabbling of a middle-class family driving to Florida for its annual vacation. Will Barrett would rather be holed up in a cave under a mountain trying to force God to show himself than live through another day of figuring out how to spend his rich Yankee wife's money. O'Connor and Percy are looking for theophany—a breaking in of the divine—to counteract the loss of density once supplied by the monumentalized past of the war that was lost. Yet to frame their problem in this way is tendentious, especially for O'Connor. It is not as though for these writers Christianity is the sudden fulfillment of a cultural wish. Rather, for both, the Gospel is the truth that was already there, obscured by the human penchant for indifference and self-deception. Fiction, for them, is one means whereby this veil can be lifted. And this pursuit of revelation as a subject naturally changes the role of the writer.

As Faulkner eloquently notes in his posthumously published introduction to *The Sound and the Fury,* the South had no use for the artist—certainly not for the kind of artist Faulkner aspired to be. ("Art is no part of southern life," he begins.) Within the conception of the artist held by Faulkner and much of modernism, there is a strong element of aestheticism—a devotion to art as its own separate and sacred sphere. Faulkner expresses this view in his description of his attitude toward *The Sound and the Fury* as being like that of the Roman who kept a Tyrrhenian vase by his bedside, wearing it away with kisses. And so, while, as I argue elsewhere, this devotion to art does not imply an indifference to society, it does eschew the directly didactic or rhetorical. Faulkner identifies his own motives in *The Sound and the Fury* as being to "indict and escape" the South. By contrast, O'Connor says in "The Fiction Writer and His Country" that she wants to "draw large and startling figures" (*CW* 806). That is, she wishes to render transparent scenes of divine mystery ordinarily invisible to world-weary modern eyes. Although O'Connor's revelations carry their own indictments of human presumption, the overriding concern is positive: to uncover God's presence in the world. Thus her art is in no wise an escape, but rather an assertion of ultimate reality. Percy, for his part, engaged in a thirty-year tug-of-war with his best friend, novelist and historian Shelby Foote, over whether art could legitimately fulfill a direct moral function. And even before he published his first novel, Percy wrote Caroline Gordon that while he might "also kneel before the altar of Lawrence and Joyce and Flaubert, it is not because I wish to do what they did, even if I could." His aim, rather, was to follow the lead of Pascal and Kierkegaard and "tell people *what they must do and what they must believe if they want to live.*"[1]

Both in the sense of content (telling people what they must believe) and in the sense of experience (providing the occasion for divine self-disclosure), O'Connor and Percy sought to practice an aesthetic of revelation. However, the two writers' relationships with Caroline Gordon point to noteworthy differences between them. Gordon was mentor to each. In fact, her success with O'Connor was one reason Percy turned to her for help with his first novel. But, as later chapters will more fully show,

1. Quoted in Jay Tolson, *Pilgrim in the Ruins,* 300.

O'Connor accepted the modernist strictures employed by Gordon to a degree not true of Percy. While O'Connor grew increasingly independent of Gordon after *Wise Blood,* she retained the disposition toward the visual and toward a Romantic understanding of symbol that Gordon embraced. Percy by contrast would turn to the more dialogic and verbal modes favored by his European models and sponsored theoretically by Kierkegaard and by Percy's own reflections upon language.

This contrast is made more intriguing by the fact that Gordon and her husband, Allen Tate, shared with O'Connor and Percy a great admiration for Jacques Maritain. Maritain was the Catholic Revival's chief spokesman for the Scholastic view of art, which at some level all four southerners accepted. Maritain's essay *Art and Scholasticism* emphasizes that the virtue of the artist lies in the skill peculiar to his kind of making, rather than in some extrinsic moral end. In arguing for the cognitive dimension of art, Maritain also endorses St. Thomas Aquinas's epistemological realism, including his claim that human language provides the means for trustworthy knowledge of God, if only by analogy. Maritain's argument that art has its own intrinsic end comported well with New Critical assertions about the "verbal icon." Thus O'Connor received from Maritain a Roman Catholic justification for much of what she had absorbed at the Iowa Writers' Workshop. Percy's hunch that language could provide a bridge between the empiricism of science and the metaphysical assertions of religion was reinforced by the recovery of Aquinas led by Maritain and other philosophers in the Catholic Revival.

These differences in interests led to distinct rhetorical strategies. O'Connor's stories typically build to a climactic image—usually that of a suffering human body—to which the rest of the story points as a kind of prophetic finger. The effect of this symbol, or tableau, is to inspire contemplation, not conversation. That is, O'Connor hopes to bring about an encounter with divine mystery that overwhelms the reader and defies comprehension. And while the content of this image is religious, the way it functions in the story is not so different from Joyce's epiphanies or other modernist examples of symbolic synthesis. The relationships her narrators establish with the reader are more likely to be aloof than intimate. Her narrators' declarations, regardless of whether we take them to be the author's own, tend to be finalizing and, in Mikhail Bakhtin's terminology, monologic.

Percy, on the other hand, strives for dialogue with the reader. Sometimes he is more successful at this endeavor than others, but the dialogic is an operating principle for him as it is not for O'Connor. This dialogue may be partly internal to a character-narrator, as it is for Binx Bolling in Percy's first published novel, *The Moviegoer,* but when Percy is at his best, it also includes an ongoing conversation with at least one significant partner. Additionally, Percy's narrators typically establish a conspiratorial bond with the reader, who is drawn into a search or quest undertaken by the central character. Thus the revelation toward which Percy's novels typically point is not captured in an image, but is posed as a question. His books include and sometimes conclude with a broken conversation—a demand or request that is not supplied by the text. Thus the novel is a kind of fragment in David Tracy's sense—a literary agent provocateur that teases a response from the reader. In this regard, Percy has much in common with Dostoevsky, the novelist he most admired, and Kierkegaard, whose method of indirect communication he emulated. The revelation Percy strives to bring about is one that happens off the page, so to speak, in an existential encounter that happens after the reader closes the book. Art at its best is a work of genius that prepares the reader to hear what an apostle has to say, as Kierkegaard might have put it.

Corresponding to these differences in rhetorical strategy are differing theological emphases from O'Connor to Percy, especially where the sacraments are concerned. For O'Connor, the reenacted sacrifice of Christ is the key to every revelatory image, just as it is the center of Roman Catholic worship life. Most of her stories can be seen as in some fashion reproducing the priest's elevation of the Host—an offering in altered form of Christ's crucified body. One thinks immediately of the blood-red sun in "A Temple of the Holy Ghost," of the pierced body of Mrs. May in "Greenleaf," of the crushed form of the innocent Mr. Guizac in "The Displaced Person," and of the decrepit lawn statue in "The Artificial Nigger." The suffering human body itself becomes her densest symbol, as O'Connor pushes a convention of literary modernism to its limit, making of it a sacramental analogue. One searches nearly in vain for such images in Percy's fiction. But also missing in Percy is that Protestant counterpart to the Eucharist, the preached Word. In fact, the sermons and prophecies are also to be found in O'Connor. Percy's orientation, like O'Connor's, is sacramental, but more allusively so. The great issue for Percy is not human obtuseness to grace, but rather doubt. Thus, instead of an unexpected and often violent in-breaking of grace that commands attention, the grace-filled events in Percy's fiction are nearly invisible and therefore easily missed. This contrast is especially stark where the sacraments themselves are concerned.

After the boy Bevel in O'Connor's "The River" has been baptized by a young evangelist, he returns to the river, seeking the Kingdom of Christ he has been promised, and while searching for it in the waters, drowns. When Jamie Vaught is baptized by a priest in a hospital room in *The Last Gentleman,* we are not even sure he is a believer, his muttered questions and ambiguous gestures understood only by his muddled companion, Will Barrett. In the churchly scene at the conclusion of *The Moviegoer,* Binx watches a black man emerge from an Ash Wednesday service and wonders if the ashes on his forehead signal an attempt at upward mobility or if instead they represent some "dim dazzling trick of grace." Percy presses such questions; O'Connor confronts us with answers we cannot ignore even if we do not understand them. And so, while both writers are deeply Catholic in their conviction that God continues to make himself sacramentally present in the world Christ died to redeem, their presentations and appropriations of divine self-disclosure differ dramatically.

Whatever their differences in strategy and emphasis, however, O'Connor and Percy are united in their conception of the artist as God's sharp-eyed witness. They stand over against what might be called the Promethean myth of the artist promulgated by many of the modern masters from whom they learned. In this view, which gained credence in the nineteenth century with the waning of religious faith, the artist becomes a stand-in for God, suffering to bring forth beauty and meaning in an indifferent universe. Indeed, *God* has become the name for an oppressive authoritarianism nurtured by institutional religion. Thus, instead of creating by analogy to God, the artist must act as successor to God, as Maurice Beebe argued in the introduction to *Ivory Towers and Sacred Founts,* a book that appeared in the year of O'Connor's death.

The Promethean alternative is posed consistently by Percy's friend Shelby Foote, who urged it upon Percy. In a particularly pointed letter written in 1954, Foote tells Percy that Flaubert had only "a very rudimentary philosophy . . . , but he had those two saving things, a good eye and a marvelous style. If a man will give all, they are enough, and what he builds will never fall or fade. The truths they set forth are universal, impervious to time." The catch, Foote says, is that the writer must surrender his entire life to his art. The great artists—Shakespeare, Mozart, perhaps Proust—"gave up love, friendship, even God, because they knew these things were less than art." Going through a painful period in his own life, Foote confides that he now knows how much suffering can teach the artist. "I have never learned the slightest truth from happiness," he observes.[2]

Foote's advice, offered at a time when he was an established novelist and Percy had yet to publish his first book, clearly sets out the artist's life as a high calling. Foote even cites the words of Jesus ("Except a grain of wheat fall into the ground and die . . . ") to support his case. Yet this religion is a religion of art, where "even God" must be abandoned; truth comes through "a good eye," which we might explain as a kind of ruthless honesty, and "a marvelous style." Although Percy and Foote were lifelong friends, Percy, like O'Connor, deeply mistrusted this creed. For the two Roman Catholics, neither a good eye nor a marvelous style could by themselves lead the writer to "universal truth." In their view, the writer needed a set of lenses and a place to stand. O'Connor and Percy found their point of certainty in the Catholic Church. Thus for them God was not the nay-saying Nobodaddy against whom the artist had to revolt in order to create, but rather the loving ground of freedom whose gracious gift makes creativity possible. Although Percy never chided his friend, he insisted that in his own case the only thing that made sense of the world was the Christian narrative. To throw over his faith in pursuit of artistic truth would have been self-contradictory.

O'Connor's summation in her lecture "Catholic Novelists and Their Readers" might serve for Percy as well:

> There is no reason why fixed dogma should fix anything that the writer sees in the world. On the contrary, dogma is an instrument for penetrating reality. Christian dogma is about the only thing left in the world that surely guards and respects mystery. The fiction writer is an observer, first, last, and always, but he cannot be an adequate observer unless he is free from uncertainty about what he sees. . . . The Catholic fiction writer is entirely free to observe. He feels no call to take on the duties of God or to create a new universe. He feels perfectly free to look at the one we already have and to show exactly what he sees. . . . For him, to "tidy up reality" is cer-

2. Foote to Percy, Memphis, February 19, 1954, in *The Correspondence of Shelby Foote and Walker Percy,* ed. Jay Tolson, 96, 97.

tainly to succumb to the sin of pride. Open and free observation is founded on our ultimate faith that the universe is meaningful, as the Church teaches. (*MM* 178)

And so, for O'Connor and Percy, the model for the artist is more Scholastic than Promethean, in that while for them art has its own integrity and object, it is still secondary and derivative as a mode of truth. The artist need not fear to make what she envisions or to report what she sees, for all truth belongs to God. Herein lies the artist's freedom. At the same time, "dogma is an instrument for penetrating reality": that is, the artist who is also a Christian has the advantage of a trained eye. The drama of salvation, otherwise invisible, reveals itself to one who has already been shown its contours. For these reasons, the artist need not defy God in order to create. In fact, insofar as creation comes at the cost of suffering, as it certainly did for O'Connor, the Christian artist actually joins God in the work of redemption, which required the agony of the Cross. Christ replaces Prometheus as the artist's model, and one might even more severely add that analogy displaces idolatry.

Thus for these Catholic writers, rather than stealing the secret of the gods for the good of humanity, the artist's role is more properly that of joining God in saving humanity—not through sacrament or proclamation, but through a special kind of making with its own restorative goodness. In the aesthetic of revelation practiced by O'Connor and Percy, the artist's gift is not snatched from heaven in an act of satanic rebellion, but gratefully received as birthright. Their work is rooted in the conviction that we make as we are made, *ad majorem Dei gloriam,* "to the greater glory of God."

1

O'Connor and New Criticism

ͽϿ

What Lewis Simpson called an "aesthetic of revelation" was a new development for literature from the American South, and Flannery O'Connor and Walker Percy were its major practitioners. In significant ways, these two writers set themselves apart from what is often called the Southern Renaissance and its "aesthetic of memory." Yet the parting was cordial. Not only did each writer voice admiration for immediate predecessors, but to some degree, both were conscious of picking up at the point where the previous generation had left off. While they might sometimes bridle at the appellation, inevitably they thought of their own work in relation to "southern literature."

The term *southern literature* itself has a history that Michael Kreyling has been instrumental in unpacking. As he has brilliantly demonstrated in *Inventing Southern Literature,* the Nashville intellectuals who were largely responsible for promoting what came to be called the Southern Renaissance had a particular and politically motivated version of the South in mind. Kreyling asserts that "the Agrarian project was and must be seen as a willed campaign on the part of one elite to establish and control 'the South' in a period of intense cultural maneuvering."[1] Although on the whole not directly racist or sexist, the evolution of "southern literature" clearly privileged the work of white males, and obscured issues of race and gender in the name of a purely aesthetic formalism. Neither O'Connor nor Percy could be counted as Agrarians, and indeed they distanced themselves from the movement. Yet they could hardly fail to feel the Nashville influence, and the literary milieu in which they found them-

1. Michael Kreyling, *Inventing Southern Literature,* xii.

selves was already shaped by its agenda. O'Connor would struggle against masculinist assumptions, Percy would reject formalism, and both would adopt a more highly principled view of race, yet each identified with the South and with "southern literature," however critically.

This issue was perhaps more acute in the case of O'Connor both because she was a woman and because she began her writing career a decade earlier than did Percy. For example, in *Revising Flannery O'Connor* Katherine Hemple Prown argues the feminist case that O'Connor repressed her female sensibilities in favor of a masculinist ideology to gain acceptance within the New Critical circles she first encountered at the Iowa Writers' Workshop. While one might challenge the accommodationist charge implicit in Prown's thesis, O'Connor certainly placed herself under the tutelage of central figures among the dominant party in southern letters and sought their blessing. Most important to her, however, was not a man of letters, but an established female coreligionist—Caroline Gordon.

Any attempt to find aesthetic ground shared by Flannery O'Connor and Walker Percy might well begin with Caroline Gordon. "Mrs. Tate," as O'Connor often refers to her in her letters, served as writing coach and literary taskmaster to both writers in the early stages of their careers. Along with her husband, Allen Tate, Gordon represented three allegiances that help us place O'Connor and Percy in context: she was closely committed to a theory of literature we may broadly call New Critical, she was a self-conscious Roman Catholic, and she was a southerner. Although Percy's philosophical interest in language theory and his inclination toward the novel of ideas would lead him away from New Critical ideals, O'Connor seems to have resonated deeply with the older writer's views on the nature of fiction. And this New Critical bent was to have consequences for her fiction, including theological consequences.

Although Caroline Gordon did not elaborate her theoretical position in print, Allen Tate certainly did, and the degree to which the two shared critical assumptions is indicated by their collaboration on *The House of Fiction,* a textbook collection of short stories with commentary published in 1950, the year before O'Connor sent Gordon a draft of *Wise Blood,* her first novel. O'Connor's relationship to Gordon and Tate, recent converts to Catholicism who already held a high place in the literary establishment, is indicative of her sympathies with the New Criticism that Tate, in particular, helped form. Indeed, O'Connor's exposure to what had already become the dominant critical orientation preceded her acquaintance with Caroline Gordon.

New Criticism and the Aesthetic of Memory

At the Iowa Writers' Workshop, where the twenty-year-old O'Connor arrived for what would be a three-year stint in the fall of 1945, New Criticism was very much in the air. During her stay, John Crowe Ransom, Robert Penn Warren, and Allen Tate all visited the workshop. Andrew Lytle supervised revisions to her thesis. Jean Wylder, one of two other women writers enrolled as students at the time, complained in retrospect that some of the men in the class were "tuned in to New Criticism theories," and that they used this ammunition to shoot down the stories of young writers.[2] For one of O'Connor's first classes, instructor Paul Engle chose as the text Brooks and Warren's *Understanding Fiction* (1943), a book that was to shape a generation of college classes and that O'Connor herself recommended to others. Although as a whole the Iowa Writers' Workshop was hardly a New Critical boot camp, and O'Connor focused on reading and writing fiction rather than philosophizing about it, clearly the atmosphere was permeated with the attitudes and the personalities of the movement.

In terms of Simpson's "aesthetic of memory," New Criticism might be said to represent at the theoretical level the same struggle with modernism to be found in the literature of the Southern Renaissance. Simpson is not alone in giving Allen Tate credit for initiating the "controlling assumption among students of twentieth century Southern literature that, fundamentally, it is a reaction to modernism."[3] In the work of these writers, historical consciousness became important as traditional, communal ways of thinking and feeling slipped away. Memory, as reconstituted through techniques perfected by modernist writers, became the bulwark against radical historicism, and the novel or poem itself could generate a community of readers to stand in for the lost historical community. Literature thus provided a modernist solution to the problem of modernity. New Criticism displayed a similar tension, asserting both that literature creates its own world and that it serves a religious function, placing us in touch with ultimate reality. The attempt to claim an independent sphere for art was in part a reaction to the apparent success of science in gaining exclusive access to truth; the formalist move "saved" literature as a legitimate

2. Sarah Fodor, "Proust, 'Home of the Brave,' and *Understanding Fiction*: O'Connor's Development as a Writer," 69–70.

3. Lewis P. Simpson, *The Brazen Face of History: Studies in the Literary Consciousness in America,* 67.

intellectual endeavor, making it the subject of its own "science." At the same time, it created room for what might be called linguistic mystery, a sacred dimension. In this way, New Criticism also offered a modernist solution to a problem of modernity, and it certainly embraced the figures and techniques of literary modernism, as the close association with T. S. Eliot indicates. The southern figures who were instrumental in formulating it were theoretically inclined literati who embraced modernist techniques.

New Criticism itself is better understood as a collection of attitudes and orientations than as a critical system, and even those most closely associated with the name (supplied by Ransom) often disagreed. Yet the loose unity was powerful. New Critics were champions of the autonomy of art, insisting on the distinctions between literary language and other uses of language. New Critics also maintained that literature had to be understood in its own terms, or at least terms suited to its unique discourse. Thus the most important activity in criticism was close textual analysis. Characteristically, interpretation was understood as a matter of sorting through the ambiguities of literary language, which was inherently polysemous or multivalent, and the literary work itself was seen as a kind of balance of reconciled opposites that reflected the complexity of human existence. *Image, symbol,* and *meaning* are terms of value in the New Critical lexicon. Equally revealing are the "heresies" or "fallacies" named in important articles by New Critics: the intentional fallacy, the affective fallacy, and the heresy of paraphrase refer, respectively, to the error of finding the meaning of a text in the author's intention, the mistake of rooting meaning in the reader's feelings, and the violation done to literature by reducing it to ordinary discourse.

That New Critics could speak of "heresies" points to their main relevance for O'Connor. In both its formulations and its goals, New Criticism leaned toward the religious. The phrase *heresy of paraphrase* itself supplies a good example. Employed by Cleanth Brooks in *The Well Wrought Urn* (1947), the phrase is not intended to carry the implications of an Inquisition anathema, yet the rhetorical punch of the phrase comes from its religious origin. In other words, *heresy* is a figure of speech that draws upon the capital of a religious practice. Written by a colleague of Brooks's, W. K. Wimsatt Jr., *The Verbal Icon* (1954) presents a similar case. As an introductory note on the title declares, *icon* refers to "a visual image and especially one which is a religious symbol. The verbal image which most fully realizes its verbal capacities is that which is not merely a bright picture . . . but also an interpretation of reality in its metaphoric and symbolic dimensions."[4]

But perhaps the best example of this tendency put to general use is to be found in John Crowe Ransom's *God without Thunder* (1930). Ransom here decries what one might call the de-naturing of God. To merge God into Reason or to do away with the supernatural entirely (as modern society has done) impoverishes poetry and threatens our humanity. John Stewart summarizes Ransom's position in this way: "We need now a God *with* thunder to represent our helplessness and induce a religious humility and a realistic relation with nature. Such a God would be the author of evil as well as good. 'This,' Ransom wrote, 'is my orthodox version of the God of Israel at the point where it is most challenging and critical.' Without Him man became a vain and fatuous monster." Yet Ransom can only speak of religion as myth—a necessary myth, but one that remains, for him, "fable."[5]

Despite the clear assertion of Brooks that "literature is not a surrogate for religion," it is equally clear that for most of the New Critics, great literature did at the very least have a religious nature and value. Wimsatt says of the verbal icon that it is "an interpretation of reality in its metaphoric and symbolic dimensions." But what can this mean except that poetry reaches out to aspects of reality beyond the ken of science and rationalism? By implication, the verbal icon has not only a religious name but a religious function, bearing out Terry Eagleton's observation in *Literary Theory: An Introduction* that the New Critics were inclined to "religious dogma."[6] In the case of Tate, this inclination eventually took the explicit form of conversion to the Roman Catholic Church.

Tate, unlike his older friend and former teacher Ransom, was not permanently content with the "mythic" religion of *God without Thunder.* One might say that he was driven to the church by the failure of the spiritual-political project of Agrarianism, the project launched by him and Ransom in the symposium that produced *I'll Take My Stand.* As Lewis Simpson remarks, Ransom, Tate, and Donald Davidson "yearned to complete the spiritualization of the secular."[7] When Agrarianism inevitably fell short of this goal, its proponents turned in other directions. Although the

---

4. W. K. Wimsatt Jr., *The Verbal Icon,* x.

5. John L. Stewart, *The Burden of Time: The Fugitives and Agrarians,* 273, 267.

6. Wimsatt, *Verbal Icon,* 276 (Brooks and Wimsatt quotations); Terry Eagleton, *Literary Theory: An Introduction,* 49.

7. Quoted in Gale H. Carrithers Jr., "Colonel Tate in Attack and Defense," 53.

question of the relation between community and religion in the South, so important to Ransom and Tate in 1930, holds great significance for O'Connor and Percy, our immediate concern is the nature of literature, and on this subject Tate's views did not change so much as intensify. That is, rather than finding in his conversion of the late 1940s a satisfying replacement for the hopes he had placed in letters, he found confirmation of them. Jacques Maritain was to play the pivotal role in this transition. But before turning to the explicitly Catholic side of O'Connor's aesthetic (a side she shares with Percy), we would do well to look more closely at the formalist views of New Criticism in relation to O'Connor's work.

Although the two are of course intertwined, for analytical purposes we might distinguish New Critics' arguments on the nature of literature from the literary models they chose. As Frank Lentricchia gives Frank Kermode credit for first pointing out in *Romantic Image,* New Criticism stands "at the end of the line of neo-Coleridgean movements in poetics, all of which in one philosophical context or another had affirmed the autonomous and autotelic nature of the single, lonely poem." The centerpiece of the poem is the symbol, which according to Coleridge "partakes of the reality which it renders intelligible." Through its use of symbol, literature is able to achieve two important goals: first, it establishes a "reconciliation of opposites"—a holding together of seemingly contradictory thematic elements in an "organic unity"; and second, it serves as a kind of metaphysical bridge between human thought and external reality. It is this second achievement that gives the poem its religious value. New Critics, as Coleridge's heirs, feel the "need to protect a quasi-religious, ontological sanctuary from all secularizing discourses that would situate literature in history."[8]

We can see this kind of transaction between critic and poem in Tate's essay on Donne's poem "A Valediction: Forbidding Mourning." The essay, "The Point of Dying: Donne's 'Virtuous Men,'" was written in 1952, the same year that *Wise Blood* made its public debut. Tate seizes upon the simile with which the poem begins—"As virtuous men pass mildly away"—to uncover the analogy between love and death that he believes the poem establishes. In death and in love, claims Tate, the poem holds up the Christian virtue of dying in order to live. For both dying men and lovers, the goal is to "die *out* of something *into* something else." But, as one would expect, given New Critical assumptions, it is not the argument

8. Frank Lentricchia, *After the New Criticism,* 3, 6.

within the poem that is important, but what it "does" within its own unique terms. Tate's concern is with "the full linguistic body of the poem which ultimately resists our analysis." And, he asserts, the poem "*is* [my emphasis] the action, the trope, the 'turning' from one thing to another." The symbol for this turning is the circle, or, more accurately, the point that is expanded to a circle in the similes of the twin compasses and the beaten gold. Corresponding to the circle is the pun "to die." In its double seventeenth-century meanings of loss of physical life and sexual orgasm, it reinforces the basic analogy between death and love, and thus between spiritual and physical ecstasy. In his conclusion, Tate sums up what he clearly considers to be the great success of the poem:

> Donne is not saying that death is *like* love, or that love is *like* death; there is the identity, death-love, a third something, a reality that can be found only through analogy since it has no name. This reality, whether of "dying" lovers or of "dying" men, is the ultimate experience. The reciprocal conversion of one into the other is the moral motion of the poem, its peripety, the "action" which eventually issues in the great top-level significance that Donne understood as the anagoge. This is nothing less, as it is surely nothing more, than the entire poem, an actual linguistic object that is at once all that our discourse can make of it and nothing that at any moment of discourse we are able to make of it.[9]

I have quoted Tate's conclusion at length because it demonstrates so thoroughly the religious nature of poetic language as the New Critics understood it. The "death-love" that is the "idea," or, one might hesitantly say, the "message" of the poem, is inseparable from the poem itself. In fact, one might almost say that the poem creates this reality; at the very least, the poem brings the concept of this "third something" into being for the discerning reader. The pronoun that begins the final sentence might easily be taken to have as its referent the "conversion" of the previous sentence, or even the "ultimate experience" of the sentence previous to that, rather than "anagoge." In plain words, Tate seems almost to imply that the poem acts the part of God in Genesis 1, speaking mystical union into being. This linguistic power of creation is of course limited to poetry. Our critical discourse is inadequate to the poem itself, which transcends ordi-

9. Allen Tate, "The Point of Dying: Donne's 'Virtuous Men,'" in *Essays of Four Decades,* 247, 249, 252.

nary language. Thus does this short essay by Tate play out all of the major New Critical themes concerning the nature of poetic language. The poem is unique, autonomous, self-contained. Through a kind of alchemy, it yokes together seemingly contradictory elements (love, death) by means of symbol and trope, yielding the reader access to religious meaning unavailable in any other linguistic medium.

"The Point of Dying: Donne's 'Virtuous Men'" is neatly illustrative of New Criticism's religious side, in part because it treats a Christian idea in a Christian poet whose own poetics coincided at important junctions with New Critical principles. But examples could be multiplied from other New Critics' writings on unlikely authors. Brooks, in order to make the point that irony is the principle of structure in poetry, famously turns to Wordsworth's Lucy poems, precisely to show that all true poetry reconciles opposites, even when on the surface it seems completely unironic. I employed the phrase *true poetry* intentionally; an important secondary theme of New Critics is that of separating excellent literature from the merely prosaic. The reason for this important distinction should be apparent: with such high claims for literature, only the truly elect can fulfill them. Eliot, who is often grouped with the New Critics, announces in "Tradition and the Individual Talent" that there is an "ideal order" of poetry, and that the living poet who aspires to it must, in effect, study to show himself approved. One of the secondary aims of the *Understanding Fiction* textbook used by O'Connor is to lead the student to distinguish "successful" from "mechanical" stories, using formalist categories to support the evaluation.

Indeed, the selection of models was central to this explication-heavy critical orientation, a feature that the craft-conscious O'Connor found attractive. As previous citations indicate, New Critics inclined to poetry, and even more specifically to lyric poetry, with its density and frequent reliance on symbol. As Eagleton notes, in their hands the poem became a spatial figure (an urn or an icon) rather than a temporal process.[10] Yet even if lyric poetry provided the quintessential literary model, fiction also qualified. As one might expect, "poetic" features of prose were important, especially symbol and irony. Aristotelian formal considerations also played a role. But perhaps the greatest single source of instruction on the proper aims of fiction were the prefaces to Henry James's novels, especially as these were synthesized in *The Craft of Fiction* (1921), by Percy Lubbock.

10. Eagleton, *Literary Theory: An Introduction,* 48.

An epigraph from James's preface to *Portrait of a Lady* opens Gordon and Tate's *House of Fiction;* indeed, the title is taken from the quotation, and O'Connor recommended it to a friend as a "profound study" (*HB* 192).

In addition to continuing a certain use of symbol perfected by Flaubert, James introduced a crucial distinction between showing and telling, or, in Tate's terms, between stating and rendering.[11] "Don't state, render!" was the dictum O'Connor was to hear from Caroline Gordon more than any other. Finally, from James came strong interest in point of view, which coincided with a Flaubertian commitment to "objectivity" or "impersonality" on the part of the author. More broadly, James was identified as the spokesman for the tradition of the novel that included Stendhal, Austen, Conrad, Woolf, and Hemingway, as well as Flaubert and James himself. Not surprisingly, most of these writers appear in a list O'Connor sent to her friend Betty Hester (called "A" in *The Habit of Being*) when recalling her reading under the direction of Paul Engle at Iowa.[12] O'Connor mentions Woolf, Conrad, Flaubert, and James (*HB* 98–99), the latter three favorably. For those who know O'Connor's stories, it is unsurprising to also find in her list writers outside this tradition, particularly Catholic writers, along with Hawthorne and Poe. Indeed, O'Connor's fiction was to be fed by a fruitful conflict between her New Critical and her Catholic sympathies, which we might describe in rhetorical terms as a conflict between the dramatic and the didactic. Before considering the second pole that generated this tension, however, it may be helpful to look for the effects of the first.

New Critical Apprenticeship: "Old Red" and "The Geranium"

New Critical assumptions influenced both O'Connor's technique and her conception of herself as a writer, to a degree not true of Walker Percy. An indication of the influence on the formal elements of her stories can be gained by looking at what must be regarded as an apprentice piece, "The Geranium," in relation to its primary model, Caroline Gordon's "Old Red."[13] Gordon's story is significant for several reasons. From first to last, Gordon served as O'Connor's unofficial editor during her professional writing years. The letters in *Habit of Being* consistently reveal how O'Connor trusted Gordon's and Tate's judgment, relying on Gordon for

---

11. Tate, *Essays of Four Decades,* 135.
12. Fodor, "Proust, 'Home of the Brave,' and *Understanding Fiction,*" 73.
13. Ibid., 74.

line-by-line suggestions in her revisions of *Wise Blood* in particular. Gordon's story is also noteworthy for being included in *Understanding Fiction,* a sign of the high regard in which other New Critics held it.

The first technical feature of "Old Red" that struck O'Connor was its use of symbol, as she noted years later (*HB* 200). Since symbol is central to the Jamesian tradition of fiction, O'Connor's appropriation of its use in Gordon at this early stage is noteworthy. The central symbol in "Old Red" is the fox named in the story's title. Formally what must have impressed O'Connor about Gordon's use of the fox is the same thing that impressed Brooks and Warren in *Understanding Fiction:* it encapsulates the protagonist's discovery about himself, a discovery toward which the entire story has moved. Brooks and Warren observe, "This realization does not come in terms of statement. It comes in terms of a symbol."[14] And of course, this remark is meant as praise on two fronts: the author has avoided "statement" while also investing an ordinary object with extraordinary meaning. O'Connor would attempt to do with her geranium what Gordon did with her fox.

Even O'Connor's choice of symbol for this story might have been suggested by her model; "Old Red" begins not with the fox, but with flowers—or, more specifically, with the absence of flowers. The roses that Mister Maury finds missing from the view he recalls from earlier years are the first indication of an important theme: loss of youth. O'Connor will use her geranium in much the same way. Old Dudley, standing at a window in a very different setting, will look longingly for the reappearance of a flower that seems out of place because of the contrast it provides to his alien urban environment. Despite the transposition from rural to urban setting, O'Connor's flower, like Gordon's, represents youth and vitality that are slipping away.

Gordon introduces her central symbol subtly, in a reverie that Aleck Maury has on the second day of his visit with his daughter and in-laws. Memory takes him to his boyhood and a foxhunt, when he first pursued the prey that was never caught. The young O'Connor hits us between the eyes with her symbol in the second sentence. Old Dudley, also visiting his daughter, is waiting for the daily arrival of the geranium that neighbors place on a windowsill across the alley. The flower obviously—too obviously, one might say—has great significance for him. In both stories, the symbol provides coherence by its recurrence as subject matter and, final-

---

14. Cleanth Brooks and Robert Penn Warren, *Understanding Fiction,* 250.

ly, as thematic hinge, joining theme to subject. Mister Maury's periodic
return to a boyhood memory, while psychologically plausible because the
topics of hunting and fishing crop up in family conversations, has no obvious connection to the subject of his own race with death until the end.
The geranium functions similarly, but again, less subtly. The second time
it appears in the story, it has its own brief paragraph, "The geranium was
late today. It was ten-thirty. They usually had it out by ten-fifteen" (*CW*
705). The function of the symbol, however, is the same. At the end of the
story, when Old Dudley sees the fallen flower in the alley, its roots in the
air, a connection is established between the old man's fate and that of
the geranium. Illusions are shattered; he, like the flower, is uprooted and
out of place.

What I have called O'Connor's lack of subtlety is, as critic Sarah Gordon suggests, a sign of her immaturity. She simply had not yet developed
her skills to Caroline Gordon's level, which no doubt explains why she
continued to work on the story even after it was published. On the other hand, O'Connor's message is less ambiguous than Gordon's, and message was always important to her. A difficulty that would prove to be perhaps the greatest technical problem O'Connor faced is already apparent.
She believed she had something of great importance to say to an audience who greatly needed to hear it, yet she was committed to a poetics
that prized ambiguity. The difficulty is pointed up by conflicting inter-
pretations of the fox in Gordon's story. In the interpretation that follows
the story in *Understanding Fiction,* Mister Maury is said to be like the fox
in that he, too, has outwitted his pursuers, refusing to be a slave to convention. He has lived life on his own terms. "[H]e is safe; he has won his
race." Sarah Gordon insists instead that at the end of the story, Maury is
faced with "the inevitability of death for even the smartest and wiliest."
The story's final sentence could, indeed, bear either reading: "He was sink-
ing down, panting, in black dark, on moist earth while hounds' baying
filled the bowl of the valley and reverberated from the mountainside."[15]
For Sarah Gordon, the "black dark" of the den represents death; for
Brooks and Warren, it signifies escape and safety.

Such ambiguity does not attend O'Connor's geranium. It is abundant-
ly clear that Old Dudley and the flower are dislocated, torn from the habi-

---

15. Brooks and Warren, *Understanding Fiction,* 250; Sarah Gordon, *Flannery O'Connor:
The Obedient Imagination,* 75–76, 73; Caroline Gordon, "Old Red," in Brooks and Warren, *Understanding Fiction,* 247.

tat where they could flourish, and immobilized in an alien environment where they are unlikely to survive. Sarah Gordon hears echoes of *The Wasteland* in "The Geranium," and Eliot might well approve of this "objective correlative" that O'Connor has found for the old man's spiritual condition. Yet we might also say that the symbol lacks the multivalency prized in the New Critical poetic. Its meaning is too close to discourse; paraphrase does too little to harm it. Thus Gordon's symbol is superior in subtlety and range of resonance, but O'Connor has a clearer message. In light of O'Connor's later work, it is surprising to note that this message is not directly religious. Old Dudley suffers from a severe case of alienation and estrangement, themes important to both the Continental existentialists and the American Agrarians, but in this story alienation is not explicitly tied to religious categories. The word *home* has a special resonance that in "The Artificial Nigger" will be given Christian specification, but in this early story we are sent no further than the circles of *The Wasteland* or, indeed, the "dissociation of sensibility" registered in "Old Red" for explanation. In this way, too, O'Connor follows her model. Caroline Gordon's story was written before her Catholic conversion, when it was not yet apparent to her that the church provided a solution to the problem of spiritual dislocation identified by the Agrarians.

O'Connor attempted to emulate Gordon in more than her use of symbol. Point of view is the second New Critical interest that this comparison highlights. Both stories are written in third-person limited, and point of view remains almost exclusively with the main character. Once again the influence of James is strong, but once again we also find O'Connor straining to do what seems to come naturally to Gordon. In "Old Red," as in the stories of a Flaubert or a Chekhov, a James Joyce or a Katherine Mansfield, we encounter a mind revealed internally, as it were, without apparent comment. The reader is led to sympathize with the character, even if in the course of the story it becomes apparent that the character is unreliable or unaware. Judgment of a character, if it is implied, is made off the page, so to speak.

In Gordon's story, the reader is led to sympathize with the protagonist with little reservation. Although we see deficiencies of sensibility and a degree of selfishness on the part of this headstrong man, we are encouraged to admire his struggle against conformity. What makes him unique is also what makes him admirable, and if we come to understand more about him than he knows about himself, what we learn is but an extension of what he senses without articulating it. The author of "The Geranium" puts much more distance between herself and Old Dudley. This distance is in part generated by evaluations the character makes that we assume the author does not share or approve; most of these have to do with race. The old man is scandalized that in New York a black man is permitted to move into an apartment next door to a white woman and her family. He is angry with his daughter for allowing such an indignity. Finally, he is hypocritical in his reliance upon this same helpful black man whom he despises for not knowing his place. But it is not only Old Dudley's unsavory racial attitudes that create distance: O'Connor also employs irony, both dramatic and situational, to separate us from her character. During a remembered incident from his past, Old Dudley refuses the good advice of his black sidekick, Rabie, to surrender his shotgun until they clear rough terrain. Sure enough, just as the white man is drawing a bead on a covey of quail, he slips and misfires, scattering the birds. Rabie wryly observes, "Dem was some mighty fine birds we let get away from us" (*CW* 710). The reader can see the criticism implied in the remark; Old Dudley misses it, as he misses O'Connor's situational irony: the decrepit white man is rescued by the spry black man he did not want for a neighbor. Additionally, this unnamed man knows more about guns than Dudley, who took pride in revealing the inner workings of his shotgun to the endless apparent amazement of Rabie back home.

Gordon does not use irony to distance the character from the reader in this way, or to call attention to his faults. We can feel O'Connor itching to make the kinds of judgments the New Critical aesthetic forbids. And it may indeed be this frustrated desire that produces the most awkward writing in the story, such as in the following passage:

> Old Dudley stared at the man who was where the geranium should have been.
>
> He would. He'd go down and pick it up. He'd put it in his own window and look at it all day if he wanted to. He turned from the window and left the room. He walked slowly down the dog run and got to the steps. The steps dropped down like a deep wound in the floor. They opened up through a gap like a cavern and went down and down. And he had gone up them a little behind the nigger. And the nigger had pulled him up on his feet and kept his arm in his and gone up the steps with him and said he hunted deer, "old-timer," and seen him holding a gun that wasn't there and sitting on the steps like a child. He had shiny tan shoes and he was trying not to laugh and the whole business was laughing. (*CW* 712)

The woodenness of the penultimate section of the story may be due to many causes. The sentence patterns are similar to those of Gordon's final paragraph, and the young O'Connor may simply have been maladroit with the exaggerated, staccato pronoun openers. Perhaps O'Connor was experimenting unsuccessfully with stream of consciousness—I am put in mind of Joe Christmas in *Light in August,* perhaps because of the racial juxtapositions. But it seems to me that the primary problem here is O'Connor's effort to go beyond her character to deliver a deeper level of meaning than he is able to achieve for himself. Having committed herself to his point of view, she had no recourse to a narrator who could elevate the tone or supply an authoritative word. Once again, the modernist forms that work well in Gordon's story are not sufficient to O'Connor's religious disposition.

The joint problem of point of view and narrative voice would remain with O'Connor throughout her writing life. In a letter to Betty Hester written in May of 1956, she complains, "Point of view runs me nuts" (*HB* 157). She holds up Caroline Gordon as a writer who has mastered point of view, following in the tradition of James. Speaking of Gordon's novel *The Malefactors,* which she faults on other grounds, O'Connor praises its "modified use of the central intelligence and the omniscient narrator" which enters the mind of only one character. This technique "gives the thing a dramatic unity that's hard to get otherwise." Thus O'Connor would continue to struggle with point of view, and she would retain the stylistic goals she had absorbed in graduate school, with Gordon as her guide. Her deeper difficulty was how to include authorial commentary while following the dictum to show and not tell. Increasingly, she would rely on the voice of her narrators to suggest commentary by way of irony. In this as in so many other writing matters, her breakthrough came with *Wise Blood.*

Irony and the New Narrator: Miss Lonelyhearts *and* Wise Blood

Robert Brinkmeyer dates the change in O'Connor's narrators to this novel, her first mature work, begun before she left Iowa. In fact, he hears a new narrator's voice emerging during the very process of revision. "Most profound was her shift from a familiar narrative consciousness to one that was strident and detached. In place of being sympathetic, this narrator distorted and intensified character and situation with severe irony."[16] As evidence for this change, we can look at a passage from the

16. Robert H. Brinkmeyer Jr., *The Art and Vision of Flannery O'Connor,* 100–101.

penultimate chapter, where Hazel Motes faces a crisis similar in severity to that of Old Dudley. Haze has announced to his landlady that he is going to blind himself. In this case, the narrator sees and judges not with the protagonist, as was true in "The Geranium," but with the landlady instead:

> The landlady sat there for a while longer. She was not a woman who felt more violence in one word than in another; she took every word at its face value but all the faces were the same. Still, instead of blinding herself, if she had felt that bad, she would have killed herself and she wondered why anybody wouldn't do that. She would simply have put her head in an oven or maybe have given herself too many painless sleeping pills and that would have been that. Perhaps Mr. Motes was only being ugly, for what possible reason could a person have for wanting to destroy their sight? A woman like her, who was so clear-sighted, could never stand to be blind. If she had to be blind she would rather be dead. It occurred to her suddenly that when she was dead she would be blind too. She stared in front of her intensely, facing this for the first time. She recalled the phrase, "eternal death," that preachers used, but she cleared it out of her mind immediately, with no more change of expression than the cat. (*CW* 119)

The passage bears out Brinkmeyer's assessment. The characters and their actions are more intense here, and so are the narrator's judgments, carried primarily by irony. Although she was speaking of a different character, Gordon thought O'Connor had gone too far in this direction, and chided O'Connor during the revision process with "taking sides" against Sabbath Lily Hawks.[17] Perhaps the best example of the new narrative voice is to be found in the observation, "A woman like her, who was so clear-sighted, could never stand to be blind." Although readers can easily credit such an opinion to the character herself, the designation "clear-sighted" comes from the narrator and is obviously ironic. The blaspheming prophet himself knows he has met defeat and must turn toward the God he cannot escape; the landlady whose smug conventionality and self-congratulation prevent her from understanding Motes now becomes the target of the narrator's satire.

Perhaps the most penetrating reading of *Wise Blood* is to be found in Frederick Asals's *Flannery O'Connor: The Imagination of Extremity,* in which Asals notes the arrival of O'Connor's new narrator also discerned by

17. Quoted in Sally Fitzgerald, "A Master Class: From the Correspondence of Caroline Gordon and Flannery O'Connor," 837.

Brinkmeyer. Given the importance of this development for her fiction, a brief excursus into its origins seems to be in order. Asals believes that O'Connor turned to a literary model she discovered during the long period of *Wise Blood*'s composition, Nathanael West's *Miss Lonelyhearts.* Evidence of this connection has been turned up by other critics, and the case for influence is strong. Asals puts the point forcefully: "Nothing is more central to [O'Connor's] mature work than the tension between the distant, ironic narrative voice and the frightening materials that voice mediates. In showing her how to achieve a greater narrative distance from her materials, West seems paradoxically to have allowed her to tap a deep reservoir of psychic energy, a darker side of the imagination—perhaps even made it safe to do so." In her feminist reading of O'Connor, Sarah Gordon gives content to this "psychic energy," arguing that the fierceness of O'Connor's narrator derives in large part from her need to distance herself from the sentimentality associated with women's writing.[18] O'Connor's sharpness indicates her resolve to be as tough-minded as the male writers to whose company she aspired. Brinkmeyer describes battling narrators in O'Connor's fiction, the fiercest of whom is what he calls a fundamentalist voice that speaks for a kind of hellfire judgment, in opposition to a Catholic sacramental counsel of grace. While these are matters that deserve more thorough treatment than a digression allows, they prepare the way for a brief comment on the theological aim of *Wise Blood* that will help place my later arguments in context.

Miss Lonelyhearts is important to O'Connor not only for its narrator, but also for the explicitness with which it treats Christian themes and symbols. Miss Lonelyhearts has removed Christ from the cross of a crucifix and nailed him to his bedroom wall; in the final section of the novel, entitled "Miss Lonelyhearts Has a Religious Experience," Miss Lonelyhearts is killed while trying to enact Christ's love. One can easily imagine the impact this scene must have had on the young O'Connor. Elements West had mastered would, of course, become O'Connor staples: characters obsessed with Jesus and religious revelation connected to death. What we find in West's novel is not only an ironic narrator, but an ironic handling of religious themes. By following West's lead, O'Connor could employ a literarily legitimate means to imply theological judgments. Situational irony could dramatize what would otherwise be mere

---

18. Frederick Asals, *Flannery O'Connor: The Imagination of Extremity,* 23; Gordon, *Flannery O'Connor,* 45.

assertion or plain discourse. To O'Connor's mind, the point of *Wise Blood* was simple, as she wrote to Helen Greene on May 23, 1952: "It is after all a story about redemption and if you admit redemption, you are no pessimist. The gist of the story is that H. Motes couldn't really believe that he hadn't been redeemed" (*CW* 897). But what makes this story of redemption a work of art (in New Critical terms) is its complexity, and the complexity is supplied through irony. Haze gains sight of his redemption only through enduring self-inflicted blindness and encountering death. So ironic is this salvation, and so deflected is news of it, that many readers miss it, or doubt it, including Asals. Yet O'Connor had found her subject as well as her means.

Additionally, O'Connor must have been impressed by West's handling of symbol. West objectifies Miss Lonelyhearts's suffering in the crucifix he defaces, and although West seems to use the image to suggest that this is a Christ who has not saved, O'Connor must have been struck by the effectiveness of this most Catholic of symbols in a serious work of contemporary fiction. Though handled ironically, Miss Lonelyhearts's death is still a kind of *imitatio Christi,* as the mutilated crucifix powerfully suggests. In her turn, O'Connor would reverse West's irony, finding redemption in human suffering identified with Christ's sacrifice. But West's use of what we might call the *imitatio Christi* symbol as the climactic, epiphany-yielding image of the story would serve O'Connor as a model. The human body in attitudes of violence and suffering would become O'Connor's chief symbol.

Although O'Connor would continue to labor within the terms of New Critical formalism, the new narrative voice recognizable in *Wise Blood* indicates one of the significant ways she would bend its rules. The Jamesian dictum to render rather than state worked against her mission to shout to a deaf world. New Critical insistence on the autonomy of art seemed to militate against addressing social problems of any sort; one can easily imagine an essay on the heresy of propaganda. More specifically, the modernist bent toward limited third-person point of view and the prohibition against direct authorial comment shut off stylistic avenues available to moralists of earlier eras. The effectiveness of the Romantic symbol held out more-hopeful opportunities, as West's use of the crucifix already began to make apparent. But it remained for the Thomist aesthetic O'Connor learned from Jacques Maritain to provide the crucial pieces her kind of revelatory fiction required.

2

Romantic Symbol and the Catholic Revival

I n one sense, the New Critical aesthetic was a box in which O'Connor's religious vision seemed not quite to fit. She had a message, and Flaubert and Henry James forbade her to "tell" it. The technical adjustment that allowed her to escape this dilemma was the detached, ironic narrator—the "fierce" narrator, as Sarah Gordon has termed her. But a second component of New Critical poetics was quite congenial to O'Connor's theological orientation, and served as a bridge between Art and Church. That component was the Romantic conception of symbol.

As we saw in Chapter 1, the New Critical generation appropriated from German Idealism by way of Coleridge a religious notion of symbol as partaking in the reality it renders intelligible. In his *Biographia Literaria* Coleridge famously deems true poetry a work of the Secondary Imagination, the Primary Imagination being the human mind's participation in God's Creation. Art, then, is essentially imitation on a smaller scale of the divine activity whereby God, so to speak, imagines the world into being. Although avoiding such a direct analogy, and without committing themselves to philosophical Idealism, New Critics retained symbol's privileged status as part of their effort to distinguish literature from ordinary discourse. Archibald MacLeish declares in "Ars Poetica" that "a poem should not mean / But be," indicating the density of the poetic symbol and its distance from ordinary language. The poem, in fact, creates its own world, and despite what the quoted lines might seem to suggest, this world is packed with meaning, in contrast to the "wasteland" that the deadly combination of science, technology, and warfare has left.

In addition to symbol, so important to New Critics and other modernists, influential theorists appealed to myth as a source of poetic power. Ransom was not the only critic to decry a God without thunder. Proponents of mythic consciousness, influenced by Ernst Cassirer but going in their own directions, argued that the health of literature depends upon its openness to a pre-rational religious awareness. Northrop Frye belongs in this category, but perhaps the most telling statement of the kind I have in mind is to be found in the work of Philip Wheelwright.[1]

Wheelwright's essay appears in a volume compiled by Allen Tate in 1942 called *The Language of Poetry*. The other contributors, who presented the essays as lectures at Princeton University in 1941, include Cleanth Brooks, I. A. Richards, and Wallace Stevens. In his preface, Tate observes that thinking on poetry is presently shifting "from poetry as emotion and response to poetry as a kind of knowledge."[2] Of the essays, Wheelwright's is perhaps most explicit in naming the kind of knowledge poetry provides. In "Poetry, Myth, and Reality" he decries Descartes' "dualistic rationalism" that has reduced religion to a "tentative and subjective validity." Wheelwright claims that poetry has likewise been marginalized, and for the same reason: post-Cartesian thought makes no room for mythic consciousness, which "may express visions of truth to which the procedures of the scientist are grossly irrelevant." Myth is the root of religion and poetry, and empirical positivism has sundered this root, ignoring or deprecating "that haunting awareness of transcendental forces peering through the cracks of the visible universe, that is the very essence of myth." Offering examples from non-Western religion as well as from poets from Aeschylus to Shakespeare, Wheelwright argues that the quality of poetry is tied directly to the state of mythic consciousness in the poet's age. Not surprisingly, he concludes that the poet of his own day is in an unpromising predicament:

> The poet of today . . . is profoundly inhibited by the dearth of shared consciousness of myth. Our current motivating ideas are not myths but ideologies, lacking transcendental significance. This loss of myth-consciousness I believe to be the most devastating loss that humanity can suffer; . . . myth-consciousness is the bond that unites men both with one another and with the unplumbed Mystery from which mankind is sprung and without reference to which the radical significance of things goes to pot.[3]

1. Lentricchia, *After the New Criticism,* 242.
2. Allen Tate, ed., *The Language of Poetry,* vii.
3. Philip Wheelwright, "Poetry, Myth, and Reality," in Tate, *Language of Poetry,* 11, 10, 32.

The difficulty here is that "myth-consciousness," like the high view of literature espoused by the New Critics, seems to require religious belief to sustain it. One who feels this need is either driven to the "as if" position of Ransom, assuming a God with thunder for the sake of intellectual and artistic vitality, or driven toward conversion, as in the case of Tate. O'Connor needed no conversion. But what she did need was an intellectual framework for her faith, and it was provided for her by a resurgence of Catholic intellectual life sometimes called the Catholic Revival. Crucial for her poetics was O'Connor's alignment with this neo-Thomist movement brought to America from France and led by the philosophers Jacques Maritain and Etienne Gilson.

Maritain's Neo-Thomist Alternative

The impact of the Catholic Revival upon American intellectuals in the 1940s and 1950s was considerable, paving the way for the conversions of Robert Lowell, Jean Stafford, Thomas Merton, and Walker Percy, in addition to Allen Tate and Caroline Gordon. Along with Christopher Dawson, a British transplant, Maritain and Gilson filled the role of public intellectual from locations at Chicago, Princeton, and Harvard, giving Catholics an academic clout that they had not previously enjoyed. In his discussion of the period in relation to Percy, Kieran Quinlan notes that Maritain and Gilson, along with the Protestant Reinhold Niebuhr, had made enough of a stir to call forth refutation in a *Partisan Review* issue of 1943 titled "The New Failure of Nerve." By 1950, this same journal invited Maritain, along with Tate, to contribute to a kind of pro and contra issue devoted to the topic "Religion and the Intellectuals."[4] The prestige of the invitation can be measured by a list of other contributors: poet W. H. Auden, philosophers John Dewey and A. J. Ayer, critics I. A. Richards and Alfred Kazin, and theologian Paul Tillich.

No doubt this success benefited O'Connor professionally, since fellow Catholics were now to be found on the boards and editorial staffs of the literary establishment. But more important was the rigorous philosophical framework she gained from the neo-Thomists as her mature work was taking shape. She seems to have read Maritain and Gilson on her own, without professorial tutelage, but she read carefully and discussed what she read with friends. From 1948 to 1950, O'Connor rented a room from

---

4. Kieran Quinlan, *Walker Percy: The Last Catholic Novelist,* 46–48.

Sally and Robert Fitzgerald in Connecticut. Upon departing the Fitzgeralds' house when illness forced her to return to Milledgeville, she inadvertently left behind a marked copy of Maritain's *Art and Scholasticism,* which she quickly requested. She often recommended this book to others, and said of it that she had "cut her aesthetic teeth" on it (*HB* 216).

This remark in itself is interesting, since she had taken a course in aesthetics at Iowa under Austin Warren.[5] What it may indicate is that despite the New Critical standards she accepted as supplying the rules of the game, it was only when Maritain gave her a specifically Catholic way of understanding art that she felt grounded in her vocation. In fact, it seems likely, as Paul Elie suggests in *The Life You Save May Be Your Own,* that *Art and Scholasticism* was essential to what we might call Flannery O'Connor's coming of age.[6] In 1947, having completed her MFA work and having won a fellowship that allowed her to return to Iowa City to work independently on her planned novel, she enjoyed a degree of freedom she had never known. Elie claims that it was during this period that she read Maritain's book and that it, together with *Miss Lonelyhearts,* launched the O'Connor we remember. It is easy to see how *Art and Scholasticism* liberated the twenty-two-year-old by giving her a sense of mission.

For Maritain, the calling of the artist is a high and noble one, although not religious in any usual sense. The artist's first obligation is to his craft. The duty of the artist is to cultivate a "habit of art"; here, *habit* is used in the sense of a disposition of mind and will established by long practice. The pursuit of art "frees from every human care, it establishes the *artifex,* artist or artisan, in a world apart, cloistered, defined and absolute, in which to devote all the strength and intelligence of his manhood to the service of the thing he is making. This is true of every art; the ennui of living and willing ceases on the threshold of every studio or workshop." At the same time, Maritain argues that the artist has an important social function, which is to provide beauty and even utility. Except by the objects they made, the Scholastics did not distinguish artisans from *artistes.* Virtue for the artist is thus faithfulness to her task. In a way reminiscent of New Critical insistence on the autonomy of art, Maritain asserts, in Aristotelian fashion, that each craft has its own standards, and is to be judged by its own rules: "This action is what it ought to be, is good of its kind, if it conforms to the rules and the end peculiar to the work to be produced: and

5. Fodor, "Proust, 'Home of the Brave,' and *Understanding Fiction,*" 72.
6. Paul Elie, *The Life You Save May Be Your Own,* 151–52.

the result to which it is directed, if it is good, is for the work in question to be good in itself."[7]

Where craftsmanship is concerned, art has its own rules; where the artist is concerned, one should separate personal morality from artistic accomplishment. Both of these assertions were important to O'Connor, and each comports well with New Critical dicta. The assertion that art has special rules unique to its particular practice reinforced O'Connor's sense of being set apart. Like many other brilliant and sensitive children, she had always stood out as different. In addition to demonstrating early talents for writing stories and drawing pictures, she was a protected only child in a family acutely aware of social convention. Flannery made her public debut as something of a character at age five when a Pathé newsreel was made of her with a chicken she had coaxed into walking backward.[8] Having her "difference" blessed by Maritain's insistence that her literary aspiration was an honorable calling must have reassured her.

O'Connor seems to have needed such reassurance, especially from an authoritative Catholic source. In the draft of a letter she wrote to Caroline Gordon thanking her for her lengthy response to the penultimate draft of *Wise Blood,* O'Connor reports that she visited a priest in Iowa City to discuss with him her fear of undermining the morality of her readers. In her account, the priest rather unconcernedly replied that she needn't write for fifteen-year-old girls, and handed her "one of those ten cent pamphlets that they are never without."[9] No doubt Maritain's more considered opinion, rooted in St. Thomas Aquinas, was a much stronger affirmation: the intellectual virtue needed for woman understood as a creature before God is prudence, which directs her to the action that serves her highest end. But the virtue of the artist, a virtue of making, is that which produces the best work. While service to God's truth is ultimately more important than service to beauty, each is necessary to human fulfillment, and art should be pursued wholeheartedly in its own terms. *Art and Scholasticism* allowed O'Connor to think of her role as a fiction writer to be a calling sanctioned by the Catholic Church. It gave her license to be different from (and misunderstood by) her fellow Catholics while still united with them in her obedience to the church. Where her work itself was concerned, Maritain helped relieve her con-

7. Jacques Maritain, *Art and Scholasticism and Other Essays,* 7, 6.
8. Elie, *The Life You Save,* 12.
9. Quoted in Fitzgerald, "Master Class," 845.

science from the fear of unintentionally corrupting her audience or herself by peering into the dark corners of human existence.

There is a strong similarity between T. S. Eliot's demand that the writer set aside his personality and Maritain's insistence that the artist devote himself to the form he envisions. Maritain explains, "The whole soul of the artist affects and controls his work, but it should only affect and control it *by the artistic habit*."[10] The purpose of art is not self-expression. By the same token, art has its own integrity and thus a kind of objectivity. In these ways, Maritain's Thomism reaffirms what O'Connor heard from the New Critics. But the new Scholastics also gave a twist to New Critical emphases—in fact, a double twist—that in effect prevented them from being formalists in the sense that term usually carries. The first twist is a teleological one, which places art within a hierarchy of interrelated goods and, though according it honor, subordinates it to other endeavors. The second twist is metaphysical. The neo-Thomists claim a cognitive or intellectual function for art that makes it a genuine form of knowledge.

By accepting that art has a place within a hierarchy of goods, O'Connor avoided the kind of isolationist thinking that New Critics are often accused of. For example, she was willing to abide by the Index of Proscribed Books, although she also thought there should be an Index of Required Books, and she was quick to ask for permission to read proscribed books when she thought doing so served some good end. Her willingness to undertake book reviews for a diocesan paper as one of the few acts of charity her illness permitted her gives further evidence of her sense of service, as does her agreeing to introduce *A Memoir for Mary Ann* in behalf of an order of nuns she admired. On the other hand, O'Connor could turn a skeptical eye on the doings of the academic and literary worlds, eager to join conversations but quick to point out pretension. More broadly, one may see—both in her determination to connect with a secular readership and in her willingness to leave the ultimate outcome of her efforts to God—a belief that art participates in larger designs. For Maritain, art is not self-referential; what he says in criticism of Oscar Wilde's aestheticism would apply to any doctrinaire formalism: "[A]rt does not derive from itself alone what it imparts to things; it spreads over them a secret which it first discovered in them, in their invisible substance or in their endless exchanges and correspondences."[11]

10. Maritain, *Art and Scholasticism*, 70.
11. Ibid., 95–96.

The phrase *a secret which it first discovered in them* leads to the second and crucial departure from New Criticism to be found in Maritain's version of Scholasticism. With Aquinas, Maritain and Gilson affirm a theistic realism that finds truth in art. To put it simply, these thinkers believed in universals. Our minds are capable of real knowledge because they have access to the real, nonmaterial substratum of the cosmos. Since art is not science or philosophy or theology, it does not have knowledge in the strictest sense as its end; rather, as we have seen, art is devoted to making. Still, art is an intellectual enterprise in that it deals in patterns that must be grasped by the mind. Thus, according to Maritain, it does offer a kind of truth: "[Art] is not itself a lie, as is commonly believed, on the pretext that its truth is not the truth of knowledge. It expresses the personality of the artist to the outside world in so far as the artist forgets his personality in his object, and in the (interior or exterior) reality which he displays transforming it."[12] The artist grasps universals. Indeed, she may grasp what is otherwise unseen, revealing the "secret" of things otherwise hidden. We may say that the artist discovers meaning, she does not create it.

In a later book, but one consonant with *Art and Scholasticism,* Maritain makes the point concerning meaning in relation to MacLeish's poem, referred to above: "A poem must only be, yes, but it cannot be except through the poetic sense; and some intelligible meaning, subordinate or evanescent as it may be, at least some atmosphere of clarity, is part of the poetic sense. . . . To one degree or another, even in the most obscure poems, even when the poet turns his back completely on intelligence, the intelligible sense is always there. No poem can be absolutely obscure."[13] The artist discerns a design and brings it to sensible form, and he does so through symbol.

Symbol with a Difference

Here we have returned to a New Critical hallmark, and once again we find a point of contact with Maritain, but with a metaphysical difference. Walker Percy, who published in philosophy journals before he published fiction, puts his finger on the Thomistic significance of symbols in one of his early essays, "Symbol as Need." Quoting from both *Art and Scholasticism* and *Creative Intuition in Art and Poetry,* Percy points to what he took to be a revolutionary breakthrough in Susanne Langer's *Feeling and Form:*

12. Ibid., 98.
13. Jacques Maritain, *Creative Intuition in Art and Poetry,* 260–61.

"The communication of meaning, positivists to the contrary, is not limited to the discursive symbol, word, and proposition; the art symbol conveys its own appropriate meaning, a meaning inaccessible to the discursive form" (*MB* 288). Percy seizes upon Langer's book because he believes her to have arrived at a vital conclusion she shares with the Scholastics, but which she reached by a completely different philosophical route. The reigning model of communication in scientific circles of the time was a behaviorist one. Language use was understood to be a biological adaptation in response to the need for sex, food, child-rearing, and shelter. In the tradition of idealist philosophy from which Langer is departing, the question of a subsistent reality beyond thought is simply bracketed. But, Percy asks, what kind of "need" can the impulse toward symbolization satisfy? Turning feeling into form serves no biological end. It would seem, then, that in this case we have an empirical phenomenon that falls outside naturalistic categories. Percy formulates the question in this way: "If the language symbol is not just a sign in an adaptive schema, and if it does not itself constitute reality but rather represents something, *then what does it represent?*" (*MB* 296).

Percy's own answer is the Thomistic one: it represents a third thing— the metaphysical substratum uniting thought and matter. Thus the symbol is neither the satisfaction of a biological need nor an end in itself, but a means of *knowing,* the "astonishing instrument by which I transform the sensory content and appropriate it for the stuff of my ideas" (*MB* 297). What this argument does, in effect, is to "defictionalize" the art symbol, removing its metaphysical "as if" status. Or, to switch metaphors, it takes art out of the realm of dream and places it in the realm of truth. Certainly, one motive behind the formalist insistence that literature creates a world of its own was the desire to protect it from the kind of reductionism Percy finds in behaviorism. Maritain says in effect that such retreat is unnecessary. His neo-Thomist account retains the meaningfulness of the Romantic symbol while restoring art to the status of knowledge. Percy would go on to make the case that symbol understood in this way can revivify science as well as art, but the point of immediate importance is that he and O'Connor had reason to place confidence in the power of artistic symbol to reveal truth. Symbol-making mysteriously puts us in touch with a level of reality otherwise unknown to us.

This understanding of symbol as the means by which human creatures of flesh and blood are brought in contact with spiritual reality is the second element, after her turn to the "fierce narrator," that allowed O'Connor to craft her mature fiction. It goes without saying that O'Connor did not need Maritain in order to discover literary symbols, since her early fiction clearly makes use of them. The term *symbol* itself has a wide range of signification; New Critical theorists diversely spoke of metaphor, paradox, or irony as the basic principle of poetry. What these terms have in common for New Critics is indication of a figural, nondiscursive use of language that could be used to distinguish literature from more pedestrian linguistic expression. But the key point for O'Connor is the metaphysical one found in Maritain: symbol connects the mind to reality and thus yields truth.

In explaining the function of literary symbols in "The Nature and Aim of Fiction," O'Connor herself calls upon the typological schema developed by the Middle Ages for interpreting scripture, with its fourfold levels of meaning: literal, allegorical, tropological, and anagogical. O'Connor maintains that all fiction writers need to have an anagogical vision, for "that is the kind of vision that is able to see different levels of reality in one image or situation" (*MM* 72). But obviously, the only writer who could have an anagogical vision in the full sense of "the Divine life and our participation in it" is the Christian one. This is yet another indication that for O'Connor, Maritain's account of art strengthened, and in effect completed, the best elements of the aesthetic of her day. Just as Gilson argued (in a book O'Connor reviewed) that for Aquinas, Christian revelation completed human reason without overturning it, so O'Connor seemed to think that Thomist aesthetics complemented those of the New Critics.

Rather surprisingly, one who reads O'Connor's thesis stories in search of the anagogical reads in vain. With the exception of "The Turkey," in which a boy prays for and receives both a turkey and a beggar to give his dime to, then loses his turkey and his pride in what would become a typical O'Connor reversal, the stories are lacking in religious resonance. And even here, the relative flatness of the story might be said to come from the fact that it is religious without being anagogical. This difference can be demonstrated by comparing O'Connor's handling of the turkey to her development of the river in the story bearing that title and written five years later.

O'Connor uses the turkey in much the same way that she employs the geranium in the thesis story that she and her teachers chose for the title piece of the collection. In both stories, the central symbol is a common object that grows in significance as it takes on layers of association that are primarily psychological, in order to illuminate the main character. In "The Geranium," Old Dudley becomes attached to the flower for reasons neither he nor the reader fully understands until the end. By then, the displaced and uprooted plant clearly represents the "transplanted" old southerner, trapped in an alien environment. As we have seen, the geranium comes to stand for the homelessness the man feels. This building of symbol by psychological association to reveal character is the principal use of it in the tradition of Flaubert and James. One thinks of Emma Bovary's wedding bouquet or of James's golden bowl. In "The Turkey," O'Connor seems to want her symbol to have a different kind of meaning, though she cannot yet steer away from the Jamesian model. The turkey is tied directly to the boy's desires; Ruller sees in the capture of the bird his chance to raise himself in the eyes of his family, and he takes his initial failure as a reason to defy God. The turkey is a mirror for Ruller's inner states. Even though it is the occasion for Ruller to expose his sinful pride and his mistaken notion of grace, there is nothing mysterious about the bird itself. In the final paragraph, when the boy has lost his turkey to three impoverished toughs, he runs home "certain that Something Awful was tearing behind him" (*CW* 752). But the Something Awful is hardly frightening to the reader; it seems entirely a bogey from the boy's imagination, for the reason that the central symbol has been framed entirely in psychological terms.

Perhaps an apt parallel can be found in Flaubert's "A Simple Heart," which Caroline Gordon and Allen Tate featured as the first story in their counterpart to *Understanding Fiction, The House of Fiction*. The saintly character described by the title becomes increasingly absorbed in another bird—a parrot, which dies, but which she has stuffed and continues to cherish. Félicité projects all her religious feeling onto the creature, identifying it with the Holy Spirit, and even praying to it. At her death, she believes she sees the heavens open and a gigantic parrot hover overhead. Flaubert's symbol is not anagogical, it is psychological. The discerning reader knows she is being shown the workings of a certain kind of mind. We learn something about Félicité, but nothing about God. The opposite is true of "The River."

In O'Connor's symbolic story written in the year *Wise Blood* appeared, the central symbol has a new kind of significance, one closer to that of the rat-colored automobile belonging to Haze Motes that she uses as her example in "The Nature and Aim of Fiction." The car, with its associations of coffin and of pulpit, becomes a symbol of "death-in-life," according to O'Connor. While this meaning certainly has to do with the character's psychology, the thrust is toward a religious significance beyond him. The same can be said of the muddy water in which Harry Ashfield ("Bevel") is baptized. Indeed, the central symbol of "The River" is one of the most freighted to be found in any of O'Connor's works. The young preacher provides the richest explication in his sermon: "Listen to what I got to say, you people! There ain't but one river and that's the River of Life, made out of Jesus' Blood. That's the river you have to lay your pain in, in the River of Faith, in the River of Life, in the River of Love, in the rich red river of Jesus' Blood, you people!" (*CW* 162). The preacher's declaration presents an overdetermined symbol, if ever there was one. The one river is the River of Life, of Faith, of Love, of Jesus's Blood, and of course it is also the red clay–tinctured stream in which he stands. Here we find room for all levels of the typological scheme—allegorically, this river is the Jordan where Israel crossed into the Promised Land and where Jesus was baptized; tropologically it points to what must be done, namely, to follow Christ in baptism; and anagogically it indicates eternal life with God. But of course, in the story the meaning of the river goes beyond these traditional Christian assertions put forth in the preacher's country rhythms. It has a unique meaning suited to the protagonist, and it does illumine his psychology. The boy's parents don't love him; he wants to "count"; he is looking for his true home. But in this story, unlike "The Turkey" or "A Simple Heart," we are not limited to the psychological. The river literally becomes the water of life and death, or—remembering what O'Connor says of Haze's blindness in "The Nature and Aim of Fiction"—the river becomes a symbol of life-in-death. The boy's simplemindedness has led him not into delusion, but into truth deeper than he understands. The preacher's words come true for him as he finds the Kingdom of Christ and escapes the clutches of the very real and very evil Mr. Paradise. The violence and death at the end of the story force us to take seriously the element of mystery in the symbol, a mystery that in O'Connor's understanding of it has to do with "the Divine life and our participation in it" (*MM* 72).

None of this is to say that the Jamesian models O'Connor began her apprenticeship by emulating aimed only at narrowly psychological concerns. To the contrary, as we have noted, at its most ambitious, the literary symbol was seen as a kind of replacement for discredited religious dogma. James Joyce suggests as much by adapting the religious term *epiphany* to literary use, famously defining it for Stephen in *Stephen Hero*

as "a sudden spiritual manifestation, whether in the vulgarity of speech
or of gesture or in a memorable phrase of the mind itself."[14] An excellent example of symbol rippling beyond the personality of a single character and providing an epiphany that draws together multiple levels
of meaning is to be found in "The Dead." In a letter to a young writer,
O'Connor praises Joyce's handling of the snow in this story, which she
had studied at Iowa (*HB* 84). While the snow is indeed a dense symbol,
the full explication of which would take us too far afield, for present purposes it is instructive to note that the snow, which is "general all over Ireland," points the reader beyond Gabriel to the history and politics of his
country—a history he cannot escape—and finally to something beyond
life itself: "[H]e heard the snow falling faintly through the universe and
faintly falling, like the descent of their last end, upon all the living and the
dead."[15] This is an inclusive image indeed, and reminiscent (or predictive)
in its scope of O'Connor's religious symbols. But despite what O'Connor seems to suggest in her lecture on the nature of fiction, this modernist symbol does not aspire to the anagogical. The epiphany here is a
moment of human consciousness, not a breakthrough of the divine. Despite the religious overtones, it provokes a kind of human insight rather
than a moment of divine grace.

Joyce's snow is an excellent example of what James MacFarlane identifies as the deepest impulse of modernism: "[T]he defining thing in the
Modernist mode is not so much that things fall *apart* but that they fall
together."[16] What Joyce is aiming for is what MacFarlane calls "super-
integration," a means to temporarily call forth a synthesis of contradictory elements from a world of flux. Thus the role of art is to provide coherence; the artist pulls together the whole range of emotional, cognitive,
and sense experience, making a kind of sense of it not available to more
reductive human enterprises such as science. But paradoxically, this synthesis is always fleeting and in a certain sense illusory, for life itself is dynamic and unfixable. The literary symbol as passed down through the
novelistic tradition in which O'Connor was trained is an ideal modernist
tool, for it universalizes what seems to be unique experience, yet in a way
that is not repeatable. The snow provides the crucial clue allowing the
reader to make sense of Gabriel's evening and his marriage and his con-

14. James Joyce, *Stephen Hero,* 211.
15. James Joyce, *Dubliners,* 223.
16. Quoted in Daniel J. Singal, *William Faulkner: The Making of a Modernist,* 10.

nection to Ireland and perhaps his place in the human race, but this moment of revelation is particular to this unique set of experiences, and the synthesis is fleeting. If the story were to go on, the kaleidoscope would shift and a new pattern would have to emerge.

Some of the things I have said of Joyce are true for O'Connor as well. The revelations in her stories are tied to the circumstances and actions of particularized characters, for example. The vast difference is that for her, the symbol reaches beyond the world of flux to that of eternity. This is part of what she means by the anagogical, and it, more than any other feature, gives her stories their startling luminosity, which is more likely to take the form of a lightning bolt than a halo. O'Connor's revelations are final and absolute—often in the literal sense of coming at the moment of death, but always in the metaphorical sense of claiming the last word. The reader may be left wondering what the epiphany means, or even whether O'Connor is of the party of God or the devil, as John Hawkes first wondered in print in 1962, but the revelation itself is fixed and unalterable. The veil between phenomenal and noumenal has temporarily been lifted.

3

O'Connor and the Body
Incarnation, Redemptive Suffering, and Evil

ಬಿ

The anagogical meaning for which O'Connor strove in her work from *Wise Blood* onward has a distinctive shape. Although the content of this vision cannot be narrowly specified—she often referred to her goal as Mystery—a definite pattern can be discerned in her handling of religious themes. Despite variations, nuances, and subtle shifts, the theological message of her work remained stable, or so I shall argue. And a good place to begin is with one of the meanings of the term *anagogical* itself, which is "having to do with the afterlife." Instructively, Dante in his letter to Can Grande della Scala illustrates the anagogical with this interpretation of Psalm 113:1–2: "[W]hat is signified to us is the departure of the sanctified soul from bondage to the corruption of this world into the freedom of eternal glory."[1] O'Connor's poetics is based not only on the metaphysical principle of the analogy of being, according to which there is no division between the sensible and the intelligible,[2] but also on the more directly theological conviction that the true meaning of life is to be found on the other side of death. This is not to say that O'Connor's fiction is otherworldly or life-denying. Rather, for her the fulfillment of this life is to be found in what lies beyond it. Indeed, it is the fullness of life beyond the natural that gives substance to nature itself.

Participation in the life of God is what gives nature its reality, and for human creatures, this participation becomes complete only after death,

---

1. Quoted in David Richter, *The Critical Tradition: Classic Texts and Contemporary Trends,* 121.
2. John F. Desmond, *Risen Sons: Flannery O'Connor's Vision of History,* 9.

through the power of the Resurrection. Thus death itself has a kind of Christian ambivalence. In one sense it is the enemy to be conquered, and the promise of Christ's Resurrection makes death's defeat certain. However, in another sense, death is positive, for when embraced as the means of self-denial it reminds us of our finitude and points us to infinite being in God. Death in O'Connor is not an escape from nature, but rather a gateway into a deeper level of being, one that transcends the body without denigrating it. In fact, as we shall see, the body is necessary to the process of redemption, both because it is inherent to our creaturely natures and because Christ's Incarnation and Resurrection took bodily form. The church, she writes a friend, places tremendous emphasis on the body, with Christians looking forward to the resurrection of a glorified body like that of Christ, in which "flesh and spirit are united in peace." This glorification is a completion of creation; indeed, "[t]he resurrection of Christ seems the high point in the law of nature" (*HB* 100).

The human body is the site at which our salvation must be worked out, so to speak. O'Connor makes this claim directly in relation to Mary Ann, a little girl whose face was grotesquely distorted by the cancer that eventually took her life. At the urging of the nuns who took the girl in, O'Connor wrote an introduction to their memoir of Mary Ann. Of this child, O'Connor says, "She and the Sisters who had taught her had fashioned from her unfinished face the material of her death. The creative action of the Christian's life is to prepare his death in Christ. It is a continuous action in which this world's goods are utilized to the fullest, both positive gifts and what Pere Teilhard de Chardin calls 'passive diminishments'" (*CW* 828). This passage is remarkable for a number of reasons. First, it metaphorically asserts that the girl's distorted face was the "material" from which her death in Christ was "fashioned." The body provides the stuff from which her sanctified self is made. Second, in the manner of the memento mori tradition, O'Connor claims that preparation for death is the purpose of life, but in exact opposition to the spirit of the Faulknerian assertion that "the reason for living is getting ready to stay dead."[3] For O'Connor this preparation is a "creative" action. Third, the girl's suffering is included amongst "this world's goods" from which the sanctified self is fashioned. Perhaps this last point is most difficult of all for contemporary readers, for it smacks of sadism and a kind of sanitizing of evil. The

3. Addie Bundren makes this assertion in William Faulkner, *As I Lay Dying,* 167.

violence done to Mary Ann's face by cancer is an example of the kind of violence that O'Connor seems to extol in her use of the grotesque.

Cruciform Counterviolence: Wise Blood and "Parker's Back"

Violence is a concept important to O'Connor's understanding of the anagogical, as she herself indicates by the title of her second novel, *The Violent Bear It Away,* taken from the Douay-Rheims translation of Matthew 11:12. As she explains to Betty Hester in a letter, "[M]ore than ever now it seems that the kingdom of heaven has to be taken by violence, or not at all. You have to push as hard as the age pushes you" (*HB* 229). Thus she suggests that violence, like suffering, death, and the grotesque, has a divine purpose. This assertion also goes against the modern grain, which may countenance violence in the form of war and even revel in it for its entertainment value on stage and screen, but condemns it from a moral point of view. For O'Connor, the violence of sin requires a divine counterviolence that receives violence and turns it against itself in the interest of peace. Again, her starting point is the cross, where Christ is, in John Milbank's phrase, "sovereign victim," inviting yet overcoming violence. As we shall see, violence in the stories falls into two categories where divine agency is concerned, revelatory and redemptive. Missing is punitive violence, God's striking down of sinners to repay them for their sins. From the standpoint of human agency, active violence is always motivated by sin, with the exception of ascetic self-violence, which is revelatory. Passive violence, on the other hand, violence endured, is nearly always redemptive.

As one might expect in the case of an overtly Christian writer whose work has accumulated a small mountain of commentary, the nature of O'Connor's message has been much debated. Early readers of a secular cast of mind tended to dismiss her work as freakish and misguided; more recent and more sophisticated critics of a similar bent have wanted to get behind or beyond theological readings to more interesting issues, assuming that since they still find her fascinating there must be more to her than Christian orthodoxy. Within the camp of those who engage O'Connor theologically, some have found her to be a champion of the faith, while others, beginning with her contemporary and fellow writer John Hawkes, have believed her to be secretly and perhaps unintentionally in league with the devil she takes so seriously. Even O'Connor critics of the stature of Frederick Asals and Robert Brinkmeyer, who are appreciative of O'Connor's stated aims, find the need to divide her work. Asals argues that *Wise Blood* is unwittingly Manichean, whereas the later stories achieve a unity of matter and spirit more in line with O'Connor's public statements; Brinkmeyer, while defending *Wise Blood* on this score, divides O'Connor's narrators into "fundamentalist" and "Catholic."

One of the chief reasons for such divisions, which extend to feminist readings as well, is the large place that violence plays in O'Connor's work—particularly violent death. Not content to display the psychological misfits and physical deformities that constitute the face of the grotesque, she insists on manifold forms of death and dismemberment. Not only do these acts often have no apparent redemptive outcome, but they seem to be part of a strategy of negation—one that denies the very goodness of life. Hazel Motes blinds himself, young Bevel drowns himself, the grandmother is shot for talking too much, Mrs. May is gratuitously gored by a bull: in none of these cases is there any benefit to the sufferer on this side of death, beyond a brief flash of insight. To make matters worse, the narrators in these stories indicate their approval, as though these terrible events are good rather than evil.

Indeed, one of the bracing first principles of O'Connor's work is that suffering is good, not evil, as long as that suffering is identified with the redemptive suffering of Christ. The violence in O'Connor is cruciform. She is perhaps more aware than any other twentieth-century American writer of the meaning of the cross: without the shedding of blood, there is no remission of sin. Our present suffering offers the opportunity for the human being to participate with Christ in the salvation of the world. One of the ways O'Connor's work is sacramental is that in it, violence becomes the occasion for the sinner to join Christ, through his or her own body. We might say that a death such as the grandmother's is a kind of Eucharist in reverse. In Eucharist, the bread and wine become Christ's body and blood in a mysterious spiritual transformation that conveys grace to the recipient. In a death like the grandmother's, her violated body becomes the means whereby she is mysteriously united with Christ's grace as she repeats his suffering. Christ's suffering produces grace; our suffering opens us to that grace. The mystery of violence is the startling recognition that by violence we are saved—not by committing it, but by receiving it. Perhaps the most startling of O'Connor's fictional assertions is that violence can be sacramental—a means by which God's grace takes saving shape in the natural world.

Closely related to the notion of violence is that of the grotesque, the category to which O'Connor frequently refers in her lectures, and which is specifically addressed in "Some Aspects of the Grotesque in Southern Fiction" (*MM* 36–50). O'Connor adopted the term in response to critics, since early in her career she was placed with Erskine Caldwell in what she called "The School of Southern Degeneracy." Characteristically, she accepted the derogatory label, but turned it to her own defiant purposes. "Whenever I'm asked why Southern writers particularly have a penchant for writing about freaks, I say it is because we are still able to recognize one. To be able to recognize a freak, you have to have some conception of the whole man, and in the South the general conception of man is still, in the main, theological" (*MM* 44). Although O'Connor acknowledged her debts to Poe and the southwestern humorists, here she calls attention to an issue deeper than literary history. A sense of the grotesque in human nature depends upon a prior sense of what is normative—and for her, what has been distorted is the image of God. And since sin mars us all, all of us are "freaks"—the anonymous organization man in the grey-flannel suit not excepted.

For O'Connor, then, the grotesque is a literary response to original sin. Distorted characters show the twist in human nature that most readers ignore, and conversely, they reveal those urges toward the good that are camouflaged from the secularized eye. O'Connor acknowledges that her kind of fiction does require a departure from realism. The subject matter of her fiction—its characters, its themes, and its action—is set against the social norm. In this way, she is doing violence to realism, and without directly acknowledging it, departing the path of Flaubert and James that Caroline Gordon had striven to keep her on.[4] She names Hawthorne as her inspiration in this essay on the grotesque, and names his style "the modern romance tradition," clearly intending to put herself in his company. Romance, as she explains, abandons everyday reality to explore mystery that is equally real, if less apparent. The prophet, she famously announces, is a realist of distances.

What is most important here for our present purpose is O'Connor's literary violence. She acknowledges that her method is one that requires distortion in service of truth. Secondarily, she names a new category previously missing from the list of her literary models—the romance. O'Connor seems to have sensed that her Thomist aesthetic, while com-

---

4. Elie, *The Life You Save,* 312.

patible with New Critical principles, was not a perfect fit. The tradition of fiction carried out by Flaubert, Chekhov, James, and Joyce produced stories that achieved epiphanies—sudden moments of individual insight issuing in a temporary synthesis. But O'Connor came to see that she aspired to revelations more comprehensive and permanent. Or, to use terms better suited to the anagogical, O'Connor aspired to rend the veil between the temporal and the eternal.

O'Connor then might be said to be on the attack on two fronts. First, she exhibits a certain fierceness toward her characters, giving moral and intellectual judgments ascendancy over feeling. In "Some Aspects of the Grotesque" she disparages as sentimentalism the kind of compassion that readers expect authors to show their wayward characters, defining sentimentality as "loving someone more than God does." And second, she is out to assault the reader's sense of propriety and normalcy. O'Connor's occasional prose is peppered with warnings to her readers: "[Y]ou have to make your vision apparent by shock—to the hard of hearing you shout, and for the almost-blind you draw large and startling figures" (*MM* 34). Most of these warnings are directed at readers who misunderstand her because they do not share her theological framework. But in fact, O'Connor intends readerly violence to all her readers, believers and unbelievers alike, not excluding herself. For, ultimately, she hopes to precipitate an act of reading that is itself a kind of *imitatio Christi,* or more accurately, an *imitatio crucis.* Of her own writing experience she says,

> I have discovered that what is needed [to make a story "work"] is an action that is totally unexpected, yet totally believable, and I have found that, for me, this is always an action which indicates that grace has been offered. And frequently it is an action in which the devil has been the unwilling instrument of grace. This is not a piece of knowledge that I consciously put into my stories; it is a discovery that I get out of them. . . . I have also found that what I write is read by an audience which puts little stock either in grace or the devil. You discover your audience at the same time and in the same way you discover your subject; but it is an added blow. (*MM* 118)

As readers of O'Connor know, the "unexpected action" is often violent, and here she names herself one of the readers who is surprised by it. And, tellingly, she calls the discovery of her indifferent audience an additional "blow," as though the subject of the story itself—the action of grace—is the first blow.

This description of both reading and the action of grace in violent terms coincides with O'Connor's statements on violence itself. "With the serious writer," she observes, "violence is never an end in itself." However, "Violence is a force that can be used for good or evil, and among other things taken by it is the kingdom of heaven. But regardless of what can be taken by it, the man in the violent situation reveals those qualities least dispensable in his personality, those qualities which are all he will have to take into eternity with him" (*MM* 113–14). Clearly for O'Connor violence has its uses, and here she directs attention to the fact that when faced with death, one may be required to abandon the trivial in favor of the essential. But the role of violence in O'Connor's stories has theological roots that run much deeper than Samuel Johnson's witty remark that "the prospect of hanging wonderfully concentrates the mind." Violence is here connected to eschatology, for the threat of death immediately places one in the context of last things, vaulting us into the realm of the anagogical. And no fewer than twelve of the twenty-one stories O'Connor published in book form (two novels and two short-story collections) include a death as the central or climactic event. But the deepest root, invisible on the surface of her remark, is the cross, for in O'Connor's world, it is only through the extension of Christ's suffering to us that we become fit for eternity.

Three interlocking theological ideas provide the framework for O'Connor's distinctive use of violence. First is the role of the body in salvation. Second is the value of human suffering. And third is her understanding of evil as privation of good. These notions correspond respectively to the Christian doctrines of Incarnation, Atonement, and Creation, all of which are necessary to make sense of stories that are otherwise not only mysterious, in O'Connor's sense, but malicious. Although it is artificial to select illustrative stories from a remarkably unified body of work, the goals of clarity and depth will be served by looking closely at *Wise Blood* and "Parker's Back" in connection with the body, for these first and last stories provide a helpful alpha and omega to O'Connor's pervasive concern with death.

Critical discussion of *Wise Blood* must begin with Frederick Asals's astute assessment, which has justly drawn widespread response and rebuttal. The theological charge Asals makes against the novel has directly to do with the body: despite O'Connor's own intentions and later work, this first book is Manichean, for through it "runs the strong current of the imagery of repulsion, a repulsion at the physical deeper than anything required by the novel's motif of reverse evolution or the satire of a secularized society." Of the body more specifically, Asals observes, "The 'blood' of the book's ironic title is no source of wisdom but the very substance that immures the self in the horror of the physical, a deadly cage and a coffin. In *Wise Blood* the self is buried alive in matter." Even given the more orthodox, medieval echoes of Hazel Motes's monklike actions in the book's denouement, Asals insists that O'Connor's protagonist thereby completes a Gnostic assault on creation: "Haze is beyond even a modern 'monkery.' The violent asceticism of his end is a thoroughgoing rejection not only of a secularized age but of life taken in through the senses at all—life in a world of matter. The grisly comic victory of Hazel Motes is exactly to escape from the world, to mortify his body, to seek out death. By the end of *Wise Blood* the chasm between inner and outer, spirit and matter, is absurdly and terrifyingly absolute."[5]

Despite the eloquence of this argument, and its grounding in elements indisputably to be found in the novel, Robert Brinkmeyer's counterpoint places us on a more revealing track. Haze's asceticism is ultimately not Manichean, but Yahwistic, an assault rooted in an Old Testament sense that everything standing between the self and God is an obstacle to be burned away. In Christian terms, this Old Testament theme allows O'Connor to balance her Manichean tendency with a more sacramental one:

> The world-ridding, body-wounding (and celebrating) motion typical of O'Connor's fiction suggests that what Asals identifies as her ascetic imagination is both Manichean (world-destroying) and sacramental (celebrating the confluence of body and spirit) at the same time. . . . That O'Connor's imagination repeatedly moves to rid the claims of the world of any significance also points to the profoundly Hebraic cast of her vision. . . . [T]he Yahwist vision . . . so devalues nature and culture before the looming, other-worldly presence of Yahweh that in a sense the world, the middle-ground between the individual and Yahweh, all but disappears.[6]

The key "sacramental" consideration introduced by Brinkmeyer is the fact that bodily mortification, of the kind practiced by Haze, accepts—indeed requires—the body as the site of intersection between God and self.

5. Asals, *Flannery O'Connor*, 50, 52, 56.
6. Robert H. Brinkmeyer Jr., "'Jesus, Stab Me in the Heart!': *Wise Blood,* Wounding, and Sacramental Aesthetics," 84.

As Elaine Scarry observes concerning one form of mortification, "The self-flagellation of the religious ascetic . . . is not (as is often asserted) an act of denying the body, eliminating its claims from attention, but a way of so emphasizing the body that the contents of the world are cancelled and the path is clear for the entry of an unworldly, contentless force."[7] One may with justice say that such a practice is world-denying, but not that it denies the body or that it demonstrates a principled animosity to matter. And in the case of specifically Christian asceticism, the body's pain is a way of identifying with the crucified Christ, just as the transcendent self to which the ascetic aspires coincides with his original self—the one made in the image of God. These two parameters of Christian asceticism, both of which are premised on the goodness of God's creation, are suggested by Geoffrey Galt Harpham's description of how St. Anthony's pursuit of spiritual perfection differed from that of his pagan contemporaries: "In place of the self-sufficient self formed on the model of the work of art, Christianity proposed an identification of the self with a text of transcendence, an experience that shattered all self-sufficiency and opened up the self both to other selves who had made this identification, and to idealization and closure. In the theology of conversion the self can be synchronized with a transcendent origin; it is invited to accede to the design that is already intrinsic to it. . . . Through conversion, one is called simultaneously to imitation and to an original condition."[8] In Haze's case, the "text of transcendence" is not the hearing of a passage of scripture, such as the reading of Matthew 19:21 produced for Anthony, but rather an act of violence, which forces him back to the biblical blueprint laid upon him in his childhood by his preacher grandfather. But in both cases, the body becomes the means to spirit, the necessary point of access to that divine grace paradigmatically joined to nature in the person of Christ.

In fact, one might say that Haze turns to the body when the overly spiritualized—in theological terms one could say docetized—form of the Word fails. We must remember that Haze becomes a "monk" convert only after he has failed as a preacher. True, his "gospel" is an anti-Gospel, and thus he himself is the agent of blasphemy, but when he sees the error of his ways, it is not to a corrected preaching that he gives himself, but to mortification of the flesh. The implication is that the path to his salva-

---

7. Elaine Scarry, *The Body in Pain*, 34.
8. Geoffrey Galt Harpham, *The Ascetic Imperative in Culture and Criticism*, 42.

tion lies in silent action. It is as though language itself has failed him, or at least that it has taken him as far toward God as it is able to go. Haze's body—the thing he has in common with all of humanity and thus the universal locus of testimony—becomes the page upon which to write the signs of his repentance, the instrument with which to perform an imitation of Christ. Asals flatly asserts that "Hazel Motes receives no revelation."[9] In a strict sense, this is true. Haze knows nothing he can say—or at least nothing he is willing to trust to words. But this is not to say that he lacks insight, to use the dominant metaphor of the book. His actions indicate that he has found a new route to God, at once more immediate and more mystical.

As even a casual reader of *Wise Blood* will recall, Haze's life at Mrs. Flood's boardinghouse after he blinds himself is monklike, a point that the landlady herself makes. And we might advantageously remember that O'Connor wrote this book during a resurgence of monastic life. Robert Giroux—the editor who published Thomas Merton and who was to become O'Connor's editor—gave her a copy of *The Seven Storey Mountain* well before she finished *Wise Blood*.[10] Even careful readers may miss how thoroughly Haze carries out the pattern of the eremitic fathers. He shows indifference to the pleasures of eating and drinking. He is free of the lure of money, throwing away whatever is left from his pension check at the end of the month. He refuses the blandishments of both his young former lover and the lonely widow, Mrs. Flood, whose advances finally drive him away. In these ways he practices poverty and chastity after his fashion. Mortification of the flesh is his specialty. He walks endless miles on gravel and broken glass; he sleeps with barbed wire wrapped around his chest. All of these are the actions of saints, extreme and (as Mrs. Flood announces) outdated though they seem.

Those few words that Haze does speak confirm, however laconically, that he is seeking to die to the old self, the "fleshly" self, in order to prepare himself to meet God. In one brief conversation with his landlady, he asserts his mistrust of speech and his own sense of sin. Having failed in other temptations, Mrs. Flood suggests that Haze indulge in his former craft of preaching; if he got a guide dog he could draw a big crowd—people will always go to see a dog, she says. But Haze refuses, saying he doesn't have time. The more urgent business he is about is suggested by

9. Asals, *Flannery O'Connor*, 53.
10. Elie, *The Life You Save*, 175.

his earlier remark to Mrs. Flood, "If you believed in Jesus, you wouldn't be so good." This dictum is not, as it appears to her, a condemnation of belief. Instead, it is evidence of Haze's recognition that those who truly believe in Jesus are forced to acknowledge their own sinfulness, and that his youthful attempt to avoid Jesus by avoiding evil has failed. As Richard Giannone observes, "The disparity between the spiritual ideal of entrusting oneself to God and His gracious guidance and the inept human groping toward the apotheosis of self depicts more than the twisting of reality that we have come to call the grotesque in O'Connor's art. This contrast conveys the theology underlying her first novel."[11]

Now Haze's task is repentance. He later tells Mrs. Flood that he walks on rocks "to pay." He sleeps in barbed wire because "I'm not clean." And in this last exchange, he indicates that his reasons are not Manichean. To the landlady's objection that his actions are unnatural, he issues a flat contradiction: "It's natural." What he seems to mean is that the journey to God corresponds with man's higher nature, which does not ignore the created self but seeks to redeem it by radically reshaping it. It is this journey to God that he surely means when in his last words he tells the young cops who are about to kill him, "I want to go on where I'm going." One might be inclined to hear this statement as a death wish, yet it is important to recognize that Haze does not kill himself. The Christian ascetic mortifies—"makes dead"—his flesh, but he does so as a means, not an end.[12] The body remains necessary to him until such time as God releases him from it to await resurrection. In Haze's case, the body maintains its significance even after death, when his corpse, returned by the oblivious policemen to Mrs. Flood, lies stretched out reverently before her on her bed, a silent sign pointing down a path she cannot take, but to which she is nonetheless lured when she stares into his dead eyes.

Haze, with his victim's death, completes his *imitatio Christi*, an imitation carried out in his body, and we might add, in silence. It is his body itself upon which he "writes" his repentance and which "speaks" his witness to Christ. And yet, an obscurity hovers over *Wise Blood*. In part, the murkiness is due to O'Connor's decision to switch to Mrs. Flood's point of view in the final chapter, which forces us to deduce the meaning of actions Haze does not explain. Further, the patterns of denigrating imagery for both humanity and landscape that Asals describes do make it

---

11. Richard Giannone, *Flannery O'Connor and the Mystery of Love,* 8.
12. Harpham, *Ascetic Imperative,* 59.

difficult for the reader to affirm the goodness of creation; Sarah Gordon may well be correct in maintaining that *The Wasteland* exerted a strong influence on this early work. But finally, it seems to me that O'Connor is unable to break through what we might call an allegorical difficulty. Christian monks do not make sense in the context of the post–World War II, Bible Belt setting of O'Connor's novel. Clearly she wants Haze to be understood in terms that neither he nor any of the other characters can supply. She seems to want Haze to "discover" Roman Catholic belief and practice without ever encountering it. Since such a discovery is highly implausible, she is forced to the level of external description to imply an interpretation of his actions he could not himself provide. Haze, we might say, is an "allegorical" monk, comprehensible only to readers who can place him in a different framework than the one he is in. And within the strict conventions of realistic fiction she has adopted, the range of clues she is permitted to leave for the reader is limited.

The obscurity of *Wise Blood* is illuminated in significant ways by "Parker's Back," O'Connor's final story. As Paul Elie remarks, the later stories are more stylized, more consciously in the manner of Hawthorne's romances, or in the terms of Scholastic hermeneutics, more openly allegorical. And in "Parker's Back," O'Connor has hit upon an image of allegorical significance that draws out the implications of *Wise Blood,* completing that novel's reflections on the body. The image, of course, is that of the icon tattoo that Parker has applied to his back, rendering him a living embodiment of Christ's face. By means of the tattoo O'Connor opens a pathway for the reader to the Christian doctrine that undergirds the world-denying asceticism of Hazel Motes—the Incarnation.

The part of the body that this story calls attention to—despite the title—is the face, for beauty is perhaps more important in this meditation on the image of God than in any other O'Connor story. There is conceptual interplay not only between divine and human, natural and supernatural, but also between the grotesque and the beautiful. The story opens with Parker sullenly watching his wife, gazing at her face and concluding that she is "plain, plain." He can't understand why he married her and is ashamed of himself for not being able to leave her. She is both ugly and pregnant, two bodily features that repel him, yet he is held by her, "as if she had him conjured." In abstract terms, Parker's puzzle at the beginning of the story is why he is fascinated by the grotesque.

This puzzle is further complicated for him by his wife's hatred of tattoos. While from one point of view tattoos represent a kind of mutilation, distorting the natural appearance of human flesh, they produced in Parker the first thrill of wonder. When he saw the tattooed man at a fair he was awed, as though he had witnessed a magical transformation. And he set about transforming himself in the same way. But from the time he begins to court her, Sarah Ruth finds his tattoos contemptible: "Vanity of vanities," she says. Yet from the fact that she marries him, we can infer that she is attracted to him despite the tattoos. From both sides of the marriage, then, we find a pattern of action that goes against inclination, but no agreement about where bodily beauty is to be found. O. E. Parker is determined to compel such an agreement—to procure a tattoo that will elicit from this wife the wonder he has felt. Sarah Ruth, for her part, seems entirely oblivious to beauty. In the course of the story, Parker's puzzle is solved, at least for the reader, by the merging of the grotesque that repels yet fascinates him with the beauty he finds in tattoos. And the theological basis of this identification is the Incarnation.

The most striking feature of Sarah Ruth's face is her "icepick eyes." They are so designated in the first paragraph, and it is exactly this feature that Parker longs for during the one night he is away from her, waiting for the new tattoo to be completed. Her eyes remind him of the ones in the icon that the artist has yet to apply to his back, eyes that penetrate, rendering him "as transparent as the wing of a fly" (*CW* 669). The icon's eyes are like his wife's, only more so, we might say. Compared to the eyes he has seen in the tattooist's book, hers are "soft and dilatory" (*CW* 669). What the two pairs of eyes have in common is the ability to see through him—to peer into his very core. Although Parker himself does not recognize it, what drew him to the icon originally was this similarity, for as becomes apparent in the story's final episode, he has a deep desire to be known.

The similarity between wife and Christ is not coincidental—indeed, in the terms the story sets up, Sarah Ruth's power might be said to derive from the source the icon represents. She is a type of Christ in this regard, and the eyes establish the connection between the beauty Parker finds in the tattoos and the grotesque power of Sarah Ruth's visage and personality. They represent the continuing presence of Christ in the world—the God within each of us illuminated and confirmed by the Word made flesh. Thus the true power of the grotesque is the hidden life of Christ, redeeming the world despite the distortions of sin. Even in the visually repulsive, this seed of redemption is present, for the image of God, though obscured, is never erased.

Parker's desire for tattoos is revealed as proceeding from an intimation of this same fact of human nature. Having once seen tattoos that turned an ordinary man into a thing of wonder, he, too, would be so transformed. His unarticulated wish is for the tattoos to grant him a kind of supernatural luminosity—to give him "color." This desire leads him to have the face of Christ permanently joined to his skin, making him the reembodiment of Christ in a very direct way. Driven to the icon by his wife's hard-edged and iconoclastic biblicism and by the unexpected religious vision that he experienced after the tractor crash, he is pressed finally toward the spiritual transformation he unwittingly desired. But as O'Connor repeatedly indicates, there is no imitation of Christ without suffering. Getting the tattoo is a crucial symbolic gesture for Parker to make, but it is incomplete. Thus is Parker, like Haze, soon beaten, but with the difference that he is made to suffer for Christ's sake, at least symbolically, and again symbolically, Christ suffers with him.

In the final scene, Sarah Ruth—Christlike in her ability to see through Parker's self-deception—turns persecutor in her iconoclasm. Having wrung from him his true name, she strikes him repeatedly once she sees the new tattoo and hears his claim that this is "God." And it is the tattoo itself that bears the brunt of her wrath, so that large welts form "on the face of the tattooed Christ" (*CW* 674). The story leaves Parker, now chastised and truly named, leaning against a tree, "crying like a baby." His condition signals repentance and rebirth, and this change is directly tied to Christ's suffering, which Parker is made bodily to share; the welts on Christ's face are also welts on his back, a direct reminder of Jesus's scourging and of the fact that by his stripes we are healed.

The process of Parker's redemption thus includes his body. In fact, we might say that it is the vehicle of his spiritual renewal, for it literally takes on Christ in the form of the tattoo, and it allows him to join in Christ's pain. Two notions are necessary to make this connection work; one is allegory and the other is participation. Clearly, O'Connor is inviting the reader to find the Christological parallels I have described. Parker's story makes sense when it is placed in the pattern of Christ's passion. It is the Christ story that gives Parker's story its meaning, even as it also takes the reader to the anagogical level of Parker's participation in the life of God. The idea of participation itself is also crucial, for O'Connor suggests that the reality of Parker's salvation lies beyond words and beyond human cognition. More specifically, she suggests that Parker does not understand what has happened to him, and that his redemption does not require what our jurisprudence would call informed consent. His salvation is able to go forward without his comprehension because his participation in Christ is more than symbolic. Thus, his suffering not only *resembles* that of Christ, it *becomes* Christ's suffering by way of his tentative but genuine cooperation with the gift of grace that draws him to the icon. Parker willingly takes the needed initial step, even if his understanding never catches up. And this identification of his own suffering with Christ's agony is in turn made possible by the Incarnation, registered in the story through the enfleshed icon. God's union with creation in the Incarnation reasserts the unity of Being that had been assaulted by sin. Because of that connection, our participation with God across time is made possible, and Christ's action can become our own.

I have paired allegory with participation to make the point that, for O'Connor, what happens to Parker is not merely allusive or illustrative. What makes her stories mysterious is her conviction that the process of redemption can take place beyond a character's comprehension. Parker, for example, means more in the total context of the story than he does in his own world because he is a type. And further, his salvation can be accomplished without his recognition through a sacramental participation in Christ. Such a background is necessary to explain the otherwise puzzling fact that Parker undergoes no "conversion" or other manifestation of the moment of grace that O'Connor seems to have intended. At the end, we observe him from the outside as we did Haze, and we are shown only brokenness. Within the terms of his own psychology, Parker seems only to desire to please his wife and to gain some relief from her insistent demands. He gives no indication of consciously identifying his suffering with that of Christ, or indeed of answering to God in any direct way at all. It is only in his attempt to do the bidding of those "all-demanding eyes" in the icon, foreshadowed by the eyes of his wife, that he can be said to have chosen Christ at all. It is not, therefore, the bare assent of his will that marks him as a recipient of grace, though this is necessary, but the mystery in which he participates, primarily through his body. One is tempted to say that he is saved and doesn't know it. Parker is at once a sacramental sign for the reader and a central player in a great drama of which he is but dimly aware. He becomes a kind of icon himself, a window by which the reader may glimpse divine reality as it interpenetrates the earthly, redeeming and restoring it.

So important is the body and the enactment of divine drama that the spoken word in this story is at most a propaedeutic. When Parker at last fixes on the Byzantine Christ, "there was absolute silence" (*CW* 667). The sight of the icon brings silence—even in the poolroom in which Parker takes refuge. When Parker examines his tattooed back in the mirror, the eyes look at him, "enclosed in silence" (*CW* 670). Parker hopes that when Sarah Ruth sees the tattoo, she will be "struck speechless," but this hope proves vain. Sarah Ruth possesses not only icepick eyes, but a "sharp tongue," which she uses to bring him to judgment. Not only does she use her words to force him into confessing his true name (which she does through the door, unseen), but her final word is a condemnation of him as an idolator and of the icon as idolatrous. She seems incapable of seeing the divine, incarnated power apparent to her husband, even if he has beheld it only in a mirror. Her word has prepared him, but not herself, and within the dynamic of the story the purpose of speech is to bring words to an end, leaving only vision and contemplation. At the end of the story, she has "hardened" her eyes, while Obadiah Elihue has opened his to weep. And these tears of a broken man have much in common with the quicklime that Haze uses to blind himself, for in both stories it is the bodily refocusing of vision that leads toward redemption.

From Suffering to Redemption: "The Artificial Nigger" and "The Displaced Person"

The link between suffering and redemption, while present in *Wise Blood* and "Parker's Back," is more plainly laid out in two other stories, "The Artificial Nigger" and "The Displaced Person." In the first story, we find perhaps the clearest example of vicarious suffering in all of O'Connor's work, the shared suffering by which Christ makes atonement for sin. In the second story, we find in Mr. Guizac the closest thing to a Christ figure to be found in O'Connor's fiction, although, surprisingly, this character does not represent one engaged in an *imitatio Christi*.

"The Artificial Nigger" confronts us both with the pride that is for O'Connor the universal source of human rebellion and with the racism that is the South's more particular sin. The complementary if conflicting presumptuousness of grandfather and grandson are shown to be the root of racist attitudes toward the black people Nelson encounters for the first time on his day trip to Atlanta. For readers unfamiliar with O'Connor's penchant for irony, even the narrator seems complicitous in supporting Mr. Head's high opinion of himself at the beginning, using the moon to enhance his nobility and crediting him with the observation that "only with years does a man enter into that calm understanding of life that makes him a suitable guide for the young" (*CW* 210). He is compared to Vergil and the angel Raphael. Nelson, for his part, wins the first battle in their daily competition by arising before his grandfather, upstaging the old man and handing Mr. Head his initial reversal during a day of reversals. Mr. Head has two goals for the adventure: to show Nelson that the big city is not for him and to prove his own moral superiority—both goals meant to make the boy want to remain at home to care for the old man in his dotage. Nelson in turn wants to demonstrate that he does belong in the city, and he means to assert his independence of his grandfather.

The struggle between them quickly moves to the arena of race when Mr. Head offers his first reason why Nelson won't like the city: "It'll be full of niggers," he warns, adding, "You ain't ever seen a nigger" (*CW* 212). Black people are here presented as negative, and Nelson's ignorance of them is evidence of his callowness. These associations continue when he sees a black person on the train and fails to identify him as "a nigger," instead calling the stranger simply "a man." When this "mistake" provokes public ridicule from his grandfather, Nelson turns his resentment on the black man: "He felt that the Negro had deliberately walked down the aisle in order to make a fool of him and he hated him with a fierce raw hate; and also, he understood now why his grandfather disliked them" (*CW* 216). The salient point here is that the white boy has turned the black man into a scapegoat, projecting onto him guilt for his own mistake. Throughout the story, blacks represent both a kind of power (usually, a kind of worldly knowledge) and a kind of moral taint. The black waiter in the dining car prevents the bumpkins from touring the kitchen, telling them, "Passengers are not allowed in the kitchen." But Mr. Head shoots back that the cockroaches would run the passengers out, implying that the waiter is hiding filth. In the same scene Mr. Head tells Nelson, "They rope them off," suggesting that segregation is a quarantine to protect white passengers from contamination. This pattern continues when the pair gets lost in a "colored" part of town. Mr. Head resolutely refuses to ask a black person for directions. The more sensible but desperate boy finally approaches a black woman standing in a doorway, to whom he feels strangely attracted. After teasing him briefly, she supplies the needed information, but Mr. Head has to drag Nelson away, for he has nearly fallen in a trance, "as if he were reeling down through a pitchblack tunnel" (*CW* 223). Nelson is drawn to what he fears, sensing something in this powerful but despised Other that he needs. Having admitted his insufficiency and turned to a black person for help, Nelson suffers the ridicule of his grandfather, who must suffer a much greater blow to his moral standing before being confronted with his own powerful symbol of the other. Mr. Head denies his grandson in a betrayal that is forgiven only after Mr. Head has cried out that he is lost, accepted the help of another stranger, and finds himself standing, with Nelson, before a piece of lawn statuary.

The "artificial nigger" itself is a dilapidated ornament, resembling both Nelson and Mr. Head yet clearly intended to represent a black man. "He was meant to look happy," but the statue's deterioration has given him "a wild look of misery instead" (*CW* 229). This figure of humiliation, which seems now to include them in its signification as well as the blacks they have both feared and despised, brings the two together: "They stood gazing at the artificial Negro as if they were faced with some great mystery, some monument to another's victory that brought them together in their common defeat" (*CW* 230). Clearly the figure refers not only to them and the black people they have feared, but to Christ as the ultimate source of reconciliation. And the key element they have in common is misery. Suffering unites sinners both with the unjustly maligned black race and also with the rejected savior. When Mr. Head arrives at home, he is given credit for understanding that mercy grows out of "agony, which is not denied to any man and which is given in strange ways to children." Further, he sees that agony "was all a man could carry into death to give his Maker and he suddenly burned with shame that he had so little of it to take with him" (*CW* 230).

Four assertions about suffering seem to be implicit in these passages. First, triumphant suffering is undeserved—the suffering of a scapegoat. What distinguishes the misery of the two white characters from that of the black person and Christ is that it is caused by their own sin. Mr. Head and Nelson are both "defeated"; the other who is victorious could be either Christ himself or the black race collectively, and victimization is the trait they share. Second, suffering is necessary to provide conviction of sin; Mr. Head's "agony" leads him to recognize simultaneously his sinful condition and God's mercy in removing it. Third, this suffering is not merely consciousness-raising. It is the crucial point of connection, or more specifically of participation, with the suffering of Christ that provides the triumph over sin. And fourth, suffering can be shared, so to speak: the suffering of another—specifically, the righteous suffering of the black race and of Christ—can be redemptive for oneself.

Each of these claims is radical in its own way, but perhaps most counterintuitive and potentially offensive is the last. Vicarious suffering seems an oxymoron. Pain is perhaps the most personal and incommunicable of human experiences. One can be sympathetic to the pain of another, but to say one suffers "for" another can only be wildly metaphorical, except in the sense of one standing in the place of another who is about to have pain inflicted upon him. But clearly, it is not this strict "substitutionary" sense that O'Connor has in mind. Blacks may be said to suffer *from* the sins of whites, but not *for* human sin in any direct way, as though God were punishing them for the crimes of others. No, the key here once again is the notion of participation. Innocent suffering, serving as an imitation of Christ, provides the Incarnational basis in current human life for our participation in the ongoing drama of salvation. Those who suffer the undeserved consequences of human sin share with Christ the divine mission of taking into themselves and so negating the brokenness that afflicts God's good creation. Like Christ, southern blacks are oppressed by corporate sin, of which they are innocent victims. And like Christ, they have not responded in kind to their enemies, interrupting the cycle of sin evident between Nelson and his grandfather. Insofar as their suffering is the price of challenging this deadly cycle, blacks may be said to suffer *for* their white brothers and sisters, making present in another form the atoning action of Jesus.

The pattern of sin exhibited by the two rural whites reveals why this suffering is necessary. As Ralph Wood points out in *The Christ-Haunted South,* Mr. Head and Nelson, in their constant and often comic battle of wills, actually carry out the ancient and universal attempt to supplant God. Their will to power, by a turn Nietzsche and Dostoevsky would have appreciated, informs even their morality, with Nelson clinging to Mr. Head's betrayal as a means to keep the upper hand on his grandfather. Without the insertion of a kind of love neither has known, the cycle of domination and revenge will know no end. The love that accepts defeat without retaliating, and that does so for the sake of the offender, is the only kind that will do, and it is this love that is symbolized by the dilapidated statue.

But one additional issue must be addressed before we leave "The Artificial Nigger": power. On the face of it, the analogy between Christ and

the black person would seem to break down here. The cross leads to the
Resurrection, when God's power over sin and death is exercised and the
"victory" O'Connor alludes to is accomplished. Yet at the time O'Connor writes (1954), blacks have very little political power in the South, the
fight against Jim Crow having barely begun. This powerlessness is trou-
bling on a number of levels. Since they lack the power to refuse suffering, blacks cannot be said to choose it, as Christ does. Likewise, it is difficult to say that black people suffer willingly for the sins of the white
man. These are serious difficulties, as is the fact that Mr. Head retains his
racist attitude after his moment of grace. But on a more directly theological level, no human victim possesses God's power to negate sin. Christ
not only accepts the consequences of sin, he defeats it, as no other scapegoat could do. He is the sovereign victim, uniquely able to conquer
through his sacrificial death. Thus there is inequality within the analogy.
The black person might more accurately be said to be a type of Christ,
and the "artificial nigger" a type of the crucifix, for only by this referent
does either figure gain its full significance.

Interestingly, power is exactly the symbolic resonance blacks have in
the story that they lack in the historical reality of the setting. In their three
encounters with black people before they stand before the statue, Nelson
and Mr. Head register power of some sort. The well-dressed "coffee colored" man on the train is clearly more prosperous than they; the waiter
forbids them entrance to the kitchen; the woman in the doorway holds
a great erotic-maternal fascination for Nelson, as well as knowing how to
direct them back to the train station. Thus is the statue shocking in part
because of the contrast, for it dramatizes the black person's humiliation. Theologically the contrast allows O'Connor to suggest Christ's self-
emptying sacrifice that enables the "action of mercy" Mr. Head feels in
the penultimate paragraph. In this humiliation, signaled by but exceeding
that of the black person, there is a hidden power that forgives as it burns
and consumes the pride that stands behind all sin.

Although in "The Artificial Nigger" we find in the black person a type
of Christ, and particularly of his suffering on behalf of humankind in order to break the power of sin, a nearer example of a Christ figure is to be
found in "The Displaced Person." Mr. Guizac, the displaced person of the
title, is more deliberately and directly linked to Christ than any other figure in O'Connor's fiction, and for our purposes the crucial analogue
is the manner of his death. However, from the outset we must note that

O'Connor is not seeking to portray a fictionalized, updated Christ, in the manner of Dostoevsky's idiot or Faulkner's corporal. As I argue elsewhere, for reasons such as those advanced by Hans Frei in *The Identity of Jesus Christ,* O'Connor scrupulously avoided direct depictions of Christ.[13] Even so, while the distinction between the Polish immigrant and the Jewish peasant is consistently maintained, the analogue is also carefully established. Perhaps rather than call Mr. Guizac a Christ figure, it would be better to term him yet another type of Christ.

Although such typology is prepared for throughout, the clearest identification occurs near the end of the story, when Mrs. McIntyre, the owner of the farm where the refugees have found a seeming refuge, interrupts the priest who is trying to work religious instruction into the conversation: "As far as I'm concerned, Christ was just another D.P." (*CW* 320). Rather than establishing this Displaced Person's Christlike disposition, what the story draws out is the similarity in external circumstances. Mr. Guizac is "extra"; he doesn't "fit in"; he is the stranger who, while doing good to others, is ultimately despised and rejected. And most tellingly, he is made to suffer a cruel death through the guilty collusion of those who resent him. In fact, at the allegorical level one might treat this story as a recapitulation of a Gospel Passion narrative, but told from the point of view of the crowds.

Mrs. McIntyre is initially an enthusiastic champion of her new tenant, declaring, "That man is my salvation!" (*CW* 294). By way of contrast, Mrs. Shortley, with her more pharisaical disposition, is suspicious of the Polish family from the beginning, hinting that Mr. Guizac is an agent of the devil. Both women, along with the men who work the farm, judge the D.P. from the standpoint of narrow self-interest. Mrs. Shortley, however, is particularly adept at supplying a religious justification for her hatred of the labor competition. She prophesies against the Guizacs, who represent a religion that "hasn't had the nonsense reformed out of it." Significantly, the "vision" that she receives supporting her view is full of bodies: "The children of wicked nations will be butchered. . . . Legs where arms should be, foot to face, ear in the palm of hand. Who will remain whole?" (*CW* 301). This prophecy bespeaks both her nightmare visions of newsreel footage from the Nazi concentration camps of World War II and, ironically, the manner of her own imminent death, but she intends it as a de-

13. John D. Sykes, Jr., "Christian Apologetic Uses of the Grotesque in John Irving and Flannery O'Connor."

nunciation of the havoc she believes the Guizacs to be wreaking all around her. Bodily violence and dismemberment will prove to be the anagogical key to the story as well, but before that culmination, Mrs. Shortley's condemnation of the Guizacs comes generally to be shared.

Mr. Shortley and the two black tenants see the economic threat; Mrs. McIntyre reverses her position once she discovers that Mr. Guizac has unwittingly violated the South's deepest taboo: he has recruited Sulk, the young black man, to marry his white niece, and so rescue her from another refugee camp in Europe. Mrs. McIntyre concludes that the Guizacs must go. Interestingly, this rejection, too, has to do with the body—specifically with joining together bodies that are supposed to remain separate. Mrs. McIntyre turns on Mr. Guizac not out of strict economic interest, but to preserve the social order. The "temple" this man threatens to destroy is the very social order that structures Mrs. McIntyre's world. If left unchecked, he will unwittingly dismember the body politic, and Mrs. McIntyre knows she must stop him.

Although there is no trial scene as such, Mrs. McIntyre does have a confrontation with Mr. Guizac, and later she presents her full case to the same priest who first brought the Guizac family to her farm, feeling afterward that she "has triumphed over him." Yet, like Pilate, she cannot quite bring herself to pronounce doom on the accused. The aggrieved Mr. Shortley, agitating to take back his old job from Mr. Guizac, can only "wait on the hand of God to strike." Mr. Guizac is indeed struck down, but only with the help of all the principals.

The Polish man's death is a kind of crucifixion, in the sense that he is innocent of wrongdoing yet undergoes a public execution of sorts, dying an excruciating and lingering death. Mr. Guizac is undoubtedly a scapegoat for sins that the four conspirators will not acknowledge. This is most clearly the case with Mr. Shortley, who nonsensically maintains that since the Polish man wears spectacles resembling those worn by the German soldier who threw a grenade at Mr. Shortley in the war, Mr. Guizac, too, is the enemy. In this comical non sequitur, Mr. Shortley neatly ties his hatred to defense of the social order. According to him, the refugee is an outsider who threatens "our way of life," and thus is no different from those armed aggressors who, in fact, displaced Mr. Guizac to begin with.

The role of the body in this entire drama is so prominent that it leads us to the story's anagogical meaning. The "passion" of Mr. Guizac completes the prophecy spoken by Mrs. Shortley. Mr. Guizac has indeed provoked the social devastation the vision forecast, and Mrs. Shortley's own death is the emblem of it, as she during her fatal stroke grabs the limbs of other family members who are jammed into their car. But it is the disruption of the body politic that is the true prophetic referent of the vision. The real reason for this disruption, therefore, is the universal rejection of the one body that is broken. That is, failure to confront their own sin has led the members of this little community to repeat that primal rejection of Incarnated grace that led to Christ's crucifixion. At the same time, this tragic reenactment also provides a renewed outpouring of grace, making possible both repentance and forgiveness.

Despite the fact that the "community" is scattered, as indeed this murderous clique deserves to be, Mrs. McIntyre is driven by guilt to physical extremity—or, more theologically put, to conviction of sin. This change, though negative in its effects on her health, is spiritually hopeful, for it shows she has accepted the truth about herself. And finally, Mrs. McIntyre appears to be on the threshold of joining the Church, which is literally the last word of the story. Beholding Mr. Guizac's broken body has led her to the body of Christ, the one true and eternal human community.

As if to confirm this pattern of imagery, O'Connor has previously had the priest administer the Eucharistic wafer—the sacramental broken body—to the dying man while Mrs. McIntyre watches. On that occasion, she was the outsider while family and priest bent over the dying man, forming an unbroken circle. Now she is invited into the circle of those who bow to the sacramentally broken body of Christ, united through him to the communion of saints. And perhaps, as Jill Peláez Baumgaertner thinks, the denouement of the story shows Mrs. McIntyre partaking of sacramental nourishment: "The final emblem of the story shows the priest arriving with his bag of breadcrumbs for the peacocks, feeding them, and then sitting by Mrs. McIntyre's bedside, expounding doctrines of the Church, feeding her bit by bit, week after week—breaking the bread of life. This is sacrament, the outward and visible sign of an inner and spiritual truth" (CW 97–98).[14]

Evil as the Privation of Good: The Violent Bear It Away

In "The Displaced Person" as in "The Artificial Nigger," we find O'Connor turning her theological attention from the penitent to the source of his or her hope in the work of Christ. As human suffering is identified

14. Jill Peláez Baumgaertner, Flannery O'Connor: A Proper Scaring, 97–98.

with and lifted up into the divine nature, it becomes redemptive, even though the characters in the stories are sometimes only dimly aware of this providential operation. In all of O'Connor's work, sin is never far in the background, constantly asserting itself in the rebellious unbelief that produces betrayal and even murder from those who count themselves "good country people." But in O'Connor's second novel, *The Violent Bear It Away,* the nature of evil comes in for extraordinary treatment. And what we find there is a working out of the Augustinian claim that evil is the privation of good. Both the boy prophet who fulfills his mission despite himself and the uncle who tries to stop him are drawn back to a good they cannot live without, and which they desperately require even as they resist it tooth and nail.

Far from being the metaphysical dualist that the Manichean charge makes her out to be, O'Connor is a powerful proponent of evil's utter dependence upon good. The very nihilists who regularly animate her fiction are typically fierce in exact proportion to their fear of what they reject. And, as we shall see in more detail, the devil himself, when he appears, has a parasitic existence, feeding on what he attempts to corrupt. Indeed, the accusation sometimes made against O'Connor that she is of the devil's party unawares springs in part from the way in which even the most twisted characters in her fiction remain susceptible to grace. Just as suffering, which both modern and postmodern temperaments take to be indisputably evil, is in O'Connor's work a means to redemption, so is evil itself presented as a deficiency to be supplied rather than a thing in its own right. Rather than reveling in evil or confusing it with good, as she appears to some readers to do, O'Connor actually denigrates evil by showing how it is constantly taken up into the good. In the strictest sense, evil does not exist; it is the "impossible possibility," as Karl Barth termed it. And in this regard, O'Connor is in accord with ancient Christian sources, which John Milbank summarizes in this way: "[E]vil for the Christian tradition was radically without cause—indeed it was not even self-caused, but was rather the (impossible) refusal of cause."[15]

For all her exposure of sin, O'Connor is opposed to what postmodern theorists, reflecting upon the Holocaust and other twentieth-century atrocities, have called "radical evil"—an evil with its own foothold in being, so that "annihilation [is] pursued perversely for its own sake, as an alternative end in itself."[16] To O'Connor's mind, not even the horror of the

15. John Milbank, *Being Reconciled: Ontology and Pardon,* 17.
16. Ibid., 1.

gas "showers" is enough to thwart the goodness of creation or the sovereignty of God. Evil is not the result either of a faulty universe or even, when properly understood, of human freedom. It is the nothing paradoxically held in place by God's "No." Thus in O'Connor's work, the emphasis falls not upon evil as a sort of opposite and equal number to good, but on sin understood as offense against God and thus as a defection from the good. In O'Connor as in Augustine, the basis of sin is precisely a turning away from true freedom into false freedom. True freedom lies in the power to envision the good and move toward it. False freedom is the self-governing autonomy that serves as the modern, Enlightenment-inspired model of moral man.

Closely allied to the conviction that evil is privation of good, therefore, is the unpopular corollary that the human will in its fallen state is neither pure, neutral, nor autonomous. Instead, it is weakened and easily distracted, lacking the vision and capacity to pursue its deepest desire, which is not for itself, but for God. Within the Augustinian Catholicism that O'Connor represents, the problem with the will is not that it has become corrupted, as the Reformers tended to say, but that it has been rendered feckless. We suffer not from excess of bad will, but from the deficiency of a diminished will. What grace supplies in order to rescue us is renewed desire—a supernaturally invigorated longing that frees the will.

In the course of *The Violent Bear It Away*, we encounter a prophet whose will is freed despite his stout resistance to the operation of grace. What may seem a compulsion is, when viewed within O'Connor's theological framework, a liberation from the false would-be autonomy that leads him temporarily to embrace an evil that is nothing. By contrast, he is measured against the great uncle who prepared him for his call and the uncle who successfully evaded his own. In the process, the measure of evil is also taken through the demonic presences young Francis Marion Tarwater encounters.

A dialectic concerning freedom is set up in the novel almost from the beginning. Upon the death of old Mason Tarwater, the fourteen-year-old nephew is faced with his first adult decision: whether to obey the injunction of his great uncle to bury him or to defy the dead man and strike out on his own. According to common usage, this decision could be expressed as one lying between obedience and freedom. But O'Connor quickly problematizes the question of freedom. In his memories of the man who raised him, the boy recalls old Tarwater insisting, "I saved you to be free, your own self!" (*CW* 339). He says this by way of discouraging the boy from seeking out his only other living blood relative, a secularized uncle who has repudiated the great uncle's teaching. Old Tarwater asserts that the free-thinking schoolteacher is actually bent on bringing others into a kind of mental bondage. For a brief time, the old man had accepted his nephew's offer of charity, only to discover that the nephew's real purpose was to scrutinize his relative in order to write up a case study of him for publication. His chagrin is registered in this recollection: "The old man had not known when he went there to live that every living thing that passed through the nephew's eyes into his head was turned by his brain into a book or paper or chart" (*CW* 341). Old Tarwater is determined that the boy will not endure a similar reduction, and that is the principal reason he kidnapped the boy and brought him deep into the woods. But not only is the boy to be free from pseudoscientific dehumanizing, he is also to be free for God. The boy "was trained by a prophet for prophecy"; "he was left free for the pursuit of wisdom" (*CW* 340). Old Tarwater gives his freedom speech a decidedly theological conclusion: "You were born into bondage and baptized into freedom, into the death of the Lord, into the death of the Lord Jesus Christ" (*CW* 342).

The other side of the argument over freedom is put forward by the nephew Rayber, who tells young Tarwater, "You don't know what freedom is" (*CW* 400). He sets out to redefine the term, offering to free his nephew from the very baptism that he himself has cast off. Rayber says he can free the boy from stultifying belief in a life beyond this life and thus a mindless obedience to the dictates of a dead father figure. But what Rayber is freeing the boy for remains much more vague. He can appeal only to the "dignity of man." He summarizes, "The great dignity of man is his ability to say: I am born once and no more. What I can see and do for myself and my fellowman in this life is all of my portion and I'm content with it. It's enough to be a man" (*CW* 437). But this freedom is largely empty of content. It amounts to a kind of brave self-sufficiency in which there is no higher good than the assertion of one's autonomy. Freedom for Rayber is its own end.

The danger of this libertarian notion of freedom is well illustrated in Rayber's struggle against the irrational love he feels for his mentally retarded son, Bishop. This love is exactly the "desire" Milbank identifies as the supernatural gift of grace that redirects the sinner to God. To Rayber, this love is "irrational," a sign of "madness" precisely because it goes against the grain of his cherished notion of autonomy. He fears that "[i]f, without thinking, he lent himself to it, he would feel suddenly a morbid surge of the love that terrified him—powerful enough to throw him to the ground in an act of idiot praise" (*CW* 401). Only by a constant effort of the will does Rayber keep himself from this "insanity." The pull is strong, not only because it strikes him as though from an outside force, but also because it brings him joy. In addition, Rayber finds himself receiving a second unwanted gift that Augustine believes was lost in the Fall: vision of the good. This irrational love begins with Bishop, but it does not end with him: "Anything he looked at too long could bring it on. . . . It could be a stick or a stone, the line of a shadow, the absurd old man's walk of a starling crossing the sidewalk" (*CW* 401). Likewise, he longs to be seen with the same kind of vision, wishing to be looked on by his deceased uncle's eyes "with their impossible vision of a world transfigured" (*CW* 401).

Since he is determined to maintain the control that this love would deny him, Rayber walks "a very narrow line between madness and emptiness" (*CW* 401). And although ideally he will maintain his balance and retain his "freedom" above these two alternatives, if forced to one side, he is determined to choose emptiness, and thereby avoid surrender to anything beyond himself. For O'Connor, the choice of emptiness amounts to embracing nihilism, and nihilism is thus the logical consequence of libertarian freedom bent on defending its autonomous kingdom at any cost. In Rayber's case, this scenario is acted out in his decision to drown his "useless" son, who has already been abandoned by his mother. The boy clearly has no prospect of becoming a fully developed, rational, autonomous human being himself, and thus according to the creed Rayber attempts to live by, Bishop is not human at all. Though Rayber never uses the word, Bishop is a candidate for euthanasia. It follows that, with Bishop removed from his life, Rayber could hope to be free of the irrational love that tempts him. The emptiness of Rayber's notion of freedom issues in the ultimate act of negation: murder. But when it comes to the deed itself, Rayber lacks the courage of his Raskolnikovean conviction. With the boy on the verge of death, Rayber has "a moment of complete terror in which he envisioned his life without the child" (*CW* 419). Bystanders on the beach help him effect a rescue, but within the terms of Rayber's philosophy, the murder of Bishop remains the deed undone.

Young Tarwater's dialectic of freedom is less cerebral and more active. Warned by the instruction of the old prophet, the teenager remains wary of Rayber's attempt to convert him to a new way of thinking. Deeper than any theoretical difference is young Tarwater's desire to be free of any personal control. He wants to defy the dead great uncle simply to show that he is his own man. He likewise bristles at Rayber's attempts to shepherd him, emphatically rejecting the school psychologist's offer to be a "father" to him now that the old man is dead. And so the struggle within young Tarwater is not so much between the opposing views of old Tarwater and Rayber as it is between self-sufficiency and submission. The main opposition to the remembered voice of old Tarwater is that of a "stranger" who soon becomes the boy's "friend," the demonic tempter who seeks to nurture the seeds of rebellion. Virtually the first thing the stranger leads young Tarwater to say is "Now I can do anything I want to" (*CW* 345) since the old man is dead. But this freedom, the freedom in which, as Ivan Karamazov might say, "everything is permitted," proves to be as dangerously empty as the freedom Rayber pursues, and it is indeed Rayber who pushes young Tarwater to decisive extremity.

When young Tarwater arrives at Rayber's door, he has already failed in one of the two commands given to him by the old prophet: with encouragement from his smooth-talking "friend," he has left Powderhead without burying old Tarwater. But the second commission still hangs over him. Mason Tarwater charged Francis Marion Tarwater with the prophet's job of baptizing Bishop. Although he is determined to flout this demand as well, young Tarwater strongly feels the force of it. On the other hand, Rayber exerts psychological coercion to break young Tarwater's will and bring him around to his own way of thinking. His most effective tactic is to isolate Tarwater in a boat on a lake, and to use fishing as a pretext to hammer away at the boy, who seemingly can't escape. "Every day you remind me more of the old man," he tells him. "You're just like him. You have his future before you" (*CW* 439). Since young Tarwater is resolved to avoid the control of both would-be fathers, Rayber's sentence strikes a nerve, but Tarwater finds a means to escape: he jumps overboard and swims for shore, answering accusation with action. What Rayber takes as a sign of his near success is actually the spur to Tarwater's own solution. During the meal following this crisis, Rayber tries to drive his point home by bringing Tarwater into the realm of "choice"—the kind of freedom that serves as his ersatz religion: "I want you to make the choice and not simply be driven by a compulsion you don't understand. What we understand, we can control" (*CW* 450). But young Tarwater, who does indeed yearn for complete autonomy, has his own notion about how to achieve it. Of his compulsion to follow the old man's bidding, the younger Tarwater says, "I can pull it up by the roots, once and for all. I can do something. I ain't like you. All you can do is think what you would have done if you had done it. Not me. I can do it. I can act" (*CW* 451).

And act he does, but in a way that curves back on himself, in just the way that Augustine demonstrated sin to operate. Tarwater lures Bishop into a boat, and, with Rayber's undiscerning permission, rows him to the other side of the lake. We learn later that out of Rayber's sight, Tarwater performs a double act. He drowns the boy, but as he holds him under the suffocating waters he also speaks the words of baptism. In this way, he carries out the fate of both earthly "fathers," intentionally completing the murder that Rayber attempted, and unintentionally completing the work of the fanatical old man. This ultimate act of "freedom" is at once radical and self-defeating. Tarwater has indeed struck a blow at the ties that bind him to anything except the dictates of his own sweet will. By killing his cousin, he slashes the bonds of blood, of animal affection, and of natural law. At the same time, he proves that his will is not sufficient to wrench him loose from the grip of God. The words of blessing come out of his mouth against his own defiant will, announcing new life even as his hands destroy the old.

It is Tarwater's failure to carry out the full resolution of his will that in the end makes possible his future redemption, just as it is Rayber's failure, and his desire for "intolerable pain" when he hears Bishop's dying cries, that provide the only hopeful signs for his future. For the will, torn from its orientation to God and thus from the good, is no longer fully free. Its true freedom paradoxically appears as compulsion—the divine grace of desire for God. And it is this desire, present in him as a literal hunger, that leads Tarwater back to his great uncle's grave, to hear and accept a new commission that will mark his having taken up the mantle of prophecy from the dead man.

So we find in O'Connor that the will itself is an example of evil as the privation of good. Diverted from its natural goal, weakened in its desire for God, and diminished in its vision of the good, it becomes liable to an ultimately nihilistic worship of its own autonomy. Even more direct, however, is the portrayal of evil in the form of the devil, who appears in several guises. The unseen "stranger" who later becomes "friend" sometimes speaks with Tarwater's own voice, representing a kind of satanic anti-conscience. He begins his tempting work by denying his own existence, saying to the boy, "No no no, there ain't no such thing as a devil. I can tell you that from my own self-experience. . . . It ain't Jesus or the devil.

It's Jesus or *you*" (*CW* 354). What this revealing passage discloses, in addition to the plug for false autonomy, is a strategy of negation. The devil insists that he does not exist, and in a certain sense this is true. Although O'Connor is straightforward in her assertion that the devil is real, this reality is of course derivative. And in his very purpose of destroying the good work of creation, he is bent on nothingness. So while he does negatively exist and thus is lying to Tarwater, in a deeper sense he is bent upon nothingness, as the "No no no" hints.

This negativity is played out in two additional episodes. Later, in the city park, where young Tarwater feels the compulsion to baptize Bishop when he slips Rayber's grip to play in a fountain, Tarwater's friend reverses religious language to dissuade him: "You have to take hold and put temptation behind you. If you baptize once, you'll be doing it the rest of your life. . . . Save yourself while the hour of salvation is at hand" (*CW* 433). The idea of drowning Bishop itself is presented to Tarwater as a perversion of baptism. Then, in his final scathing encounter with the demonic, this time in the form of the man in the lavender shirt who offers him a lift, Tarwater suffers the bitter consequences of perversion. Drugged by spiked liquor that he declares to be "better than the Bread of Life!" (*CW* 471), Tarwater becomes the victim of a homosexual rape.

Certainly for O'Connor, as for Dante, homosexual intercourse is itself unnatural, a turning of the right desire for bodily and procreative concourse with one's sexual other into a sterile union with one's own kind, in this case, an unconscious and thus corpselike boy. The man's act is thus necrophiliac as well as sodomitical and pedophiliac. But the greater wrong here is Tarwater's violation: he is literally used against his will in the most intimate of ways. Having spiritually seduced Tarwater into murder, in this final encounter he seduces him sexually, concluding the meeting with what we might call date rape. Having initially gained Tarwater's cooperation, he incapacitates his will entirely, rendering him a volitionless object of pleasure. When the stranger leaves, his skin has "acquired a faint pink tint as if he had refreshed himself on blood" (*CW* 472), a final parasitic image implying that, like a vampire, the devil sustains his own life only by preying upon the life of others.

It is hardly coincidental that in her most direct depiction of personified evil O'Connor should progress from disembodied to embodied form. The devil begins as a voice, but he ends as a yellow-haired man wearing a lavender shirt and a thin black suit. Evil exists as the privation of good, but its particular nothingness takes both spiritual and physical shape, for it is a distortion of creation. And for O'Connor, all of earthly creation is affected by evil. Just as Tarwater's rebelliousness issues in a violent act of his own hands, so does his seduction into evil culminate with his own physical violation. And on the other side of his humiliation, it is the fire that purges the woods, the earth of his great uncle's grave, and the hunger within him that serve as points of connection between him and the God he will now serve. He throws himself to the ground and presses his face into the dirt of the grave where the old prophet's corpse lies. Only then does he hear the words of command that commission him and cause him to rise to a new life. The message comes not audibly but palpably: "The words were as silent as seeds opening one at a time in his blood" (*CW* 478). As we have seen in other representative works, in her portrayals of redemption as well as of evil, O'Connor displays the body as the site on which the drama of salvation is played out.

4

O'Connor on Divine Self-Disclosure
Eucharist as Revelation

ΩΩ

A
s I have tried to show, O'Connor's notions of suffering, redemption, and evil are tied inextricably to the body through her
understanding of the Christian doctrines of Incarnation, Atonement, and Creation. But even more crucially, her work points to the central sacramental instance of Christ's body, the Eucharist. One could helpfully see all of her work as pointing to that mystery that was the focus of
her own life and worship: the consecrated bread and wine that have become the body and blood of Christ. She could hardly have been more
blunt than in her declaration to a friend in a letter that the Eucharist "is
the center of existence for me; all the rest of life is expendable" (*HB* 125).
In considering O'Connor's work, it is revealing to note that, for the
church fathers, the word *mystery* itself, so important in her occasional
prose, refers to the Eucharist by way of its Greek derivation *musterion,* "secret rites." Of course the term has a wider designation in her usage, but
it seems to me that this ancient reference is the heart of the matter for
her. In a famous epistolary outburst on the Eucharist, O'Connor report-
ed saying to Mary McCarthy at a literary cocktail party, "If it's just a symbol, I say the hell with it" (*HB* 125). We might say that the whole of her
work seeks to provoke the conviction that the Eucharist is indeed the core
of earthly reality—the "place" where God is most fully and palpably present in daily life. "This is Christ's body broken for you"—these words of
consecration might stand as the motto for O'Connor's fiction.

The Eucharistic nature of O'Connor's fiction manifests itself in three
ways: in attention to broken bodies, as we have already begun to see; in
its emphasis upon mystery as transformation; and finally, in its privileging
of sight over hearing as the means to revelation. The roots of this dispo-

sition to sight run deep in the history of Western theory (a word that is itself derived from a Greek term for *spectator*), but they are also present in O'Connor's biography and especially in the Roman Catholicism of her formative years. During the performance of the Tridentine Mass of pre–Vatican II Catholicism, the lay worshipper took in meaning principally through her eyes, watching the priest, who officiated facing the altar with his back to the worshippers. The liturgy was said in Latin. At certain points in the rite, as in the praying of the secret prayer and the fraction of the Host before the priest's communion, the priest actually prayed silently. The mystery of the consecration was "revealed" not with words, but with a gesture, when the priest lifted the Host up to God in plain sight of the congregants. Sounds provided context for the moment that was taken in visually: the familiar yet foreign words ("*Hoc est enim corpus meum*," "This is my body") and the ringing of the sanctus bell directing attention to the climactic event, which for the worshipper was visual.[1]

This drive to the visual and the imagistic is also to be found in the modernist aesthetic that shaped O'Connor in its New Critical form, as we saw in an earlier chapter. In fact, although it has been overlooked, the conversation O'Connor reports in her letter actually hints at exactly this point of connection. McCarthy says that the Host, which as a child she believed to contain the Holy Ghost, she now believes to be a symbol, and "a pretty good one." O'Connor hears this comment as a rejection of what for her is the central fact of Christian worship and devotion. But one might also hear it as an affirmation of the literary value of the concrete image. While O'Connor is understandably angry over the theological implications of the remark, McCarthy's aesthetic distancing of herself from religious commitment is also an example of investing the literary with religious overtones. In other words, behind the comment lies McCarthy's modernist allegiance to the Romantic Image, an allegiance O'Connor shared with her.

We might think in this regard of another sometime Irish Catholic, James Joyce, in his use of Eucharistic imagery in his early fiction. In "Araby," a story that O'Connor studied at Iowa from the New Critical textbook *Understanding Fiction,* Joyce uses the religious sensitivity of his ado-

---

1. Latin and English texts of the Tridentine Mass may be found on the Internet Web site encyclopedia.thefreedictionary.com. This site also contains a link to serial photographs of this liturgy being said. Although services in the vernacular are the norm for Roman Catholic practice since the Second Vatican Council (1962–1965), the Tridentine or "traditional" Mass still has its staunch adherents among Catholic traditionalists.

lescent protagonist to heighten the boy's romantic illusions about girls. He imagines himself bearing the image of the girl he cherishes like a chalice through the crowded streets of Dublin, a detail to which Brooks and Warren draw attention. In "Araby," Eucharistic imagery is used to highlight the way the boy has employed religious symbolism to sublimate sexual desire. What O'Connor does in the story she had in mind when she recalled the literary cocktail party is the reverse of Joyce. In "A Temple of the Holy Ghost," O'Connor follows a young protagonist for whom the mystery of sex is ultimately explained in terms of the Eucharist. By so doing, O'Connor appropriates the techniques of modernist aesthetic into her own Christian orthodoxy.[2]

The Eucharistic cast of O'Connor's fiction is thus most evident in this, the one story where the Mass is directly described. The epiphany of the story occurs at precisely the moment when the Host is elevated, when the twelve-year-old girl from whose point of view the story is told connects the consecrated wafer with the hermaphrodite in the freak show she has heard about from her older cousins. At this moment, the story establishes a link between the present, earthly bodies that have attracted the girl's curiosity and the body of Christ, of which other stories, notably "The Displaced Person," provide a type. The link is the Host.

"A Temple of the Holy Ghost": Two Sexes, One Body

The particular feature of bodily human life that comes to the fore at the beginning of "A Temple of the Holy Ghost" is not suffering, but sexuality. The two fourteen-year-old second cousins visiting for the weekend from their convent school are preoccupied with boys, a subject that has never interested the younger girl. Sex becomes a metaphor for knowledge in this coming-of-age story, but not in the usual way. Here, sexual experience does not provide awakening, but rather discovery of sexual difference leads to new insight into God's nature. The transformation that takes place in the protagonist begins with new knowledge about sex, but

2. The point I am making here is similar to one made by Carol Shloss in *Flannery O'Connor's Dark Comedies* in connection with epiphany. Shloss notes that for Joyce, Woolf, and other modernists, revelation is not an insight conveyed from outside by a transcendent God, but rather a sudden connection made by human consciousness. The power to generate such epiphanies is the power of the artist, who in Stephen Dedalus's words in *A Portrait of the Artist as a Young Man* "converts the daily bread of experience into the radiant body of everlasting life" (240). My contention is that O'Connor is intentionally reversing this process of subjectivizing both the Eucharist and revelation.

more importantly, it is a moment of grace—a change triggered by the sacred transformation of the Host.

The girl's curiosity, like the story's title, is drawn from the inside joke the giggling teenagers invoke by calling themselves temples. A nun has told them they can stop the untoward advances of boys in the backseats of automobiles by telling them, "I am a Temple of the Holy Ghost!" This Pauline allusion (1 Cor. 6:19), itself metaphorical, makes an assertion that will be amplified at the conclusion—the body is holy, indwelt by God. The nun sets this assertion in the context of sex. Unfortunately, she makes the mistake of "setting the spiritual in opposition to the sexual," as Richard Giannone points out.[3] Holiness, she seems to say, makes girls sexually unattractive to boys, or at least it prevents boys from acting on their sexual impulses. Sexual contact would be a defilement of the bodily temple. The girls understandably think this advice naïve, as is the nun's assumption that the girls have no interest in boys on their own accounts. Yet the nun's assertion is in the long run justified, albeit in a manner the nun would be unlikely to approve, for it is echoed by the hermaphrodite. The hermaphrodite's explanation provides the grounds for affirming the holiness of the body in whatever form, and in whatever sex or combination of sexes. The hermaphrodite's condition of containing both sexes within him/herself also offers a powerful analogue to the unity of humanity as represented in the single body of Christ.

The first movement of the story might be characterized as one of disruption and division in the life of the unnamed girl whose consciousness serves as the story's center.[4] The cousins' visit is itself a disruption of routine and a challenge to her position as household favorite. Since the convent girls are older, they represent a threat to what the girl is used to thinking of as her superior knowledge. And since there are two of them, the cousins make an alliance that excludes the younger girl. The focus of divisiveness is, of course, sex. The girl places the cousins' interest in boys in the same category with the boarder's courtship: the lonely Miss Kirby having as her only friend an older man who drives her around in a car he uses as a kind of unregistered taxi for black people. Initially, the girl mischievously suggests to her mother that the aptly named Mr. Cheatam could squire the teenagers around as well. The problem of how to enter-

---

3. Giannone, *Flannery O'Connor and the Mystery of Love,* 77.
4. Frederick Asals discusses the story in these general terms in *Flannery O'Connor: The Imagination of Extremity.*

tain the guests is finally solved by arranging a double date with the grand-
sons of a neighbor, but here again divisions emerge. These boys are so-
cially inferior to the girls—"They're only farm boys," says the mother—
and they plan to become Church of God preachers, making them of a
starkly different religious orientation.

On the date itself, the differences threaten to break into conflict. The
girl eavesdrops as the two couples sit on the porch, the boys serenading
the girls with gospel songs and the hymns "I've Found a Friend in Jesus"
and "The Old Rugged Cross." The girls strike back with "*Tantum Ergo,*"
St. Thomas Aquinas's Latin Eucharistic hymn. "That must be Jew singing,"
observes one of the startled boys. To twist Mark Twain's observation about
Britons and Americans, the boys and girls seem to be fellow Christians
separated by a common religion. And when the cousins return from their
trip to the carnival with the yokels, the theme of difference is manifested in the form of physical misshapenness. When the younger girl asks
what the older ones saw, Joanne answers, "All kinds of freaks" (*CW* 205).
But initially, the cousins refuse to tell about the greatest freak of all, because to do so would require discussion of sex, which they think the
younger girl is not ready for. After persuading the older girls to tell their
tale by falsely claiming that she has witnessed the birth of rabbits, the girl
hears the revelation that will push the momentum of the story in the direction of unity.

The chief freak was a man and a woman both, the cousins say. The cu-
rious girl thinks they must mean that the freak had two heads. But no,
only when the freak pulled up its dress could you tell what it meant, answer the cousins. In other words, the revelation is couched in terms of a
unity of two natures—not a divine-human union, as in the Christological assertion of Chalcedon, but a male-female one. Shockingly, this male-
female difference, so pervasively driven home to the pubescent girl as the
great divide within humankind, is in this one case overcome, although in
a disturbing, emotionally painful way. For the remainder of the story, we
find images of painful unity. The girl dreams about the freak, imagining
him/her preaching in a kind of Protestant worship service, but concluding with the biblical words originally quoted by the nun: "I am a temple
of the Holy Ghost." This declaration is a painful one for the freak, who
says that "God made me thisaway and I don't dispute it." Yet the freak
praises God, even for what he/she clearly sees as a calamity. The revelation of unity over division is completed during Benediction at the con-

vent, the cousins now restored to their usual place and the girl and her mother having become the visitors. When the priest raises the monstrance, with the very "*Tantum Ergo*" hymn the cousins had sung for the Church of God boys sounding in the background, the girl's thoughts go to the freak and his/her words "I don't dispute it. This is the way He wanted me to be" (*CW* 209). Here Protestant and Catholic, male and female are united in a single moment. But as though to underscore the pain in the freak's accepting declaration, the girl feels a crucifix "mashed" into her face as she leaves the service, an exuberantly affectionate nun having grabbed her in a surprise hug.

The dominant resonance here is that of Christ's cross as the center of unifying sacrifice. The nun's crucifix and "The Old Rugged Cross" testify to the same reality made present in the monstrance, and made vivid to the child in her recollection of the freak. The freak is a legitimate type of the crucified Christ for two reasons. First, he/she is of two natures, though of course in an imperfect and disturbing way. Second, the freak is a willing sufferer, one who has accepted God's will as his/her own. Thus the freak presents his/her body as a living sacrifice, fulfilling another Pauline injunction, and again establishing a connection with the body of Christ present in the Eucharistic offering. Although the second similarity is the more important, echoing as it does all the other cases of re- demptive suffering in O'Connor, the first analogue is perhaps more difficult to accept. But it explains, I think, the implications of O'Connor's remark that this story was her one attempt to come to grips with the virtue of purity, as she told Betty Hester in the aforementioned letter (*HB* 124). Clearly she has in mind the cousins' initial snickering at the nun's expense over her advice on keeping boys at bay with scripture. But more deeply, the story attempts to sanctify sexuality itself by placing it in a context where it can be offered as a sacrifice to God in imitation of Christ. The hermaphrodite is an ingenious symbol because he/she can suggest both the unity of the human race and the unity of human nature with the divine by way of sacrifice.

Feminist critics such as Louise Westling and Sarah Gordon have taken O'Connor to task for avoiding the subject of normal sexual interaction, claiming that in this story O'Connor has in effect unsexed her protagonist. But while it is true, as O'Connor herself admitted in correspondence, that she had an aversion to imagining romantic relationships, it seems to me that her theological emphasis in this story is daringly sexual and decidedly anti-Manichean. As Anthony Di Renzo puts it, O'Connor "plays with sacrilege" in this work.[5] The story suggests that not only are the fourteen-year-old convent virgins temples of the Holy Ghost, but so also is a traveling-freak-show hermaphrodite. Although O'Connor has not addressed the topic of sexual intercourse, she has forthrightly affirmed the holiness of our sexual natures, and she has done so in a manner consistent with her understanding of redemption.[6] Bodily suffering is our Incarnational connection to the history of salvation. And within earthly life, the one perfect embodiment of that sacrifice is the Eucharist.

We have seen ways in which in "A Temple of the Holy Ghost" differences are held together within a greater unity, but it is important to add that this unity neither erases difference nor cancels hierarchy. Between the sexes, O'Connor does assert an equality of dignity and holiness by way of our bodies' common status as "temples of the Holy Ghost." Yet Gordon is right in her claim that O'Connor makes no challenge to whatever gender inequity might exist within the church or larger society. For O'Connor, the larger and necessary inequity is that between humanity and God. The earthly points to its source and end in the heavenly; the human is dependent upon the divine. The ultimate puzzle of the hermaphrodite's nature is one that is at home only within the mystery of Christ's nature as human and divine without confusion.

Where the contrast between Protestant and Catholic is concerned, although that difference is not so stark, for O'Connor, a hierarchy nonetheless remains. In this story as throughout her work, O'Connor's respect for the faith of her fundamentalist neighbors is deep,[7] and surely O'Connor regards the songs sung by the Church of God brothers as testaments to the ecumenical faith to be found also in Aquinas's Latin. But for O'Connor, Protestantism is incomplete, and what it lacks is the Mass and thus the church that administers it. She once hyperbolically remarked in a letter that if a solitary man found a Bible in the woods, he would eventually become a Catholic (*HB* 517). In a kind of historical reversal, O'Connor seems to have regarded Bible-thumping Protestants as proto-

5. See Westling, *Sacred Groves and Ravaged Gardens,* 138–43, and Gordon, *Flannery O'Connor,* 152–64; Anthony Di Renzo, *American Gargoyles: Flannery O'Connor and the Medieval Grotesque.*

6. Giannone, following up on suggestions made by other critics, helpfully declares that this is "a story of confirmation" in *Flannery O'Connor and the Mystery of Love,* 76. Thus, the girl might be said by implication to participate in a second sacramental rite.

7. Ralph Wood makes this point powerfully in the first chapter of his book *Flannery O'Connor and the Christ-Haunted South.*

Catholics. The logic of many O'Connor stories follows a pattern by which faithful Protestant witness leads to the Roman way. And in this story, the pattern leads specifically to the Eucharist. "*Tantum Ergo*" is a Eucharistic hymn; theologically, it trumps "The Old Rugged Cross" in the sense that it is in the consecrated host, not the emotions stirred by a song, that the cross finds its truest embodiment, by O'Connor's reckoning. And as we have seen, the girl's revelatory dream in which the freak leads a church service and declares its body a temple of the Holy Ghost, discloses its full significance only in the light of the raised monstrance, a point that is underscored in the final sentence of the story, when the setting sun is "a huge red ball like an elevated Host drenched in blood" (*CW* 209). The imagery of the story moves to this Eucharistic symbol as its goal and completion, the auditory revelation finally absorbed into revelatory vision.

"Revelation": From Word to Vision

This pattern is nearly universal in O'Connor's stories: Protestant preaching leads to Catholic sacrament; prophecy gives way to vision; the heard Word is succeeded by blessed sight. "A Temple of the Holy Ghost" points us to the Eucharistic center of O'Connor's theological world; the story "Revelation" further discloses the process of insight that in all her fiction O'Connor hopes to lead readers through.

The title "Revelation" itself might seem to give the lie to the thesis that sight ultimately replaces hearing, revelation having often been conceived in the history of Christianity as being conveyed by the written and heard Word. O'Connor herself was working, of course, in a medium of words. But we might well remember that the great Dante concluded *The Divine Comedy* with a vision that he said no words were adequate to convey. And of more recent interest, critics influenced by Mikhail Bakhtin have called attention to ways in which O'Connor's own language seemed to be at odds with itself. That is to say, O'Connor seemed to be sensitive to what we might call the fallenness of language—the gap between transcendent Being and those human signs that seek to convey it.

One needs to be careful here—O'Connor was no proponent of indeterminacy for its own sake reveling in the free play of language. And she certainly believed that the analogical language conveys real meaning. But, for her, language was revelatory in only a provisional way. Recent discussion of whether O'Connor's fiction is dialogical or monological within the Bakhtinian lexicon is instructive on this topic. Robert Brinkmeyer argues in *The Art and Vision of Flannery O'Connor* that a dialogue emerges between a Protestant fundamentalist voice and a Catholic sacramentalist one that represents O'Connor's own considered stance. Both feminist critics such as Sarah Gordon and theological proponents such as Ralph Wood have found the stories to be monological, with O'Connor using the prophetic voice of authority for good or ill, depending on one's position, but using it without qualification. My own position is that O'Connor used the monologic against itself, not to contradict the prophetic word, but to surpass it. In this way, her work became dialogic in an apophatic sense: for her, the highest use of language was to prepare us to encounter something beyond language.[8]

The story "Revelation" deals directly with these issues. As the title suggests, it has as its central event God's disclosure of previously hidden truth. This truth is coherent, but complex. To be more precise, there is a doubleness about the revelation Ruby Turpin receives. In fact, the revelation itself comes in two stages. The first stage is one of judgment, with a message directed specifically to her, both initially destructive in its effect, and delivered by means of the spoken word. The second stage is one of grace, with a vision of the wider human community, edifying in its effect, and conveyed by means of sight. But these stages, although distinct, are not contradictory. Indeed, there is an overlapping of the visual and the aural in the course of the story.

The first revelatory stage culminates in a message. Those familiar with the story will have no trouble recalling the single imperative line "Go back to hell where you came from, you old wart hog" (*CW* 646). It is delivered by an emotionally disturbed Wellesley coed ironically named Mary Grace. The words have special impact because Mary Grace has seized Mrs. Turpin's attention by hitting her just over the eye with a tome on human development and by choking her hard enough to leave a bruise over her windpipe. Mrs. Turpin thinks of these words as "the message" sent directly to her from God. She had even elicited this declaration by asking the seemingly clairvoyant girl, "What you got to say to me?" Once she hears it, Mrs. Turpin has no doubt about the message's authenticity, only its appropriateness.

---

8. Bakhtin's theological side, including his own interest in apophatic thought, is suggestively explored in a recent volume of essays. See Susan M. Felch and Paul Contino, eds., *Bakhtin and Religion: A Feeling for Faith*.

Three aspects of this revelation are important, one of which is theological and two of which have to do with the interplay of speech and sight. Theologically, the point the reader is meant to see in Mary Grace's utterance is that Mrs. Turpin is a sinner, not the paragon of virtue she believes herself to be. Mary Grace's outburst was brought on by Mrs. Turpin's self-righteous announcement, "When I think who all I could have been besides myself and what all I got, a little of everything, and a good disposition besides, I just feel like shouting, 'Thank you Jesus for making everything the way it is!' It could have been different!" (*CW* 644). This smugness that blinds her to her complicity with evil and her utter dependence upon God while feeding a pious false gratitude is exactly what stands between Mrs. Turpin and salvation. She is in desperate need of a revelation that shatters the lie she believes about herself, a word that wounds in order to heal.

Rhetorically, something very similar happens. This revelatory word is the result of a dialogue, but is intended to bring dialogue to an end. In Bakhtinian terms, we might say it is a monologic intrusion into dialogue. Yet the eventual outcome of this intrusion is not an end to dialogue, but rather the beginning of a dialogic interaction previously unavailable to the self-involved Ruby. When Mary Grace speaks her word to Mrs. Turpin, she is not expecting a reply. The finality of her declaration is inherent in its authoritativeness. In other words, part of what it means in the story for this word to be a message from God is that it cannot be refuted or answered. As Bakhtin says of authoritative discourse in general, "It is not a free appropriation and assimilation of the word itself that authoritative discourse seeks to elicit from us; rather, it demands our unconditional allegiance."[9] In this way it is a conversation stopper, an antidialogic utterance. On the other hand, this word is elicited by a conversation, and it needs that context to become intelligible. The revealing utterance is an answer to a question raised but unrecognized by Mrs. Turpin. Without the revelation, Mrs. Turpin would never have grasped the meaning of her own words, for the interrupted conversation is nothing if not circumscribed and repetitive. Thus Mrs. Turpin's conversation is itself un-dialogical. The circle in which it operates is so tight that no truly new discourse can enter it. Every voice, every idea gets absorbed into hers, and that circle must be broken before she can "hear" at all. And the ma-

9. Mikhail Bakhtin, *Discourse in the Novel,* excerpted in David Richter, *Critical Tradition,* 784.

jor rhetorical force holding this circle together is convention—clichés of thought and speech of which Ruby is past mistress.

Ruby Turpin is remarkable for her skill at enclosing others within the loops of her conventional wisdom. Her basic attitude toward potential interlocutors is suggested in the story's second paragraph. As she enters the waiting room of the doctor's office, she "put a firm hand on Claud's shoulder and said in a voice that included anyone who wanted to listen, 'Claud, you sit in that chair there . . .'" (*CW* 633). She speaks to "anyone who want[s] to listen," but with no intention of altering her speech or her mind to suit her audience. She speaks to reaffirm opinions she already holds, decisions she has already taken. Her poker-faced husband, Claud, is her comic sidekick, who reinforces her authority by silently doing her bidding.

With strangers, Mrs. Turpin has other strategies for keeping the conversational upper hand. Until Mary Grace attacks, the unnamed "white-trashy" mother is Mrs. Turpin's sole opponent in the waiting-room dialogue, and Mrs. Turpin handles her by appropriating and subverting her speech, even if for propriety's sake she must do some of the subverting silently. The white-trashy woman attempts to seize control of the conversation when the origin of the waiting-room clock comes up. You can get one with Green Stamps, says the woman. She adds, "That's most likely where he got hisn. Save you up enough, you can get you most anythang. I got me some joo'ry" (*CW* 637). Mrs. Turpin retrieves the initiative by completing this line of thought, but in a way that turns it against the speaker: "Ought to have got you a wash rag and some soap," she thinks. With the "stylishly dressed" lady who proves to be Mary Grace's mother, Mrs. Turpin's strategy is one of complicity. Both women seem determined to put the best face on things by praising the conventional, and are united in their conviction that no personal quality ranks higher than having a "good disposition." Such esteem for conventionality and approval of the status quo naturally issue in an extreme social conservatism, which is reflected in their attitudes toward race.

Although Mrs. Turpin avers that she would rather have been "a neat clean respectable Negro woman, herself but black" than to be slovenly white trash, her sense of social class is racist, completely compatible with white community norms. The black delivery boy on his bicycle appears through the window as "a grotesque revolving shadow," an unacknowledged sign of difference that Mrs. Turpin ignores. When she delivers the little self-assured speech that provokes Mary Grace, Mrs. Turpin is summing up a view of herself, the community, and God that she has tightly packaged, deftly defended, and falsely believed to be impregnable. What we might call bad faith, to borrow an existentialist term, lies behind Mrs. Turpin's seemingly inclusive stance toward the social cross section represented in the waiting room. She does not really want dialogue partners; instead, she wants everyone to speak up so that she can put their words to her own use, which is primarily a kind of ideological self-justification. Thus when Mary Grace makes her drastic pronouncement, Mrs. Turpin has, in more senses than one, asked for it. But this word, unlike the others, cannot be appropriated. It breaks the conversational circle Mrs. Turpin has drawn. It is impolite, unconventional, personal, and damning.

The healthy irony in the assaulting word Mrs. Turpin elicits from the inspired lunatic is that by bringing an end to the self-congratulatory waiting-room conversation, the "message" makes it possible for Mrs. Turpin to pay attention to something outside her verbal circle for the first time. This is a word that ends all words, at least for a time, and the transition from Mrs. Turpin's self-deceiving volubility to a truth-giving encounter with God is conveyed by means of a switch from the aural to the visual. After the assault, Mrs. Turpin has no word left except "Why?" She asks God how she could be both her and a hog. And she can see no justification for the accusation that she is from hell—a daughter of darkness rather than an angel of light. She can as yet make no connection between the smug declaration that preceded Mary Grace's attack and the words of judgment that followed it. These questions, which she formulates in private, are genuine, unlike her pseudo-conversational sallies in the waiting room. The authoritative, monologic utterance thus opens up the possibility of dialogue with God for the first time.

The answers Ruby receives are not verbal, however. Indeed, the visual supplants the aural. This is a process that begins in the first half of the story. I have already alluded to one example: the black teenager on the bicycle casts a "grotesque . . . shadow" that flits as a warning at the periphery of the white-dominated social space. The gospel song that is playing when Ruby takes her seat is "When I Looked Up and He Looked Down"—an invitation to see God rather than hear him. When Mrs. Turpin wonders at night about the different classes of people and where she fits in the scheme, her musings first take the form of questions—she *asks* Jesus not to make her white trash. She drifts off to sleep *naming* the classes, but the dream she has in the night is visual: she *sees* the people of all classifications packed in boxcars and carried away to gas ovens, an in-

dication of the truly fascist and hellish nature of her scheme. What begins
as a series of questions is answered with a vision.

The reader's attention is constantly directed also to characters' eyes,
most arrestingly to the eyes of Mary Grace. It is the look of Mary Grace's
eyes that proves to Mrs. Turpin that she is touched by the preternatural:
"The girl's eyes seemed lit all of a sudden with a peculiar light, an unnatural light like night road signs give" (*CW* 637). These "fierce, brilliant"
eyes transfix Ruby until she is ready to receive the truth. When she is first
attacked, it is her vision that is affected; it is "narrowed," as though she is
seeing everything through the wrong end of a telescope. The blow Ruby
receives is just above her eye. In fact, this blow could serve as an emblem
of the whole process of revelation in the story: a book, full of explanato-
ry words, is used as a weapon to strike the eye of Mrs. Turpin, silencing
her and focusing her attention so that her vision will be clarified. To re-
inforce the change, Mary Grace chokes her, thus cutting off the very air
that makes the words with which Ruby fashions her false world.

After the attack, Ruby's vision is altered, and the altered vision is the
beginning of a reconstructed world. When the doctor has examined her,
Ruby looks "straight ahead at nothing," as though her mental screen has
been cleared. The next time we are told what she sees, we find her "suspicious" at the familiar sight of her own house, for in the light of what
has happened she wouldn't have been surprised to see "a burnt wound
between two blackened chimneys" (*CW* 647). When she and Claud lie
down to recover from their traumatic excursion, Ruby stares at the ceil-
ing, "as if there were unintelligible handwriting" there. She has stopped
talking her world into being and begun to look for divine signs. Further
indication of her new dissatisfaction with the mannered sophistry of conventional conversation comes when she tells the black hired hands what
has happened to her. For these women are more masterfully evasive than
Ruby herself. Their reaction when they hear the girl's message to Ruby
is brilliant: "You the sweetest white lady I know," says one. "She pretty,
too," chimes in another. "Stout as she can be, and sweet. Jesus satisfied with
her!" (*CW* 650). These declarations are of course filled with double en-
tendres, so that the black women's sympathetic utterances could be either
insults or flattery. Either way, Ruby is not comforted. The same kind of
congratulatory utterance she once deftly employed now leaves her angry,
for she knows it to be empty. Conventional speech has failed her.

When Ruby receives her vision, it comes after she has finally exhausted her linguistic possibilities. Left alone at the pig parlor, she plays out in

private a drama similar to the one she endured in the doctor's waiting room, only now she metaphorically hurls in God's face the accusation leveled against her: "What do you send me a message like that for?" (*CW* 652). But this attempt to refuse the word she has been given rebounds on her own head. Her final challenge, "Who do you think you are?" which she roars out in fury, literally returns to her as an echo, changing her assault on God's sovereignty into an affront against her own false autonomy. This time Ruby has been silenced not by the word of another, but by her own word. She receives no verbal reply to her questions; she seems to have talked herself out, to be in a failed dialogue with one who will not answer. It is only when she enters this reduced state, having abandoned both self-justification and angry accusation of God—indeed, having exhausted all her linguistic resources—that she gets her silent sign. It is conveyed not by sound but by sight, after a "visionary light" settles in her eyes and she lifts her eyes from the hogs to the sky, where a single purple streak remains in the gathering dusk. She sees herself, not as a "wart hog" from "hell," but as one of the heavenly band rumbling toward heaven. Only, in stark contrast to her earlier vain imaginings, she and those like her come at the end of the line, marching in good order as always, but with shocked expressions, as even their limited, word-borne virtues are burned away. This, then, is Ruby Turpin's positive revelation—the divine vision of human community ordered by God's love and redeemed through God's mercy—a revelation that sees with the soul's eye, as the medieval mystics might say.

This vision in effect completes a circle in O'Connor's fiction first begun with *Wise Blood*. There, the antiprophet blinded himself in repentance and in a final desperate effort to acquire spiritual truth. Here, the soul's eye sees through the bodily eyes, and the door that opens is not the portal of death but the highway to heaven, a human parade having replaced the thin ray of light that Mrs. Flood thinks she can discern in the dying Haze. Thus, appropriately, the vision of "Revelation" has content, the content of the heavenly city: the gathered humanity on its way to God. While this sight is not the ultimate beatific vision of God, it is truly revelatory, and it is in an important sense Eucharistic. Ruby Turpin ushers in the "visionary light" by raising her hands "in a gesture hieratic and profound" (*CW* 653), just as the priest raises the monstrance in "A Temple of the Holy Ghost." And the vision itself is the fruit of her own painful judgment, as well as her reluctant identification with the hogs. The sanguinary colors—the crimson sky with its purple streak and the red glow suffusing the hogs—are reminders to the reader, if not consciously registered by Ruby, that the basis of this loving interconnectedness of humanity and nature is the blood of Christ.

In this story as in O'Connor generally, the purpose of words is to prepare for divine encounter. With only slight exaggeration we might say that when O'Connor wrote, she was hoping that her stories would become the words of institution that transform the stuff of earthly life into the body of God. Her model in this artistic endeavor was the Eucharistic celebration. And as in the Mass she daily attended, the climax for the worshipper is a silent beholding of a mystery with which we are in a communion beyond speech. The Word has become embodied; we taste it and see it, but we do not speak it.

Thus might we say that for O'Connor the ultimate aim of fiction is not dialogue, but communion. The role of words in revelation is to bring us to the state where, in the presence of the crucified God, we do not answer so much as participate in the divine Being. What Rowan Williams says of the apophatic tradition generally applies to O'Connor's fiction in particular: she uses a "strategy of dispossession"—"a dispossession of the human mind conceived as central to the order of the world, and a dispossession of the entire identity that exists prior to the paschal drama, the identity that has not seen and named its self-deception and self-destructiveness." Ultimately, however, this negation is replaced by a great gift: "The fruition of the process is the discovery that one's selfhood and value simply lie in the abiding faithful presence of God, not in any moral or conceptual performance."[10] And this state is a silent state, although one necessarily made possible by words. To return to Bakhtin, we might say that the silence that accompanies revelatory sight in O'Connor is generated by a dialogic situation in which the verbal pointing of "This is my body" can be effective in the hearer. Just as for Bakhtin's beloved Dostoevsky the silent kiss of Christ is the appropriate answer to the monologic diatribe of the Grand Inquisitor, so in O'Connor the work of fiction prepares the reader for the sacramental gesture that embodies divine grace.[11]

A retrospective glance through O'Connor's fiction ("Revelation" being the next to last story she wrote from scratch) shows that a sacramen-

---

10. Rowan Williams, *On Christian Theology,* 10–11.
11. Caryl Emerson suggestively comments on silence in Bakhtin in her afterword to the Felch and Contino volume previously cited.

tal image is presented for the silent contemplation of character and/or reader in most of the stories. Sometimes, the image is crucifix-like, the violent death of a character aligned somehow with that of Christ. Thus in "A Good Man Is Hard to Find" the grandmother is shot in direct rejection of her spontaneous offer of love and acceptance, her legs "crossed" under her in death in the final image we and the Misfit have of her. In this way, she, like Hazel Motes, provides an analogue to Christ's innocent death, despite the sin of pride that marked her previously. A more purely innocent death is to be found at the conclusion of "The Lame Shall Enter First," where reader and father are left with the sight of the victimized son hanging dead from the rafters in a desperate attempt to be united with his mother in heaven. We may add to these images those of the artificial nigger, the scapegoated displaced person, and, most directly, the icon on Parker's back. O'Connor also gives us climactic images of the principal sacraments, both associated with suffering bodies. The boy Bevel drowns as he gives himself over to the waters of baptism in "The River"; the Host is associated with the freak in "A Temple of the Holy Ghost." Although some of the stories leave us with visions of unmitigated judgment, as do "A Late Encounter with the Enemy," "Good Country People," and "A View of the Woods," the direction of O'Connor's work as a whole is toward the ultimate image of embodied redemption. And having presented us with the image sacramentally rendered, O'Connor seems to have hoped that her reader would in turn read sacramentally, absorbing directly an intuition of divine mystery that would operate as a source of grace. She strove to produce an ineffable moment that could be embraced or spurned but not understood, and for which sight, not speech, is the best vehicle.

5

Helen Keller and the Message in the Bottle
Percy on Language

༄༅

I f the drive of Flannery O'Connor's fiction is toward silent Eucharistic vision, Walker Percy's work might be said to begin and end with conversation. While his commitment to a sacramental understanding of the world is as strong as O'Connor's, Percy is more acutely attuned to *analogia entis* as it is linguistically manifested. His entry into the Roman Catholic Church was in part due to apologetics, and he never lost his appreciation for the give and take of argument as a means to truth. At a deeper level, for Percy, the mystery most patently present in the sacraments of the Catholic Church found its clearest echo in the common miracle of human speech. His version of the aesthetic of revelation is rooted in a set of convictions about language.

Percy's preoccupation with language predates his fiction, and what he came to believe about the implications of the way human language works was the philosophical linchpin of his Christian belief. If the paradigm moment of revelation for O'Connor is a vision of Christ crucified, the crucial instant for Percy is one in which a word establishes a connection between a solitary individual and the world of meaning outside herself. O'Connor gives us artificial niggers and blood-red suns; Percy offers Helen Keller signing at the water pump and a message in a bottle.

No doubt this difference in theological orientation has its roots in biography and personal disposition. From her childhood, O'Connor drew as well as wrote, and in college she was known for the cartoons she contributed to student publications. She was accomplished enough in this medium to submit a cartoon to the *New Yorker,* although none of her work was ever accepted.[1] One of the best-known photographs of O'Connor is one that she uncharacteristically asked to be taken, and it features her sitting in front of her painting of a pheasant cock. In addition to this inclination toward the visual, O'Connor was, as we have seen, deeply formed by the Tridentine Mass through lifelong practice. Since she was a "cradle Catholic," the Mass was there as the root of her spiritual life before she could understand it, and even in adult years it remained for her a mystery that surpassed explanation. Percy, by contrast, was a convert who was nearing thirty when he attended his first Mass; his prior interest in language had given him his initial push toward Catholicism. In later interviews he mentioned philosophy of language along with European novels as the staples of his reading during the convalescence that preceded his conversion (*CWP* 106). While Jay Tolson is certainly right to stress the spiritual and emotional motives that were paramount in Percy's conversion,[2] no one doubts that Percy was prepared for this step by an intellectual awakening that had fascination with language at its core. Within his family life, Percy's interest in speech would only intensify when a hearing-impaired daughter, Ann, was born in 1954. But perhaps the best way to gauge the religious import of language within his thought is to recall his response to the book that provoked his first publication.

Breakthroughs: Susanne Langer and Helen Keller

Miss Lonelyhearts seems to have provided O'Connor with the final stimulus she needed to generate her authentic voice. *Philosophy in a New Key* served a similar function for Walker Percy. While Susanne Langer's book had no effect on Percy's style, it did for his vocation as a writer what West's book did for O'Connor's: it galvanized his own nearly formed thought into its final shape. Percy described the experience in a number of interviews as inspiring his first successful foray into serious writing. For example, he tells Barbara King,

> I was reading a lot and found a book which got me excited. You know, that's the whole secret to writing. You have to get excited about something either for or against it. It doesn't matter which, really. Otherwise, I don't see how anybody ever could set pen to pa-

1. Jean Cash, *Flannery O'Connor: A Life,* xvi.
2. Tolson, *Pilgrim in the Ruins,* 198–200.

per. . . . Anyway I read a book by a . . . philosopher named Susanne Langer, called *Philosophy in a New Key,* which concentrates on language. I thought she had gotten hold of something and then turned around and let it get away from her. I wrote an article saying what was right and what was wrong with her book. You see, to be a writer you have to be conceited, you have to think you know more than anybody else. So I wrote it and sent it off to a journal called *Thought* and they *accepted* it, they *published* it. (*CWP* 93)

This article, "Symbol as Need," which is ostensibly a review of Langer's *Feeling and Form,* successor to *Philosophy in a New Key,* actually sets out the central idea of Percy's entire corpus: man's symbolic activity is the key to his nature, and this phenomenon can be explained only through a new science freed from physicalism. The reason that this idea became so important for Percy the Catholic and the novelist is that he saw it as the basis for a new synthesis of knowledge that made Christianity intellectually plausible and human estrangement explicable. In other words, it was no longer true, as Percy himself had earlier believed, that science discredited religion. Rather, science itself had now bumped up against a natural phenomenon that its metaphysical assumptions prevented it from understanding. And these assumptions, compatible with Christian assertions, were alone adequate to deal with this phenomenon. For Percy, the development of a new science and the recovery of the wrongly discredited "news" of Christianity were the best hope for overcoming the deep human sicknesses that the twentieth century had exposed: sanitized violence, alienation, and despair.

This case is not, of course, the one argued by Langer. Percy's excitement in reading her work was generated by his belief that she had independently confirmed conclusions he had arrived at by other means. While insisting on "naturalist orthodoxy" and crediting "physical science, logical positivism, mathematics, Freudian analysis, German idealism" as her sources (*MB* 293), Langer had, according to Percy, arrived at a theory of the symbol remarkably like that of St. Thomas Aquinas. In her account, a symbol gives "form" to "feeling," which is not a mere emotion, but rather sentience itself. The symbol thus simultaneously represents the inner, felt life of the artist and the subject or theme of the art work. The symbol "becomes" both the feeling and the subject matter for artist and audience alike, despite the fact that in a literal sense it is neither. In effect, this relationship is the one that the Schoolmen had described, Langer having reached by an alternate intellectual route "the mysterious analogy between the form of beauty and the pattern of inner life" (*MB* 290). Percy points out that this description of aesthetic symbol—Langer concentrates upon music, painting, and poetry—is very close to the realist epistemology of the Scholastics.

For thinkers such as Aquinas, a symbol, such as a noun in human language, does not simply refer to an object; it also names a concept, which indicates a universal, a real though immaterial entity. Scholastic realism claims that this tertium quid is the metaphysical bridge between mind and physical reality. However, Langer resists the metaphysical conclusion, maintaining instead that symbol simply satisfies a human "need" for making. It is precisely here that Percy believes Langer lets the truly revolutionary import of her insight get away. To say that symbol is "natural" to human beings because it arises out of a "human need" is to beg the truly important question. As Percy notes, saying that human beings use symbols because they satisfy a need is like saying bees make honey because it is part of bee nature to do so. While such a statement may be true, it fails as an explanation, offering only a tautology. Langer has not said what a symbol does or what it is for. By implication, Percy suggests that the purpose of symbol—what Aquinas might have called its final cause—is to serve as the medium between human mind and reality, both material and immaterial. To borrow Paul Ricoeur's phrase, the symbol gives rise to thought; it is the key to all things distinctly human, from cave drawings to science itself. And for Percy, as we shall see, symbol offered the key to overcoming both the impasse he believed science had reached when it came to explaining the human condition, as well as the deep alienation besetting that condition in its modern form.

Thus, according to Percy's assessment, Langer had reached by means of mid-twentieth-century secular philosophy an insight lost since the rise of nominalism in the theological debates of late Scholastic thought, but she had failed to follow up on her breakthrough. Percy was to gain more direct help in formulating his own theory of symbol from the work of an eccentric nineteenth-century American philosopher and scientist, Charles Sanders Peirce, whom he had begun to read by the late 1940s.[3] Peirce, sometimes called the father of modern semiotics, made little impact on his own time, and died in destitution. Years after his death in 1914,

3. Patrick Samway, *Walker Percy: A Life,* 148–49.

his efforts to develop a science of signs gave impetus to an increasingly important academic field. While semioticians were drawn to Peirce's more scientifically directed researches, Percy was most taken with Peirce's metaphysical argument, as John Desmond has masterfully demonstrated. Using his own terminology, Peirce had argued that only a realist metaphysic (of the sort advanced by Aquinas) could account for symbol. In the final years of his life, Percy would be absorbed by Peirce's thought, corresponding extensively with Peirce scholar Kenneth Laine Ketner. Only illness prevented him from following through on the audacious plan he described to Ketner in 1989 for "using CSP as the foundation of a Catholic apologetic, which I have tentatively entitled (after Aquinas) *Contra Gentiles*."[4] But while Percy increasingly turned to Peirce as his staunchest ally in forging a new anthropology that rejoined science and theology, it was his response to *Feeling and Form* that first opened his eyes to what he might do as a writer.

If Langer's book provided the catalyst for the central argument of Percy's thought, Helen Keller provided the telling example. Throughout his career, he referred to the crucial breakthrough recorded in her autobiography, quoting from it most freely in "The Delta Factor," the essay he placed first in his one nonfiction volume dedicated entirely to theory. In Percy's account, the eight-year-old Helen enters the well-house as a responding animal, capable of using hand signals to satisfy biological needs, and but she leaves it a full-fledged *Homo symbolificus,* who wants not water, but the *name* of water.

> We walked down the path to the well-house, attracted by the fragrance of the honeysuckle with which it was covered. Someone was drawing water and my teacher placed my hand under the spout. As the cool stream gushed over one hand, she spelled into the other the word *water,* first slowly then rapidly. I stood still, my whole attention fixed upon the motion of her fingers. Suddenly I felt a misty consciousness as of something forgotten—a thrill of returning thought; and somehow the mystery of language was revealed to me. I knew that "w-a-t-e-r" meant the wonderful cool something that was flowing over my hand. That living word awakened my soul, gave it light, hope, joy, set it free! There were barriers still, it is true, but barriers that could in time be swept away.

4. John F. Desmond, *Walker Percy's Search for Community,* especially pp. 5–6; Percy to Ketner, February 27, 1989, in *A Thief of Peirce: The Letters of Kenneth Laine Ketner and Walker Percy,* ed. Patrick Samway, 131.

> I left the well-house eager to learn. Everything had a name, and each name gave birth to a new thought. As we returned to the house every object which I touched seemed to quiver with life. (quoted in *MB* 34–35)

Percy finds in this description nothing less than testimony to the birth of human consciousness and the establishment of a world, in contrast to a mere environment (in Heidegger's terms, *Welt* rather than *Umwelt*). And of course, it serves as confirmation of the theory of symbol he believed Langer had arrived at through the unlikely paths of physical science, logical positivism, and German Idealism. But perhaps even more importantly, the example indicates the human implications of the intellectual problem confronting Percy. Neglect of what we might call the symbol problem renders us incapable of understanding our greatest—and seemingly intractable—difficulties. In his novels, Percy makes us acutely aware of our contradictions: that the triumphal age of science was also the age of holocaust; that technological mastery is attended by boredom and malaise; that people often feel better in a bad environment (a hurricane) than in a good one (their quiet suburban neighborhoods on an ordinary Wednesday afternoon). Need satisfaction of a strictly biological sort does not fulfill us, but in fact, seems to make us miserable if other needs are not taken into account. The nature of these other needs is exactly what Percy finds Helen Keller's awakening to hint at.

As a person reduced by circumstance to her merely animal nature, Helen Keller before the well-house experience might be said to represent humanity as an object of what Percy, borrowing the term from Peirce, called "dyadic" science. Her actions could be explained in terms of stimulus-response models, and her motives were explicable as those of an organism adapting to her environment. But once she becomes a symbol-user, a new set of joys and sorrows are open to her as she becomes a creature capable of "triadic" interaction. Her own account speaks of "light, hope, joy" she had not previously known. She later speaks of tears of repentance she shed for a doll she had previously broken in a fit of temper, her awakening to words having given her a new purchase on what we might almost call her preconscious life. The world established by words seems to bring with it the possibility of good and evil as well as joy and sorrow. Though this connection is certainly important to Percy, the fact that symbol establishes for Helen a *self* has even more vital significance for him.

From Symbol to Self

If any notion plays a larger role in Percy's thought than symbol, it is that of self. His first book of nonfiction (*The Message in the Bottle*) is devoted to language; his second and last (*Lost in the Cosmos*) is subtitled "The Last Self-Help Book." The self is the "strange new creature who *symballeins,* throws words and names together to form sentences," as Percy says in his National Endowment for the Arts Jefferson Lecture, which he gave in 1989 (*SSL* 288). Calling on the vocabulary of the early semioticist Peirce, Percy records that the words *interpreter, interpretant, asserter, mind, I, ego,* and even *soul* suggest something of the self's nature, though each is deficient in some measure. Percy thinks it indisputable that the self is real, that its existence follows from the use of symbol, and that science has ignored it.

In "A Semiotic Primer on the Self," the theoretical core of *Lost in the Cosmos,* Percy lists the properties of this "I" that arises simultaneously with the symbol: it is social, since a symbol require both an utterer and a hearer (Helen Keller must "share" the name of water with her teacher for it to be valid); it has two sorts of relationships open to it, intersubjectivity (I-Thou) and depersonalization (I-It); it makes use of the naming function Helen Keller discovers, whereby a thing "is" its name, and not simply itself; and finally, the self has a world and not merely an environment, with even the unknown aspects of a world also having a name, such as "the unknown" (*LC* 96). For Percy, these are exactly the characteristics that science in its present form cannot explain, despite the fact that they are the most distinctive, troublesome, and therefore important things about us. What our culture at large lacks and desperately needs is a "theory of man," or philosophical anthropology. Without it, we have no hope of grasping our true situation or of avoiding the catastrophes, both global and personal, of which we are now capable and which already beset us.

Percy is at his most brilliant in exposing the lacunae in our understanding of ourselves, drawing often on the more phenomenological vocabulary of such thinkers as Heidegger, Kierkegaard, and Marcel to describe what "dyadic" science had left out. Many of Percy's examples might be said to be inspired by a remark made by Kierkegaard, who said that Hegel (the reigning figure of a totalizing *Wissenschaft,* to Kierkegaard's mind) was like a man who built a mansion but lived in the porter's lodge. Hegel could explain everything except himself. Repeatedly we find in Percy's work victims of what he calls the fateful flaw of human semiotics: "that of all the objects in the entire Cosmos which the sign-user can apprehend though the conjoining of signifier and signified (word uttered and thing beheld), there is one which forever escapes his comprehension—and this is the sign-user himself" (*LC* 106). Thus the final feature of the self is its unsayability—its utter and irremovable elusiveness.

A common target of Percy's satire, as evidenced by his parody of self-help books, is the therapy culture. The problem he finds is that objectively formulated advice always misses its subjective target. Thus in Percy's second novel, *The Last Gentleman,* Will Barrett abandons Freudian psychotherapy once he discerns that he and Dr. Gamow are playing a kind of game in which the psychiatrist proposes a diagnosis and the patient does his best to conform to it. The "real" Barrett slips away from the Barrett defined by a set of symptoms, joining the doctor in a kind of dance, where each partner performs a series of accepted moves. While the young man is genuinely troubled, and although the treatment he receives may do him some small good, analysis will never cure him since his deeper problem is one of the self.

Another example of a dis-ease in the self is that of a symbol losing its "life" through overuse and excessive abstraction. "The Loss of the Creature" offers the observation that the sight of the Grand Canyon that so amazed its Spanish discoverer, Garcia Lopez de Cardenas, can only be recovered by the contemporary American tourist through the most strenuous efforts. Although the landscape has changed but little, we ourselves have changed a great deal, with the result that we have "lost" the Grand Canyon. It has been emptied of significance for us. Percy offers suggestions for "rescuing" the Canyon, including strategies he will employ in his novels. He recommends recovery by ordeal, whereby a visiting family might be able to reclaim the wonder of the sight by being quarantined during a typhus outbreak, for example. But of greater theoretical interest are the reasons Percy advances for how we "lost" the Canyon. He claims we are unintended victims of a triumphant scientific worldview. Experience is swallowed up by experts with their authorized categories. No actual sighting of the Canyon can compete with the pictures in the guide book; the visitor arrives wondering if she will see what she is "supposed" to see. The experience has been taken away from us before we have it. What we get instead is an abstraction (the guide book, the slide show, the statistics, the maps), which walls us off from the thing itself and bores us as well. We actually suffer a double loss, loss of sovereignty and loss of the world. The Canyon is not "ours"; our role in relation to it is passive. Nor do we "have" it even when the experts "give" it to us. It has been absorbed into theory. In other words, the self is displaced, deprived of its freedom and its location. To return to those characteristics of the self that Percy lists in his "Primer," the self is deprived of its power as co-namer and loses its intersubjective connection to the world around it.

Intersubjectivity itself is more nearly the focus of "The Man on the Train," with its attention to alienation. This essay, Percy's third published piece, deals with the special kind of isolation represented by a bored commuter making his daily round. Percy describes two different but related reversals. The first is similar to the one he noted in describing strategies to defeat the "invisibility" cloaking a famous wonder such as the Grand Canyon: ordeal. The man on the train can be pulled out of his anxious ennui by truly dreadful news. Fear that the Russians might actually drop the Bomb temporarily cures him of his alienation, and thus the commuter paradoxically feels better when he is threatened than when he is safe. The second reversal is one that Percy calls "aesthetic." When an alienated writer writes an alienated novel, the result is not suicide, but liberation. Both he and his readers find a release that may even lead to hilarity, as it did when Kafka read his work to his friends. Percy suggests that alienation is a sickness of the self that science as currently conceived cannot address. In fact, another reversal of common assumptions is revealed when art seems better able to deal with the self's afflictions than does medicine. Percy insists that art is cognitive—Kafka's fiction is not an escape from thought—and it somehow engages those aspects of the self that science cannot see. More specifically, the alienated novel allows writer and reader to "name" their malady, thereby granting them a kind of power over it. Further, the work of art creates a virtual community, a site of intersubjectivity in which a connection is established that counteracts the alienated condition itself.

This line of thought is evident in Percy's first published novel, *The Moviegoer,* which began to take shape soon after "The Man on the Train" appeared. Both the male protagonist and the woman he eventually marries are afflicted by a malaise that has no discernible cause. Their marriage, which comes as a surprise to many readers, has brighter prospects than at first appear because they inhabit a common network of signs, symbols, and strategies for placing their despair. During their odd courtship, sex fails to dispel the gathering psychic gloom. What does rescue them is the bond created by the private vocabulary they have created for describing their predicament. This pattern also obtains in the novel Percy wrote twenty years later, *The Second Coming,* in which we find the female character Percy was most proud of. The romance that blossoms in this book depends even more directly on a new language, the speech that Allie forms as her way of emerging from an acute depression left untamed by the best medical care. While not quite as prominent, in Percy's fourth novel, *Lancelot,* this pattern emerges when the title character begins to make contact with the traumatized and mute woman in the room next door by means of taps on the wall that are eventually returned. Lance plans a new life with this woman, one that will represent a clean break from the past and the end of their literal isolation in a mental institution. It is no accident that the new life begins with a new language.

As we shall later see in more detail, this theme of intersubjectivity as the creation of language extends to the full range of social relationships. For example, the crucial rhetorical consideration in reading *Lancelot* is that Lance is speaking to his best friend, who utters but a single word and that at the very end of the novel. Thus throughout Percy's work, language is the key to overcoming alienation, regaining sovereignty, and receiving the world again. But before tracing how these themes play out in the novels, a further word needs to be said concerning the theological underpinnings of Percy's notion of the self. For just as his theory of the symbol has its roots in Aquinas as well as Peirce, so his theory of the self takes its inspiration from Kierkegaard and Aquinas. Two other essays, one early and the other late, confirm the continuity of Percy's conception.

From Knowledge to Faith and Back Again

"The Message in the Bottle," which provides the title for Percy's first volume of nonfiction, addresses the nature of "news" in relation to faith. First published in 1959, it begins with epigraphs from Aquinas and Kierkegaard that seem to take opposing stands on the relation between faith and knowledge. The position that Percy himself works out might be said to represent a kind of compromise favoring the Catholic saint: faith is knowledge, but of a different sort than that provided by science or philosophy. It is knowledge directed to aspects of the self that Kierkegaard illuminated, aspects that correspond with the model of the self that emerges when one starts with a notion of man as *Homo symbolificus.* Percy employs two categories to distinguish two types of knowledge: knowledge *sub specie aeternatatis* and news. The first kind of knowledge is universal; it applies to every time and place, having to do with the essential nature of things. News, on the other hand, applies to a particular time and place, being directed to a situation or predicament. Science (understood in the broadest sense captured by the German word *Wissenschaft*) supplies us the first kind of knowledge; news could come from anywhere. The determining factor in whether a piece of information is knowledge or news is the situation of the hearer. If I am on an island and someone tells me there is fresh water in the next cove, this datum could be the next entry in my geological survey. Alternatively, it could be the news that saves my life. The difference lies in whether I am visiting the island with a full canteen and a research vessel anchored offshore, or I am marooned and dehydrated.

This difference in the conditions under which information is received leads to a difference in the verification and acceptance of a message. In the case of the fresh water, one can verify the report by empirical means, as one might well do no matter whether he received the report as knowledge or as news. However, the prior question is not one of verification but of trust. Before one checks on the truth of the claim, one makes a judgment about its reliability. If I am conducting a geological survey and have a reliable assistant, I likely will see no reason to verify her report at all. If I am a thirsty castaway and the reporter seems sincere, I hasten to follow her. In either case, whether I act or not depends upon whether I trust the reporter. But the action I take, even if it looks the same in both cases, will serve different purposes. In the case of the survey, I verify in order to make the knowledge more secure, perhaps because I do not trust the reporter. If I am a castaway, I do not go with verification in mind at all; I go to drink, and I go because I do indeed trust the newsbearer.

The issues of trustworthiness and action become more acute as news grows more urgent. For the most urgent cases, verification may be out of the question. When an announcement comes over the loudspeaker that the theater is on fire, no sensible person asks for proof. Where news is concerned, Percy claims, what matters are its relevance to my situation and the credibility of the newsbearer, not whether it can be tested by external criteria. News, then, is a message directed to someone in a particular situation, who acts if he accepts the news as relevant and the newsbearer as credible. In this way it is an inescapably personal transaction, one requiring faith.

Faith, with its religious connotations, leads to the real point of Percy's philosophical exercise, which is that Christian belief can in principle be rationally justified even if its claims cannot be scientifically certified. According to Percy, Christianity (with Judaism) asserts that certain contingent, historical events have the most urgent importance, and that these events and their true meaning cannot be deduced or discovered; they can only be witnessed to. Percy paraphrases Kierkegaard approvingly on the particularity of Christianity: "[T]he object of the student is not the teacher but the teaching, while the object of the Christian is not the teaching but the teacher" (*MB* 140). Percy in fact owes to Kierkegaard the major insight that Christianity is not a species of knowledge *sub specie aeternatatis*. Where Kierkegaard went astray in Percy's view was in claiming that faith is an absolute scandal, and thus a logical absurdity. News of the Gospel sort only appears absurd when one overvalues knowledge of the broadly scientific type. In other words, Percy believes that despite his attacks on Hegel, Kierkegaard gave away too much to him in allowing him to define knowledge. Percy clearly sides with Aquinas in concluding that faith is a kind of knowledge (that is, it is not absurd), but that it does depend upon revelation (news) rather than reason alone.

Percy's effort to clear intellectual space for Christian belief follows from his understanding of the symbol-using self in several ways. First, the dominant metaphor of man as castaway—one who is not living in his true home—is another representation of the restless and "left over" self who cannot be captured within its own purview. Second, "news" itself as a category is, as Percy says, "a mode of communication." It depends upon speakers and hearers; it is necessarily intersubjective. In other words, we must return to the activity of language as the clue to our place in the cosmos. Finally, Percy hints of the self's incompleteness in "The Message in the Bottle." Even after he has gained the acceptance of the islanders he has landed among, the castaway feels something is missing. And the "something" is not only a message, but also a *someone*. Percy's argument seems strained when he asserts that for the castaway a message alone is not sufficient to qualify as a piece of news (*MB* 136). True news, Percy insists, must be delivered by a newsbearer. But while it makes sense to say that a message must have a sender, it is difficult to see why news must be delivered in person. It seems to me that the real reason for Percy's insistence on a newsbearer is theological: he believes that the original sender of the most important of messages is God.

Kierkegaard's comment about the teacher being more important for the Christian than the teaching falls within the same line of thought. Faith is not merely cognitive assent (though for Percy and for Aquinas it is that), but also trust in a person. In Percy's understanding, the self is only completed in God. In interviews, Percy confided that this insight hit him as a result of reading Kierkegaard's *Sickness unto Death,* and that it made an in-

delible impression on him (*CWP* 110, for example). And although Percy
pulls up short of such a declaration in a non-apologetic piece such as
"Message," the implication is plain. The essay does conclude with the
hope that if any castaway hears news from across the seas delivered "in
perfect sobriety and with good faith and perseverance to the point of
martyrdom" by a newsbearer, he will, "by the grace of God, believe him"
(*MB* 149).

That the self made necessary by the birth of the symbol can be completed only in relation to God is also suggested in *Lost in the Cosmos*. Percy thus describes a "semiotic fall" in which the self is exiled from the Eden
of its symbol-world. He characterizes the fall in this way:

> You are not a sign in your world. Unlike the other signifiers in
> your world which form more or less stable units with the perceived
> world-things they signify, the signifier of yourself is mobile, freed
> up. . . .
> The signified of the self is semiotically loose and caroms around
> the Cosmos like an unguided missile.
> From the moment the signifying self turned inward and became
> conscious of itself, trouble began as the sparks flew up.
> No one knows how such a state of affairs came to pass, except
> through the wisdom (or folly) of religion and myth. (*LC* 107)

According to Percy, the rise of the symbol was very quickly followed by
an estrangement of the self from its own world of signs. Now, alas, "The
self perceives itself as naked. Every self is ashamed of itself" (*LC* 108). Percy even speculates that this process may repeat itself in the human life cycle, ontogeny repeating phylogeny. He cites a child development textbook to give a common view of three stages through which the child
passes. By age two, the typical child has discovered language. At four, she
is outgoing, positive, enthusiastic. But by seven, the child has grown self-
conscious, private, and sensitive to criticism. Percy wonders whether this
change is the necessary and inevitable result of "the sudden emergence
of a triadic organism into a dyadic world" or a catastrophe following "a
bad move in the exercise of [the self's] freedom," "a turning from the con-
celebration of the world to a solitary absorption with self" (*LC* 109). Although in such a book, meant to pique and tease the reader toward her
own conclusions, Percy does not state his own position, even a passing acquaintance with his other work leaves little doubt that he favors an Augustinian interpretation of this event. The semiotic fall, which he believes

to be an empirically verifiable fact, is a "catastrophe" that in turn leads to all the distinctly human trouble in the world. While he avoids the word, it is clear that Percy is pointing to the theological category of sin.

Some of the most arresting passages in *Lost in the Cosmos* are those in which Percy explores strategies that the self uses to hide its "nakedness." Displaced from its own world and unable by its very nature to get a purchase on itself, the self seeks stability by attaching itself to other selves or even to other things. Percy believes this is the true dynamic driving practices as seemingly diverse as totemism and the fashion industry. The totemist identifies religiously with a bird or a bear; the shopper identifies with a style. What does a friend mean, for example, when he says, "That shirt is you"? And why does the shirt or haircut that seemed so "me" twenty years ago now look so quaint and "un-me" in the old photograph?

This need to identify the self in order to avoid a kind of ghostly nonexistence is balanced by another pole of the self that revels in its freedom. The fully autonomous self that has emerged in Western society in the wake of weakened religious and mythic consensus prizes its freedom but finds it difficult to handle. The success of science, which has completely transformed our world, has led us to value the kind of detachment and abstraction science seems to require. Science gives the self a means of transcending and mastering the world, thus allowing the self to assert its autonomy. The difficulty is that such exaltation cannot last; one must return to earth sooner or later. The artist faces the same problem, even though his mode of knowing is different. And so one finds scientists and artists, along with many members of their "lay" audiences, attempting by various means to negotiate between the transcendent stance of the knower and creator on the one hand, and the immanent life of bodily needs and concrete commitments on the other.

The male scientist at work in Los Alamos on the research that will produce the atomic bomb descends weekly for vigorous sex with his wife, whom he hardly talks to, ignoring both her and the kids while he eats ravenously and watches TV until time to go back to the lab. The novelist who has finished a modernist masterpiece first gets drunk for a week, then begins hanging out at the county courthouse square, pretending to be just another idle farmer. In both cases, the self that has successfully transcended the world seeks desperately to "come back home," literally and metaphysically. This return, however, is seldom fully satisfying and always temporary. In his section on reentry difficulties of writers, called "Why Writers Drink," Percy describes a southern exile who leaves Valdosta,

Georgia, as soon as he can get away, but who grows weary of his writerly companions in the Northeast and decides to return to his roots. After fifteen minutes of listening to the drone of his fellow townsmen and contemplating a prolonged future of the same, he can think only of fleeing or plunging himself into drink. But in his list of reentry options, Percy does include one more-hopeful alternative that avoids the violent swings between transcendence and immanence, and it is one that returns us to Kierkegaard.

The self can achieve reentry "under the direct sponsorship of God." Percy notes, "It is theoretically possible, if practically extremely difficult, to reenter the world and become an intact self through the reentry mode Kierkegaard described when he noted that 'the self can only become itself if it does so transparently before God.' This is in fact, according to both Kierkegaard and Pascal, the only viable mode of reentry, the others being snares and delusions" (*LC* 156). The phrase Percy quotes from *The Sickness unto Death,* which he referred to in interviews throughout his career, sums up his own take on the self, just as it also provides the final, missing piece in the puzzle of the semiotic self. The reason the self "caroms around the Cosmos like an unguided missile" is that it has cut itself off from God and, conversely, it can find balance only when its connection to God is reestablished. On the short list of twentieth-century writers who seem to have managed to live their lives "transparently before God," Percy reserves the highest place for Flannery O'Connor, who he says has "even outdone Kierkegaard and seen both creation and art as the Chartres sculptor did, as both dense and mysterious, gratuitous, anagogic, and sacramental" (*LC* 157).

Seeing creation as sacramental takes us beyond Kierkegaard, Percy claims, and it brings us full circle as far as this study is concerned. The self's problem is the loss of the world and the consequent disorientation of itself through sin. Healing of the self comes through returning to God and coming to see the world sacramentally. The self is not autonomous—it is incomplete without God. And the physical ("dyadic") world is not Descartes' *res extensa,* but the living form of God's eternally creative power. Here lies the formula for curing the self of its despair and for making the world meaningful again. Self and world have value by their common origin in God, and by honoring God, the self is liberated from its demonic emptiness and its false transcendence. Yet the category of the sacramental also points to a difference between O'Connor and Percy.

The very problem that Percy is dealing with in this section of *Lost in the Cosmos* is that of receptivity to sacramental reality. Percy indicates that because of her faith, O'Connor is not alienated, as are nearly all modern writers, and thus she avoids the artist's particular kind of despair. Percy, both in his ironic self-help book and in his novels, is primarily concerned with those obstacles that make O'Connor's kind of faith so difficult at the end of the twentieth century. Percy attacks those obstacles by shining a sudden, bright light on them, hoping that reason and grace will take over after the reader's shock of recognition wears off. When confronted by sacramental reality in Percy's fiction, the reader is teased and provoked into entertaining a proposition that she is nonetheless free to doubt, as do most of Percy's own protagonists. Will Barrett witnesses Jamie Vaught's baptism and has to ask Sutter, "What happened back there?" and the reader thus is forced to take up his question. By contrast, when Bevel drowns in the baptismal waters of the river, O'Connor's narrator leaves us in no doubt that he has been redeemed by the Lamb and gone to join God. Percy's job is to make a sacramental universe plausible; O'Connor's mission is to assault the reader with a divine irruption that can not be ignored. While Desmond is persuasive in arguing that a Eucharistic understanding is central to Percy's work,[5] it is central as a principle rather than as an action. The sacraments themselves are often peripheral to the action of his novels, the deeper problem being characters' inability to adopt a sacramental perspective. In O'Connor's work, divine action is inescapable, theophany unavoidable. And this difference is most stark when it comes to O'Connor's fictional *imitatio Christis.*

As we have seen, O'Connor repeatedly employs violence as a means whereby her characters are allowed to participate in the suffering of Christ. Although these actions are not always sacramental in the precise sense of belonging to one of the rites of the church, they are means whereby God's grace is made present in the material world. They are also christocentric, pointing directly to Christ's Passion. While Percy's protagonists suffer, their anguish is typically psychological and spiritual. And insofar as their mental suffering prepares them for redemption, they hardly suffer in the manner of a willing victim, as the grandmother or Mr. Guizac or even Parker might be said to do. In Percy's novels, the physical suffering of characters—a Lonnie Smith in *The Moviegoer* or a Jamie Vaught in *The Last Gentleman* or a Samantha in *Love in the Ruins*—may take on a Christlike quality, but the roles of these cases in their respective

5. See John F. Desmond, "Walker Percy's Eucharistic Vision."

plots is never central. They take their significance from the effect they have on doubting or lapsing protagonists. The metaphorical crucifixes to which O'Connor points at the end of so many of her stories as a kind of final punctuation mark are rare in Percy's fiction, which is much more likely to end with a question.

In part, this difference has to do with Percy's strategy of indirect communication: Percy believes that in a time when religious language is worn out, meaning cannot be restored through a frontal assault, as we will see more thoroughly in the next chapter when we look more closely at Percy's novels. But one result of Percy's approach may be seen at the end of *Lost in the Cosmos,* when Percy comes closest to stating the conclusion of his semiotic apologetic.

As the final section of *Lost in the Cosmos,* Percy writes a brief apocalyptic space fantasy that owes much to *A Canticle for Leibowitz,* a novel he admired. Percy calls one of his own characters Liebowitz, making him a Jew who has embraced Christianity and become the abbot of a Roman Catholic monastery. In explaining himself to fellow survivors of nuclear war, he becomes Percy's spokesman:

> I believe that God exists and that he created the Cosmos . . . , that he created man through evolution, in the latest moment of which, perhaps the last Ice Age, man became ensouled and came to himself as man, body and spirit; that God created man as a person who had gifts of knowledge and love but most of all freedom, that he somehow encountered a catastrophe, God alone knows what, used his freedom badly, and chose badly—perhaps chose himself, the one thing he can never know of itself, rather than God—and has been in trouble ever since. That, as a consequence, God himself intervened in the history of this insignificant planet, through a covenant with an even more obscure tribe, the Jews, through his son, a Jew who actually lived as a man on this earth, him and no other, through founding a church, the Catholic Church based on a very mediocre, intemperate Catholic, Peter, also a Jew; that he, God, is somehow inextricably and permanently, even hopelessly, involved with the two, the Jews and the Catholic Church, until the end of time. (*LC* 248)

This account, which serves as a succinct statement of the position that Percy has hinted toward throughout the volume, is straightforwardly Catholic and Christian, but strangely silent when it comes to the work of Christ. Later in his speech, the abbot will say that "Christ, having come once to save us from the death of self in search of itself without any other self, will also come again at the end of the world" (*LC* 249), but no mention is made of Christ's death. And despite Liebowitz's own practical concern for administering the sacraments—the question of ordination is a pressing one because there are few people and a dangerously small number of priests—no direct connection is made between those sacraments and the work of Christ. Of course, both Percy and his spokesman take it as a given that Jesus's sacrificial death and resurrection are the basis of sacramental practice, but that fact itself is not part of the explanation.

This omission has nothing to do with Percy's orthodoxy, but it does illustrate the nature of his apologetic project. Each of the doctrines listed can be tied to the epistemological question, how do we know? As we have seen, Percy's dissatisfaction with science was piqued by his discovery, by way of the existentialists, that the one thing the scientist could not explain was himself as thinking, feeling, truth-asserting individual. For Percy, the nature of language opens the door to this self that Kierkegaard called the Individual. Likewise, each of the items in Liebowitz's list has to do with the particularity as it stands over against the generalizable. Sin is the violation of a norm, the assertion of self over against God; the Incarnation is God condescending to a particular time and a single human body—Christ's; the Jews and the Catholic Church are likewise undeducible and unique historical entities, as is the Parousia. Likewise, these truths are carried forward through intersubjectivity by a (sacramental) community, as Peirce insisted. Thus Percy's credo, as expressed by the abbot, follows from his apologetics, the centerpiece of which is his theory of language.

Apologetics Malgré Lui

My use of the term *apologetics* to describe Percy's project in *Lost in the Cosmos* and *The Message in the Bottle* would not sit well with him. When he does use it himself, as in the title essay of the earlier volume, it is to disassociate himself from the enterprise. And it is certainly true that many apologetic topics, such as the historical accuracy of scripture, hold no interest for Percy. But apologetics in the broader sense of providing a rational case for the plausibility of Christianity serves as a good description of the general purpose of Percy's nonfiction. Although he insists that his theory of language is based upon empirical science, it is clear that for Percy the Delta factor has metaphysical implications as well. Language is important to him because he believes it exposes a gap in current scientific thinking—one that should lead to a new kind of science—and because it opens the door to religious faith. The seriousness with which he viewed this mission can be gauged by his remark to Shelby Foote that if he was remembered in a hundred years, it would be because of his contribution to semiotics, and that his essay on the theory of language was "the most important I'll ever write."[6] Clearly, although Percy believed art and philosophy to be distinct activities, along with Maritain and O'Connor, he thought them both to be inherently cognitive, and believed that ideally they should reflect a unitary truth, thus the importance of theory in his version of the aesthetic of revelation.

Given the importance Percy attached to the philosophical side of his endeavor, it is worth noting that his arguments have not gone unchallenged. Linguists and philosophers have taken issue with his language theory; recent studies of animal behavior pose objections to his case for the uniqueness of man. So far, his prediction to Shelby Foote has not been borne out. Despite continued interest in Thomistic language theory and Peircean epistemology,[7] an honest review of Percy's philosophical claims shows that, some fifteen years after his death, weaknesses in his account are at least as apparent as strengths.

A good place to begin is with two reviews of *The Message in the Bottle* written by academic theorists. Thomas Nagle and Walter Benn Michaels are philosophers of language with a Wittgensteinian orientation, and it is their Anglo-American approach to ordinary language that Percy largely ignores. In his essays, Percy does battle with behaviorists such as B. F. Skinner and transformational grammarians such as Noam Chomsky, and he applauds the underappreciated insights of phenomenologist Susanne Langer, touting his own neo-Thomist appropriation of Peirce as a way of bridging the gap between language as behavior and language as meaning. But as Nagle points out in his *New York Review of Books* essay, Percy has left out Wittgenstein and a whole set of twentieth-century thinkers who have mulled this issue.

Wittgenstein's conclusion might be put in this way: meaning does not come from some mysterious connection between mind and external re-

6. Percy to Foote, May 23, 1974, in *Correspondence of Foote and Percy,* 184.
7. See Farrell O'Gorman, *Peculiar Crossroads: Flannery O'Connor, Walker Percy, and Catholic Vision in Postwar Southern Fiction,* 117n19.

ality, but from "forms of life," the patterns of social interaction and work by which language is learned and in which it is used. That is, what we need in order to understand how meaning works is not a new, metaphysically attuned science, but a new point of view. In the past, (some) philosophers have mistakenly thought that language could be explained from the outside, so to speak, with all of its elements and processes laid bare as one lays out the bones of a skeleton. But language can only be understood from inside—by its use.

Both Nagle and Michaels point out that Percy lands himself in a contradiction generated by his missing precisely this point. Nagle notes that while Percy affirms the intersubjective nature of language as the crucial element the linguists miss, he himself diminishes the sociality of language. For example, although Percy can analyze the interchange between boy and father over the connection between the word *balloon* and its referent to show that the naming function includes more than treating the word as a mere sign of the thing, he does not linger over the social context of toys, parent–child relationships, and the conversation itself that place this naming function. Percy's approach is what we might call atomistic; by analyzing the individual case, he wants to find the principle that will explain the general phenomenon. But when it comes to language, one has to begin with the whole to understand the parts.

A second, related point concerns scientific method. Nagle argues that Percy reproduces what he rejects in the scientific approach to language. Percy constantly adopts what Percy himself calls a "Martian's" view of human communication, when in fact the distinctive features of language cannot be seen by this method. That is, just as Percy claims that science leaves out the individual, so Nagle claims that a scientific approach to language of the kind Percy wants would leave out the very intersubjectivity that Percy most values. Thus Percy tries to replace one external view of language with another: "To believe that a Martian could understand the workings of human language better than we can and that the best way to achieve understanding is to become like a Martian is, in extreme form, to elevate scientific objectivity and detachment into a universal method."[8]

Michaels makes a similar case, arguing that Percy's theory of language is insufficiently social. However, he dwells upon the more literary features of Percy's work, finding a disjuncture between form and content. According to Michaels, Percy's theory, in stressing intersubjectivity, rightly

8. Thomas Nagle, "Sin and Significance," 55.

takes American behaviorists to task for ignoring it, yet Percy's own stance is that of a detached observer theorizing about what he sees. Percy as author-essayist has the same relation to language as the protagonists in his novels have toward their lives and relationships: detached, ironic, theoretical. Percy's method is thus at odds with his message. In Michaels's words, there is a "penetrating and interesting contradiction which underlies [Percy's views]: the face-off between the social theory of meaning the book proposes and the anti-social *Moviegoer*-like character of its proposer."[9] This internal inconsistency also has implications for Percy's understanding of community, as we will see when we consider the existentialist themes of the novels. But simply as a theory of language, Percy's stance creates difficulties. As Michaels concludes, "We are left in a predicament. On the one hand, meaning and understanding are possible only within community; on the other hand, the community represents a sinister form of domestication. The business of the essayist (the professional amateur) is to resist community, 'to see things and people as if he had never seen them before,' but the mark of his success is the creation of a community of readers who subscribe to his vision and so, on its own terms, defuse it."[10]

A final issue important to Percy on which his views seem less and less plausible is that of symbolic language use as belonging uniquely and exclusively to human beings. Although he sometimes qualified this claim, he consistently maintained it, as this passage of his Jefferson Lecture indicates: "This strange capacity [to use symbols] seems to be unique in Homo sapiens. And even though there is nothing unscientific about assigning a 'species-specific' trait to this or that species . . . many scientists, including Darwin, find this uniqueness offensive" (*SSL* 281). Percy goes on to declare that though much effort has been exerted to teach language to other primates, these efforts have failed. He specifically mentions Washoe as the chimpanzee who was supposed to have broken this barrier when she learned American Sign Language, but Percy claims that a later investigator, Herbert Terrace, effectively overturned this conclusion by showing how a chimp he adopted was actually following subtle clues from his trainers rather than signing spontaneously. And so, according to Percy, nonhuman animals remain in a dyadic world where there are signals but no symbols. To a dog (or, Percy would say, a chimp) *ball* may mean an object, but

---

9. Walter Benn Michaels, review of *The Message in the Bottle,* 973.
10. Ibid., 975.

it does not mean itself, so to speak; it does not have a place in a symbolic world. In one of Percy's favorite illustrations, if I say "ball" to my dog, he starts looking for it; if I say "ball" to you, you say, "What about it?"

The problem with Percy's position on this issue is that, since his death, evidence against his conclusion has mounted. One convincing counter story is that of Roger Fouts, a graduate student of the husband and wife team who trained Washoe, and the man who became her keeper and an important researcher in his own right. In *Next of Kin* (1997), Fouts provides a thick description of years of intimate contact with primates who, having been exposed to ASL, passed every test for symbolic language. Washoe clearly possessed concepts—of *tree,* for example, applying the sign to all successive trees after first learning the signal. Washoe as a youngster was observed lounging in a tree and signing to herself while she looked through the pages of a magazine, clearly using her language as a means of self-expression. Fouts and his coworkers have observed chimps cursing in sign language, and have seen them generate creative names for newcomers, names that they continue to use. In an experiment designed to test a grasp of syntax, a chimp named Ally showed she could consistently distinguish "toothbrush on blanket" from "blanket on toothbrush." Washoe has taught signs to adopted offspring, thus showing that chimps can spontaneously pass on language to the next generation. Fouts has known chimps to lie to him—about who defecated on the floor, for example. These examples all seem to indicate that chimps are capable of generating a symbolic world, including a universe of discourse where they can curse, tell lies, and make jokes. Against Terrace's claims that the chimps who demonstrated language use were simply responding to subtle cues from their human trainers, Fouts provides thorough and emphatic refutation.

Ironically, much of Fouts's credibility on these matters comes from his having to a considerable degree participated in the chimps' community over a period of years. That is, he has increasingly modified the detached observer role in favor of befriending the animals and allowing them, insofar as possible, to develop their own community, in part by way of response to the success of his friend Jane Goodall with wild chimpanzees. Thus has Fouts abandoned Percy's "Martian" perspective and "gone native," with striking results. This is ironic because, just as Nagle might have predicted, Fouts has made his breakthroughs by reversing the procedure Percy recommends, yet confirming what Percy asserts about the communal nature of language.

As I have explained elsewhere, although I disagree with his tendentious claim that Percy was the "last" Catholic novelist,[11] Kieran Quinlan is surely correct in his assessment that Percy was neither current nor convincing in his language theory or his science. And it would seem, as Quinlan would like to suggest, that one set of errors might lead to another. If Percy was wrong about language, given the importance he attached to his views, are his theological conclusions not also discredited? My answer in short is no. Although Percy's philosophical positions do create theological difficulties for his understanding of self and community, his commitment to a neo-Thomist sacramentalism, which he shared with O'Connor, served to balance the dangers of an epistemological individualism that he failed to escape. Such sacramentalism is also inherent in his theory of language, in the form of a metaphysical realism that posits a real connection between mind and reality by way of symbol. That is, while Percy's theory of meaning is skewed by his failure to grasp the full implications of the sociality of language, this failure does not refute the metaphysical claim that supplies the essential theological point.

This essential point is the one insisted upon by such Percy proponents as John Desmond and Patrick Samway. As Desmond frames it, "Percy said, during Samway's last visit shortly before the writer's death in 1990, that he felt it crucial to believe in a 'realistic' philosophy and theology that could lead to absolute certainty, such as the certainty that the Eucharist was not a symbol but a reality, and that God was genuinely present as a person in the consecrated bread and wine. Samway regards this, as I do, as 'the central intellectual intuition' of Percy's life."[12] The difficulty, as I see it, is not with this central intuition, or with the realist aspect of Percy's philosophical position, but with the degree to which he failed to escape the limitations of important dialogue partners. Kierkegaard alerted Percy to the dangers of scientism and the need for faith as antidote to despair, but he also reinforced Percy's native tendency toward solitariness and thus opened him up to a kind of individualism. And Peirce, whom Desmond sees as Percy's most important conversation partner, encouraged Percy's tendency to a kind of totalism that could outweigh the wholesome effect of Peirce's emphasis on intersubjectivity and a realist view of meaning. Percy's existentialist tendencies will be more fruitfully explored under the topic of community in the final chapter. But the

---

11. Sykes, review of *Walker Percy: The Last Catholic Novelist,* by Kieran Quinlan.
12. Desmond, *Percy's Search,* 5.

temptation represented by Peirce has to do with Percy's apologetic project as a whole, and thus deserves attention before we leave his philosophical nonfiction.

Desmond has provided the most careful and thorough account of why Percy was attracted to Peirce and of what Percy borrowed from him. But he also notes two points on which Peirce's Idealism was incompatible with Percy's Catholicism. The first is Peirce's penchant for absorbing the particular into the general, most especially as that tendency is registered in Peirce's remark that matter is only "effete mind." In his enthusiasm to show that relation is the most basic reality, fully as real as the material world, Peirce went the full Idealist distance, claiming that matter is actually an instance of mind. No doubt Desmond is correct in concluding that Percy resisted this move because of his commitment to the Christian doctrine of the Incarnation. Percy called this side of Peirce a kind of Gnosticism. Likewise, according to Ketner, Peirce held that "individuals are not basic. They are derivative." Indeed, as Ketner says in explaining Peirce's position, "the term 'individual' merely denotes a being who is essentially a particular unity of signs," the makeup of which is constantly shifting.[13] Percy again took issue, this time on the basis of the Christian conviction that each human being is unique before God, just as God the Son became a unique, enfleshed self in Jesus of Nazareth.

Desmond observes that Percy's objections "reveal a deep tension within his own mind . . . the tension between reason and faith, which he had addressed in his 'The Message in the Bottle.' On the one hand, from a scientific viewpoint Percy searched for a natural explanation for the role of the interpretant in the act of communication, one that was empirically demonstrable. . . . On the other hand, from a Christian metaphysical and theological viewpoint, rooted in the Incarnation, Percy affirmed the absolute uniqueness of the person as a hypostatic mystery." One reason for this tension is the implicit acknowledgment that if reason is sufficient unto itself, faith becomes unnecessary. Peirce, like that earlier nineteenth-century, Idealist system-builder Hegel, had a penchant for absorbing the particularities of faith into a universal reason. And indeed, any exhaustively descriptive science would have the same effect. Percy resisted the Idealist extremes of Peirce's thought, but he continued to search for the kind of definitive, empirical scientific explanation of human language that if successful would in effect either render Christian theology an adjunct

13. Quoted ibid., 24.

of scientific reason or make science a branch of theology. My point, in opposition to Desmond's presentation of Percy, is that the tension between faith and reason was bound to be relaxed in favor of reason so long as Percy used Peirce to establish "no less than an anthropological basis for the creation of a revitalized organon of truth."[14] The goal itself was problematic.

Percy's temptation, which he shared with his brilliant character Tom More, was to attempt a grand synthesis of science and theology that would be so rationally persuasive as to restore a Christian worldview to intellectual dominance. As Weldon Thornton puts it, "For Percy . . . as essayist, it seems that man's present malaise is largely a matter of cultural and intellectual events of the past few hundred years that eroded the traditional Judaeo-Christian view of man, and that when corrected will permit our return to some such happy union of methodology and faith."[15] But this rationalist solution to what is at root the problem of sin is, to use Thornton's kind word, too sanguine. Such an apologetic project is doomed from the start, for it strives to produce a kind of universal science that would swallow all of reality. Ironically, such hegemonic system building was exactly what originally sparked Percy's critique of scientism and led him into the church. However, Percy at his best is aware of the recurring temptation, and repeatedly the probing particularity of his novels points beyond detachment and system to the divine, unifying mystery lying within the quotidian. Most tellingly, Percy finds in the provoking word, the dialogic confrontation with another, the possibility for revelatory encounter where the word becomes the means not simply to knowledge, but to grace. This quest first takes lasting fictional form with Binx Bolling's search in *The Moviegoer.*

14. Ibid., 25–26, 23.
15. Weldon Thornton, "Homo Loquens, Homo Symbolificus, Homo Sapiens: Walker Percy on Language," 189.

6

Percy's Novelistic Quest for Faith

ௐ

W hen *The Moviegoer* began to attract attention after it won the National Book Award in 1962, most readers regarded it as fresh in a number of respects. In addition to speaking with a distinctive new voice, Percy's first novel crossed the grain of several expectations. Here was a southern book void of southern literary paraphernalia—no family sagas, no decayed mansions, no sexual degeneracy or colorful dialects. Instead, there was a sparseness and archness about the narration that seemed to fly in the face of the rhetorical display often associated with southern writing. Further, the musings of the wry protagonist were decidedly philosophical in a precise, closely observed way that reminded one more of a scientist than of a windy lawyer or cynical aristocrat. The ideas themselves were not passed down from the Greek stoa, but imported from modern European thinkers whose terms were so adroitly Americanized and woven into the fabric of contemporary New Orleans that they seemed newly minted. Finally, the main character himself was a different kind of bird—the scion of a noble stock, as his aunt liked to say, but one who stood oddly apart from his family, indeed from his entire environment. This difference was not due to a family curse or a rebellious nature, but rather to some deeper estrangement that seemed to have more to do with metaphysics than history. Binx Bolling suffered from a kind of detachment having no obvious cause, but which was large in its effects, leaving him curiously disconnected from a world that seemed to him not evil or even hostile so much as artificial and flimsy.

In this way, Percy's character stands in a very different place from the typical O'Connor protagonist. Although the world surrounding Hulga Hopewell or the Wellesley student in "Revelation" or Julian in "Everything That Rises Must Converge" or Asbury Fox in "The Enduring Chill" contains its hidden dangers and unseen depths, it is solid and real. As O'Connor was fond of saying, her characters are *from* somewhere. Her disaffected intellectuals may strain against backwardness and ignorance, but their social environment also gives them a reassuring counterweight to abstraction and anonymity. And the natural world in O'Connor's stories is often the vehicle of divine disclosure. The solidity of the social and natural contexts is matched by certainty on the part of characters. In fact, O'Connor's characters are too sure of themselves—they are victims of a pride that must be broken before they can be redeemed. Percy's protagonists by contrast are constantly at risk of losing their grip on the world. Their surroundings seem insubstantial, and correspondingly, they themselves are always in a state of doubt.

This combination of insubstantiality and doubt is evidenced repeatedly in Percy's novels. An early, memorable, and oft-cited passage from *The Moviegoer* (inspired by a scene from Sartre's *Nausea*) has Binx trying to "see" the pile of personal items on his bureau. They have been rendered invisible to him by overfamiliarity. He labors to find an angle that will restore to them the reality that a dung beetle held for him as he lay wounded on a Korean battlefield. Will Barrett, in both *The Last Gentleman* and *The Second Coming,* actually suffers from an illness that sends him into fugue states and delusions, giving him added reason to doubt himself. Dr. Tom More serves time as a patient in the psychiatric ward of his hospital; Lance Lamar confesses to his priest friend from a cell in a prison for the criminally insane. But these unstable men are onto a truth that has eluded the more comfortably adjusted: the world is indeed slipping away from a humanity that grows increasingly ghostlike.

A honeymooning couple in New Orleans is sunk in boredom until the film star William Holden unexpectedly turns up on their street and needs a light for his cigarette, which the young husband can casually but confidently supply. The sudden visitation from a stellar being representing the unreal realm of movies has mysteriously supplied density to a washed-out, used-up locale: the honeymoon is saved, but only by a kind of trick that will itself wear out over time. In *The Thanatos Syndrome* Tom More cannot shake the impression that many of the people around him—including his wife—are turning into soulless hominids who only ape human motions. He turns out to be right. These examples, taken from the first and last of Percy's published novels, bracket a host of fictional glimpses into unreality. Some of these have to do with being displaced from history—as in Will Barrett's status as "the last gentleman." Others expose the unraveling social fabric, as consensus breaks down and ideological warfare heats up, notably in *Love in the Ruins.* Yet another concern is the flattening effect of scientism and the cult of the expert, which Binx discovers when he rejects what he calls the vertical search, the hope to "solve" life's mysteries through detached observation and theory.

The Rhetoric of Faith: Indirect Communication

The twin themes of unreality and uncertainty, largely lacking in O'Connor's work, led Percy to entirely different theological-literary strategies. The antidote to doubt is faith, and while Percy, like O'Connor, found in St. Thomas Aquinas his primary theological saint, he drew heavily from another source that O'Connor was only cursorily acquainted with: Søren Kierkegaard. As the previous chapter laid out, Percy plays Kierkegaard off Aquinas on the question of faith in his important essay "The Message in the Bottle." Percy insists that faith does not require a leap beyond the rational, siding with Aquinas in claiming that faith is a form of knowledge. But in Kierkegaard he found a convincing phenomenology of faith that seemed to describe the condition of modern man. This phenomenology had to do with the reception of faith—the conditions under which faith becomes possible—and it led directly to distinctive rhetorical strategies, which would in turn shape Percy's novelistic work.

The importance of what we might call the rhetorical side of Kierkegaard is suggested by a remark Percy made to Bradley Dewey: "The most important single piece that Kierkegaard wrote is something I seldom hear about and a lot of people don't know too well. It's his essay called 'The Difference between a Genius and an Apostle.' That was tremendously important to me" (*CWP* 113). This essay loomed so large for Percy as a Christian writing fiction because it describes the limits of art for communicating faith. Faith is called forth not by the immanent insight of the poet or the scientist, but by what Percy called "news from across the seas"—an announcement or revelation from God that not even a genius could have predicted. But this circumstance makes the job of the Christian writer problematic from the theological point of view, especially if that writer shares O'Connor's conviction that he must rouse a deaf world. In short, the novelist cannot proclaim the truth directly. However, what does lie open to the novelist is the circuitous path Kierkegaard calls indirect communication.

The religious writer who practices indirect communication attempts to lead the reader to the verge of a discovery that the reader may or may not make. This discovery is one that the writer has already made, and in that sense the writer has led the reader directly to it. But in a deeper sense, the revelation by its very nature is private and invokes the agency of the reader. In fact, for Kierkegaard, this "discovery" is primarily the recognition of a relationship, and thus cannot occur without the participation of the subject. The name of the relation is of course faith, which for both Kierkegaard and Percy is a bond between the individual and God. One might say that the novelist's job is to remove the obstacles between the reader and God so that the connection can take place. But the connection itself can never be forced. Indeed, the author is under obligation to step aside at the final stage of the process for at least two reasons. First, he or she has no authority to make a direct pronouncement—only an "apostle," one called by God, has such a commission. Second, since the faith relationship is private, the writer would himself become an obstacle if he tried to intervene.

Kierkegaard discusses these matters in a number of places familiar to Percy, most searchingly in *Philosophical Fragments, or a Fragment of Philosophy; Concluding Unscientific Postscript to Philosophical Fragments;* and *The Point of View for My Work as an Author.* In the first two works, his primary concern is not with the writer, but rather with Christ as historical embodiment of truth, and with the ordinary believer who witnesses to his faith. Even the Christian proclaimer must avoid "the meddling busyness of a third person" between his hearer and God.[1] But in the case of the imaginative writer, the same issues arise and become more acute, for fiction by its very nature is in a tangential relationship to fact. Though there is some dispute about how accurately he represents his own work,[2] Kierkegaard near the end of his life claimed to have arranged his whole pseudonymous corpus along these lines, inventing authors as well as characters and using multiple genres to distract the reader from his real purpose at the same time that he led him toward the goal of faith:

> [F]rom the total point of view of my whole work as an author, the esthetic writing is a deception, and herein is the deeper significance of the *pseudonymity.* But a deception, that is indeed something rather ugly. To that I should answer: Do not be deceived by the word *de-*

1. Søren Kierkegaard, *Concluding Unscientific Postscript to Philosophical Fragments,* 77.
2. Alasdair MacIntyre, *After Virtue,* 41.

ception. One can deceive a person out of what is true, and—to recall old Socrates—one can deceive a person into what is true. Yes,
in only this way can a deluded person actually be brought into what
is true—by deceiving him. . . . Thus one does not begin . . . in this
way: I am a Christian, you are not a Christian—but this way: You
are a Christian, I am not a Christian. Or one does not begin in this
way: It is Christianity that I am proclaiming and you are living in
purely esthetic categories. No, one begins this way: Let us talk about
the esthetic. The deception consists in one's speaking this way precisely in order to arrive at the religious. But according to the assumption the other person is in fact under the delusion that the
esthetic is the essentially Christian, since he thinks he is a Christian
and yet he is living in esthetic categories.

Percy adopts a very similar strategy, "deceiving" the reader out of his delusions in the name of truth, and in order to preserve the possibility of faith
without "the meddling busyness of a third person." His method is at once
dialectical and, to use a word from Kierkegaard's vocabulary, teleological.
Yet it is not, at its best, didactic, for "direct" communication is forbidden.
Nor is it inherently condescending, as it may at first appear. Kierkegaard
makes a typically striking remark, which Percy might have echoed: "I regard myself as a *reader* of the books, not as the *author*."[3]
    The attitude Percy takes toward his reader is that of a fellow searcher
who is perhaps one step ahead of his companion but liable to stumble at
the next turning. Unlike O'Connor, Percy was a convert whose belief was
hard won. The uncertainty that plagues his protagonists continued to as-
sail him in ways that sometimes paralyzed him, but it also helped him
maintain a dialectic tension in his work that prevented his manipulation
of the reader. Typical of Percy's authorial stance is the one he adopts in
his "interview" with himself, "Questions They Never Asked Me" (*SSL*).
The format itself is dialectical, though the dialogue is of course internal:
Percy projects himself into the kind of questioner he had by this time
(1977) faced far too often, answering through a persona much less polite
and accommodating than the man whom interviewers encountered. In
perhaps the most revealing self-description he ever published, Percy comments on his authorial self at the end of the piece by way of analyzing a
portrait of him painted by his friend Lyn Hill. The painting, he says,
"shows me—well, not exactly me, a version of me." This figure is "cold-

3. Søren Kierkegaard, *The Essential Kierkegaard,* 467, 454.

eyed and sardonic." He looks "straight at the viewer, soliciting him ironically: *You and I know something, don't we? Or do we?* Or rather: *The chances
are ninety-nine in a hundred you don't know, but on the other hand you might
be the one in a hundred who does—not that it makes much difference. True, this
is a strange world I'm in, but what about the world you're in? Have you noticed
it lately? Are we on to something, you and I? Probably not"* (*SSL* 422). The dialogic element in this excerpt is strong: Percy is interpreting himself to
himself by means of a visual artist's interpretation of him and his work,
with the reader of the mock interview clearly in the field of vision. Yet,
balancing this give and take is a powerful teleological pull: the figure in
the painting "knows something"—or appears to—something important
that he wants to let the viewer in on. This something is a "secret" in the
sense that even though the viewer may have an inkling of it, he's not quite
sure what it means. And despite the figure's apparent diffidence, the secret is of the greatest importance, having to do with nothing less than the
collapse of an old world and the beginning of a new. The figure is cagey
and "smart-assed," and thus not above leading the viewer on. But finally,
there is about him a kind of doubtfulness that he shares with the viewer—
"*Are we on to something, you and I? Probably not.*" This note of uncertainty
is repeated at the inconclusive conclusion of the interview when the
"real" Percy turns the tables on the "interviewer" Percy and asks, "Do you
understand?" The interviewer answers, "No."

One might take this final exchange to be Percy's parting shot at critics who fail to grasp what he's about, but it also reinforces the impression that Percy himself is never free of doubt. Nor is it merely coincidental that this exchange should come after the "real" Percy has reluctantly
explicated the painting in Kierkegaardian terms. For not only has Percy
used one of Kierkegaard's categories—the aesthetic stage of life—to analyze the painting, he has used rhetorical strategies very similar to those
Kierkegaard employed in his pseudonymous works: deception in behalf
of truth at the same time that the writer acts as a reader of his own work
rather than as its author. In a more traditional interview, conducted ten
years later (1987), Percy himself connects these techniques to Kierkegaard: "[T]he novelist is entitled to a degree of artifice and cunning, as
Joyce said: or the 'indirect method,' as Kierkegaard said; or the comic-
bizarre for shock therapy, as Flannery O'Connor did" (*SSL* 385). Joyce
and O'Connor may have given Percy inspiration and validated his poetic license, so to speak, but it is Kierkegaard who developed the "method"

of eliciting from the reader a faith that cannot be otherwise communicated.

An insistence on the Kierkegaardian source of Percy's novelistic practice is necessary both to be faithful to his intentions and to open up the theological dimensions of his work. Percy stands, we might say, between Joyce and O'Connor on the scale of dogmatic assertiveness. Joyce avoids assertion entirely, in part because he has abandoned the Catholic Church, as Julian Hartt argues in *The Lost Image of Man*. For him, religious language is either a means of naturalistic display or a tool of irony. O'Connor likewise is a master of irony in matters religious, but her narrators also advert to full-fledged theological judgment. Percy has Joyce's cunning and archness but shares O'Connor's theological agenda. I have tried to suggest as much by insisting that Percy's method is not only dialogical but also teleological. This, incidentally, is the major point of divergence between Percy and his friend Shelby Foote, who as a staunch modernist in the Faulknerian mode was always pushing Percy to read Proust and avoid didacticism. To have taken such advice would have been for Percy to abandon his entire project and return to the "aesthetic of memory."

The issues at stake can be made clearer by yet another comparison. Criticism of both O'Connor and Percy has been enriched by analysis drawn from the categories of Mikhail Bakhtin. For example, Michael Kobre's chapter on *The Moviegoer* in *Walker Percy's Voices* tellingly charts the ideological discourses that Binx mimics, adopts, engages, appropriates, and rejects in the course of his search.[4] Percy's ear for the nuances of voice and the processes of internal dialogue becomes eminently more transparent within the framework of Bakhtin's dialogism as Kobre employs it. But working under the heavy hand of Soviet censorship, Bakhtin came to regard conversation and carnival, especially in their verbal manifestations, as goods in themselves. Finality and closure, which he saw all around him in the form of state oppression, were evils to be resisted. And although there is reason to believe the Russian theorist retained deeply held Christian commitments, the major Western appropriations of his work have emphasized his championing of a kind of anarchical open-endedness. Where Percy is concerned, such emphasis is misleading because Percy's work, however dialectically complex, is always directed toward an end.

4. Michael Kobre, "Out of the Evening Land: *The Moviegoer*," in *Walker Percy's Voices*, 21–80.

While he always grappled with what we might call the phenomenology of faith, whereby the obstacles to our appropriation of the Gospel are taken with utmost seriousness, Percy remained convinced that truth lay somewhere on the other side of our questions—truth faithfully if precariously carried along by the historic witness of Jews and Christians.

The larger dialectic in Percy's novels, then, is a dialectic of faith, a kind of agon between unbelief and belief where the first obstacle to be overcome is indifference. Faith requires a restored relationship between the self and its world, and therefore the process of faith is always intersubjective—or, as Bakhtin would style it, dialogical. But in Percy's understanding of it, intersubjective connection conscientiously pursued leads to trust in God, and thus the journey of faith is complete. We might also formulate this general project in terms of specific virtuous ends: faith, hope, and love. Faith realized gives hope, which leads ultimately to love. Thus what we might call the noetic dimension of Percy's concerns—his effort to point us to truth—is bound up with issues of character and thus the virtues necessary to undergird our quest for personal solidity and certainty. Percy's protagonists struggle not only to know, but to be. And while for the most part they lack the needed habits of heart and mind, their failures themselves are instructive. If O'Connor's protagonists often undergo an edifying process that takes them from self-confident volubility to shocked silence before the overwhelming power of God, Percy's characters must move in the opposite direction: from private observations and intuitions into speech.

The existentialist, the psychologist, and indeed the Catholic in Percy all directed him toward sustained consideration of the inner workings of the soul, and especially those conditions under which knowledge of God may take hold of us. Thus, although Percy did not set out to illustrate the three theological virtues, we may employ them to see more clearly the deeper dynamic of his work, remembering always that the themes intertwine, one being incomplete without the others. Percy's attention to these issues does seem to follow a rough pattern. His first published work grows out of a sense of dislocation that can be described as a largely unacknowledged crisis of faith. This is Binx's problem. By the time Percy comes to write *Lancelot* some fifteen years and two intervening novels later, he is seeking to break through his pessimism about the American social order in the aftermath of the Kennedy and King assassinations, the scandals of Watergate, and the loss of the Vietnam War. Thus is hope the virtue noticeably lacking in this most jaundiced of Percy's protagonists.

The Second Coming, Percy's penultimate novel, includes paradoxically a character's most direct assault upon God and what some have regarded as Percy's most successful love story. In these ways, Percy might be said to fulfill the motto Jay Tolson insightfully supplies for him in the epilogue to *Pilgrim in the Ruins.* It is the reversal of the motto Joyce's would-be artist adopts at the end of *A Portrait of the Artist as a Young Man* in imitation of Satan, announcing his intention to serve no church of God but only the religion of Art. Percy's art has its own integrity, but it is not autotelic: "*Serviam,*" it declares.

Faith Intimated: The Moviegoer

Binx Bolling's response to the sense of unreality and uncertainty felt by all of Percy's protagonists does not at first glance appear to be a problem of faith. In fact, three other subjects seem much more pertinent to his malaise. Scientism, or what we might also call the triumph of theory, has isolated the self and evacuated the world of real significance. In a similar way, the social world seems fragile. It is a kind of façade held together by people acting out parts that they don't fully understand and seem only partially committed to. Finally, this general air of insubstantiality has taken a toll on the human soul, rendering the people Binx meets strangely out of touch with themselves, although they are generally oblivious to their disjointedness. Yet as Percy hints throughout his book, these problems in fact have a religious origin. World, society, and self lapse into incoherence when displaced from a sphere of transcendence.

The loss of the world through science is suggested by Binx's recollection of what happened when he became interested in a biology problem in college:

> I had a hunch you might get pigs to form oxalate stones by manipulating the pH of the blood, and maybe even dissolve them. . . . But then a peculiar thing happened. I became extraordinarily affected by the summer afternoons in the laboratory. The August sunlight came streaming in the great dusty fanlights and lay in yellow bars across the room. The old building ticked and creaked in the heat. Outside we could hear the cries of summer students playing touch football. In the course of an afternoon the yellow sunlight moved across old group pictures of the biology faculty. I became bewitched by the presence of the building; for minutes at a stretch I sat on the floor and watched the motes rise and fall in the sunlight. (*MG* 51–52)

Binx's fascination with the sunlight and the sounds of touch football do not represent the distraction of a bored student unsuited to the tedium of hard work. Rather, they illustrate what Percy in the title of an article calls "the loss of the creature." Science, at least as Binx has received it, has eliminated mystery and thereby rooted out personal connection.

What Binx feels in the lab is an example of a phenomenon he describes elsewhere in connection with his search. For a long time, he says,

> I read only "fundamental" books, that is, key books on key subjects. . . . During those years I stood outside the universe and sought to understand it. I lived in my room as an Anyone living Anywhere and read fundamental books and only for diversion took walks around the neighborhood and saw an occasional movie. . . . The greatest success of this enterprise, which I call my vertical search, came one night when I sat in a hotel room in Birmingham and read a book called *The Chemistry of Life*. When I finished it, it seemed to me that the main goals of my search were reached or were in principle reachable. . . . A memorable night. The only difficulty was that though the universe had been disposed of, I myself was left over. There I lay in my hotel room still obliged to draw one breath and then the next. (*MG* 69–70)

Percy is here incorporating a lesson drawn from Heidegger's exposition of *dasein* and Kierkegaard's critique of Hegel: the objectification of the natural world into discrete phenomena about which generalizations can be made has the effect of rendering the individual phenomena themselves worthless—the husk left over after the kernel of knowledge has been extracted. The sundering of the world into subject and object, which with Maritain Percy traces to Descartes, has deprived the physical world of meaning and left the knower to wander like a ghost. This process of abstraction goes a long way toward explaining Binx's sense of unreality. The only way he can preserve his sanity is to undertake what he calls his horizontal search, where the general is forsaken for the particular. "What is important is what I shall find when I leave my room and wander in the neighborhood. Before, I wandered as a diversion. Now I wander seriously and sit and read as a diversion" (*MG* 70). Binx's wanderings, like his daydreams in the college lab, bump him up against mystery and, in John Desmond's phrase, "inspire a genuine search for being and communion with others."[5] But Binx's glimpses are fleeting, and bring him no lasting

5. Desmond, *Percy's Search*, 50.

answers. The malaise growing from the feeling that nothing matters inevitably returns.

Loss of the natural world through Cartesian sundering of subject and object is complemented by fragmentation of the social order. Binx is made aware of this loss through his encounters with his formidable aunt. Binx's two interviews with Emily Cutrer are hugely important to the structure of the novel, since they frame the action of the entire book. In the novel's first paragraph he is musing over a summons from her, and the oratorical highlight of the book comes in the final chapter with her denunciation of his treatment of Kate. She is a commanding presence who speaks for a daunting heritage. When Binx observes that confrontation with her is "enough to scare the wits out of anyone," he speaks from Percy's personal experience.

The Percy family had been in the Mississippi Delta since the eighteenth century and could show a remarkable record of accomplishment, which Bertram Wyatt-Brown has detailed in *The House of Percy: Honor, Melancholy, and Imagination in a Southern Family*. After losing first his father and then his mother under tragic circumstances, Walker and his brothers were adopted by an older cousin, William Alexander Percy. "Uncle Will," as the boys affectionately called him, was one of the most distinguished southerners of his era. The similarities between the literary character and the man are manifest: Aunt Emily's views and even her phrasing can be found in Will Percy's memoir, *Lanterns on the Levee*. Walker Percy called this attitude Southern Stoicism, and in *The Moviegoer* Binx labors under its weight, as critics such as Lewis A. Lawson have repeatedly demonstrated.[6]

To Aunt Emily, the old order is slipping away, with aristocrats of her generation fighting a rearguard action against irresistible decline. She tells Binx that "among certain people, gentlefolk I don't mind calling them, there exists a set of meanings held in common, . . . a certain manner and a certain grace [that] come as naturally as breathing" (*MG* 222). She's unapologetic about her elitism: "The charge is that people belonging to my class think they're better than other people. You're damn right we're better. We're better because we do not shirk our obligations either to ourselves or to others." But she lives in a time when greatness is mocked. "Ours is the only civilization in history which has enshrined mediocrity as its national ideal." She has nothing but scorn for the elevation of the "common man" as a cultural ideal, for "it has always been revealing to me

6. See "*The Moviegoer* and the Stoic Heritage" in Lewis A. Lawson, *Following Percy*.

that he is perfectly content so to be called, because that is what he is: the common man and when I say common I mean common as hell" (*MG* 223).

We might say that Aunt Emily's critique has two parts, ideological and sociological. The values she has lived by are no longer accepted, even by the nephew who has drawn her ire. At the same time, the social class that sustained those values is disappearing. Emily seems to believe the "enemy" is the average man on the street, whose herd mentality threatens to swallow even her own kind: "Let me tell you something. If he out yonder is your prize exhibit for human progress in the past three thousand years, then all I can say is that I am content to be fading out of the picture" (*MG* 224). But Binx is aware that the neat class system his aunt believes in has always been illusory. His own mother is far from patrician, having married his father after coming to work for him as a nurse in his medical practice. In her second marriage, his mother is happily middle class. Binx is also tuned in to the complicated set of roles played by Mercer, his aunt's butler. As a black man in a white household, Mercer knows he is expected to play the role of faithful family retainer, and does so to his own advantage. At the same time, he styles himself a man on the rise, proud of his independence. Binx muses over Mercer's self-understanding:

> When he succeeds in seeing himself, it is as a remarkable sort of fellow, a man who keeps himself well-informed in science and politics. This is why I am always uneasy around him. I hate it when his vision of himself dissolves and he sees himself as neither, neither old retainer nor expert in current events. Then his eyes get muddy and his face runs together behind his mustache. Last Christmas I went looking for him in his rooms over the garage. He wasn't there but on his bed lay a well-thumbed volume put out by the Rosicrucians called *How to Harness Your Secret Powers*. The poor bastard. (*MG* 24)

While Mercer is losing his sense of identity as his social role disappears, Aunt Emily is living in the midst of a greater dissolution than she knows. For her, "even the dissolving makes sense" (*MG* 54), but for Binx, Aunt Emily's explanation misses something crucial. Mercer is not failing in his loyalty to the old ideals through any dereliction of duty; his old role simply no longer makes sense in the changing social order. Likewise, Binx himself cannot take up the burden of noblesse oblige as his aunt wishes him to do, for she is more right than she knows—not only have the old values been forsaken, the class itself—the old planter class she calls "gentlefolk"—has disappeared except as an idealized memory. To call attention to the social basis of this worldview, historian Richard King chooses the term *Catonism* over *Southern Stoicism,* for in fact the dying of civilization it envisions is tied to the threatened status of a particular aristocratic class.[7] And in *The Moviegoer* the planter class has already in effect been erased by a new economy. Aunt Emily's own husband owns a brokerage business. While race and family certainly continue to provide a degree of privilege, Aunt Emily's South is increasingly dominated by money. To further complicate matters, Binx finds he cannot adopt the values she has so nobly upheld, much as he admires them.

Binx believes that the social dislocation he and Aunt Emily both recognize has a source deeper than sociological change. He notes the general dis-ease people feel in their interactions, an uneasiness not limited to those like Mercer who straddle social roles. In friendship and love, Binx sees and experiences a similar breakdown. He muses on the subject of friendship after a conversation with an old fraternity brother, now engaged to his cousin Kate. The two were once close, and Walter is now on the verge of entering Binx's family. Yet Binx reports that "I've always been slightly embarrassed in Walter's company. Whenever I'm with him, I feel the stretch of the old tightrope, the necessity of living up to the friendship of friendships, of cultivating an intimacy beyond words. The fact is we have little to say to each other. There is only this thick sympathetic silence between us. We are comrades, true, but somewhat embarrassed comrades. It is probably my fault. For years now I have had no friends. I spend my entire time working, making money, going to movies and seeking the company of women" (*MG* 40–41). At first sight, this passage seems to be a common story of people who drift apart as they age. But Binx's disclosure that he has no friends—despite being well connected, single, prosperous, and sociable—strikes a warning note. It is "the necessity of living up to the friendship of friendships" that holds him back, rather than aversion to companionship itself. He feels a pressure to meet expectations that he finds to be false, and therefore he avoids them.

Binx is no more at home in the role of "friend of friends" than Mercer is in that of grateful family retainer. The gap between what he is and what he is expected to be is too great. The fact that Binx's problem has

---

7. Richard H. King, *A Southern Renaissance: The Cultural Awakening of the American South, 1930–1955,* 51–57.

to do with the state of the world rather than with his private quirks is suggested by an earlier exchange. Walter tells Binx to call him sometime. Binx sincerely asks, "What would we talk about?" To which Walter responds, "No, you're right. What would we talk about. Oh Lord. What's wrong with the goddamn world, Binx?" But rather than leave this rejoinder as an elegy to lost youth, Binx begins an honest answer: "I'm not sure. But something occurred to me this morning. I was sitting on the bus—" (*MG* 39). Walter cuts him off. One implication of this exchange is that whatever is interfering with their interaction has more to do with the common ethos than with them. But further, in the guise of bemoaning the paucity of intimacy, Walter is foreclosing it. This is the one point in the conversation when Binx is speaking honestly about a matter of common concern around which they might actually build a friendship. The quest for friendship seems to defeat itself.

Likewise with love affairs, or what in Binx's case might more accurately be called dalliances. He has a series of secretaries whom he pursues romantically, and although he does not abuse them, or even break their hearts, his affairs with them run their course and end. It seems that once the excitement of the chase wanes, so does Binx's interest—as indeed does the interest of the woman. Two features of Binx's descriptions of these courtships are notable. First, they involve a large number of references to movie stars. And second, his maneuvers with these women always include a strong element of indirection. At one point in his cultivation of Sharon he stages an evening work session in order to change the dynamic between them. This allows him to get a look at her boyfriend, whom he labels a Faubourg Marigny type, after the New Orleans neighborhood he takes him to hail from. As they work, Binx projects himself into another role: "It is possible to stand at the window, loosen my collar and rub the back of my neck like Dana Andrews. And to become irritable with her: 'No no no no, Kincaid, that's not what I mean to say. Take five.' I go to the cooler, take two aspirins, crumple the paper cup. Her friend . . . turns out to be invaluable. In my every tactic he is the known quantity. He is my triangulation point. I am all business to his monkey business" (*MG* 105).

This role playing in imitation of assorted characters and scenes from films reveals another aspect of the general sense of unreality Binx feels. This moviegoer finds the projected world of films to be more substantial than his own, a feeling that seems to be general, as judged by the reaction Binx observes on a New Orleans street to the unexpected appearance of

William Holden one otherwise ordinary day. The greatest beneficiary of this visitation is a young man on his honeymoon, who manages casually to offer the celebrity a light for his cigarette, as though they were old chums. The action certifies his honeymoon as something extraordinary, allowing him to turn confidently to his bride, satisfied that he now has a right to a good time and to her admiration. Binx is likewise using the movies to validate his maneuvers. It is important to him, as it is to the honeymooner, to gain his object obliquely. To approach William Holden directly and ask him for an autograph would cancel out the validation the movie star could convey. The trick is to make the exchange seem casual and routine, thus conferring on the ordinary a blessing it normally lacks. And so Binx combines his pursuit of Sharon with the making of money, playing one chase off against the other in order to add excitement to both.

The shortcoming of Binx's erotic exercises is that his brief successes never last; understood as an attempt to overcome the isolation and detachment he feels, they are distractions that relieve the symptoms of malaise but provide no cure; indeed, they worsen the disease. His relationship with Kate is more hopeful because it is notably different from his romantic liaisons. They conveniently come from the same social set and even enjoy a family connection through marriage, and they are friends before they are lovers. But these conventional signs of compatibility should not obscure their deeper similarities. While others seek to treat Kate's "illness," Binx "appreciates [her] authentic rejection of everydayness."[8] They recognize in one another the same malady, and they evolve a common language to name it. And as they do so, they reveal both the damage the self has endured in the modern shift and the means to its salvation.

Percy's name for their condition, again borrowed from Kierkegaard, is despair. It is a condition shared by the general population, but unknown and unnamed by them. In Kate the symptoms are acute, part and parcel of a configuration to which the psychiatrist Dr. Mink gives his own names. Kate suffers from depression and is prone to self-destructive behavior and suicidal tendencies. Her stepmother fears a crisis, and enlists a host of helpers, from psychiatrist to old family friends, including Binx. Kate's private reports to Binx about her state of mind are indeed unsettling. She describes intentionally overdosing on nembutal to get herself "off dead center" (MG 181), flirting with death to make life more vivid.

8. Janet Hobbs, "Binx Bolling and the Stages on Life's Way," 42.

Later, she discusses suicide more generally: "They all think any minute I'm going to commit suicide. What a joke. The truth of course is the exact opposite: suicide is the only thing that keeps me alive. Whenever everything else fails, all I have to do is consider suicide and in two seconds I'm as cheerful as a nitwit" (*MG* 194). The emptiness that Binx sees around him and records in its myriad manifestations takes a clinical form in Kate. A brush with death can have the same effect as a chance encounter with a movie star: it breaks the grip of meaninglessness.

In fact, Kate's episodes closely mirror those of Binx. The drug overdose followed her finishing a good book, after which she wondered, "What next?" (*MG* 181), just as Binx, having finished *The Chemistry of Life,* found he was "still obliged to draw one breath and then the next." Kate is subject to paralyzing fits of anxiety, during which she relies on Binx to tell her what to do, but Binx also has fits of disorientation that incapacitate him, as happens when the two of them arrive in Chicago and Binx feels "the genie-soul of Chicago flap down like a buzzard and perch on my shoulder. During the whole of our brief sojourn I am ridden by it. . . . All day long . . . I stand sunk in thought blinking and bemused, on street corners. Kate looks after me. She is strangely at home in the city, wholly impervious to the five million personal rays of Chicagoans and the peculiar smell of existence here, which must be sniffed and gotten hold of before taking a single step away from the station" (*MG* 201). In Chicago, she does for Binx what she later asks him to do for her when she agrees to marry him: "It seems to me that if we are together a great deal and you tell me the simplest things and not laugh at me—I beg you for pity's sake never to laugh at me—tell me things like: Kate, it is all right for you to go down to the drugstore, and give me a kiss, then I will believe you" (*MG* 234). Marriage represents the best chance for these two to break the grip of despair because they come to an understanding of their situation through shared experience and a common vocabulary. Kate can talk about Binx's "search," his "repetitions" and "rotations," and apply such categories to her own condition. But the final requirement is a step of commitment and an act of faith in pledging themselves to each other. Commitment breaks the hold of theory and structures the vertiginous expanse of possibility. But commitment also requires faith. As Kate says, she may not ever change. The marriage may not work.

The faith needed for the commitment of marriage is not necessarily religious; neither Kate nor Binx speak of either God or church as they make their promises to each other. But there is a kind of faith between them that Lawson describes in "Walker Percy's Indirect Communications": "[Binx and Kate] literally depend upon the recognition of themselves they see in each other's eyes for their feeling of authenticity."[9] In the world of Percy's novel, this trust is an analogue of religious faith, for faith in God is the only resource capable of sustaining this marriage or defeating despair. Percy suggests as much by concluding the marriage discussion (and the novel proper) with what appears to be a digression. Binx watches a black man emerge from a church. It is Ash Wednesday. For Binx, the scene is filled with ambiguity. Did the man receive ashes? What is he looking at on the car seat next to him? Why is he here? "It is impossible to say. . . . Is it part and parcel of the complex business of coming up in the world? Or is it because he believes that God himself is present here at the corner of Elysian Fields and Bons Enfants? Or is he here for both reasons: through some dim dazzling trick of grace, coming for the one and receiving the other as God's own importunate bonus? It is impossible to say" (*MG* 235). The repetition of "impossible to say" draws out what Kierkegaard called the inwardness of faith—its inaccessibility to outsiders. Its presence can't be proved or demonstrated. But in the epilogue, Binx gives indication, albeit indirectly, that he himself has come to faith.

When his half brothers and sisters ask him if their fatally ill brother, Lonnie, will be able to water ski in heaven, Binx answers, "Yes," to the cheers of his siblings. This exchange, which Percy said he borrowed from a similar affirmation in *The Brothers Karamazov,* was meant to cue the reader to Binx's new faith (*CWP* 66). Despite his faults, Binx never lies. Binx's simple "yes" is also a sign that he has embraced a particular discourse—that he has found it internally persuasive, to use Bakhtin's term. Until this point, Binx's use of phrases and inflections from the competing discourses of science, Southern Stoicism, therapy, and church have been in quotation marks, so to speak. His appropriation of these ways of speech has been provisional, holding the ideological aspects of the discourse at arm's length. But now, the language of the Catholic Church, which he has spoken knowledgeably but noncommitally with his half brother Lonnie, is the discourse for his own oblique but sincere assertion of faith.

Indeed, it may be the case, as Desmond suggests in "Walker Percy's Eucharistic Vision," that Lonnie's earlier promise to offer his communion for Binx has borne fruit. According to Desmond, the belief Binx states to the

9. Lawson, *Following Percy,* 23.

children "implicitly affirms the incarnation, redemption, and resurrection of the body, the *real,* living substance and mystery of the Eucharist, connecting the transfigured material world of the here-and-now to its mystical center in eternity."[10] Although it is also important to recognize that Percy's protagonist is never able to adopt Lonnie's unselfconscious directness, his actions indicate an inward amendment.

When immediately after this conversation with the children Binx gives Kate the reassurance she needs to complete a simple errand that has temporarily paralyzed her, we see the successful carrying out of the pattern Kate had described when they decided to marry. The connection between these events—Kate's hope that Binx might give her the understanding and direction she needs if they marry, Binx's observation of the man who may or may not have gone to church in faith, the affirmation in answer to the children's question about heaven, and the successful fulfillment of exactly the pattern Kate had described before their marriage—suggests that faith in God is what makes the marriage work and what has brought Binx to the end of his search. But Binx can communicate this message to the reader only indirectly, for at least two reasons. The language of the church, which he can now affirm, is in Binx's words "worn out." Without rehabilitation, it often fails to convey meaning. In addition, faith as we have seen is a matter of inwardness, and can't be elicited by direct assault, so to speak. This problem is illustrated by Binx's response to another discourse that has lost its hold on him, that of his aunt.

By far the most dramatic speech in *The Moviegoer* is that delivered by Emily Cutrer upon Binx's return with Kate from Chicago. As Kobre argues, "Binx's struggle with his aunt's values is ultimately the novel's dialogic core,"[11] and Binx's response to this speech represents the climax of that struggle. She is moved to eloquence by Binx's behavior, for by her lights, he has run off with a mentally unbalanced woman, removing her from the care of her family and physician in order to enjoy a brief fling. Binx finds he can neither explain his actions to his aunt nor accept her philosophy, which prizes "gentleness toward women" as well as a defiant, aristocratic honorableness. To his aunt's charges, he can only reply, "You say that none of what you said ever meant anything to me. That is not true. On the contrary. I have never forgotten anything you ever said. In fact I have pondered over it all my life. My objections, though they are

10. John Desmond, "Walker Percy's Eucharistic Vision," 221–22.
11. Kobre, *Walker Percy's Voices,* 35.

not exactly objections, cannot be expressed in the usual way. To tell the truth, I can't express them at all" (*MG* 224–25).

We might try to supply the explanation Binx cannot muster by saying that, for him, the form of life that his aunt represents has eroded. In fact, Percy, through his character, might be said to be picking up where Faulkner and the modernist writers of the Southern Renaissance left off. Binx is not paralyzed by the burden of his heritage, as is Faulkner's Quentin Compson; he is detached from it. And his emotional and intellectual estrangement has a metaphysical basis that, for Percy, requires an ontological solution rather than a historical one. Too much of what Binx knows of his world simply is not captured by the net of his aunt's discourse. She understands neither Kate's malady nor his willingness to go along with her scheme of escape as something meant for her good. And the Binx of the search could never say with his aunt that he will look whatever high gods there may be in the eye without apology. In Aunt Emily's philosophy, there is no room for faith and no need for it. Yet this speech is crucial to Binx's double decision to marry Kate and to embrace the religion of his mother's family, for it shows Binx the failings of his present life and the inadequacies of his inherited ethical framework for dealing with that failure. He registers this recognition in a single word. His aunt asks him what he thinks the purpose of life is—to go to the movies and dally with every girl that comes along? He answers, "No." This "no" follows his rejection of Southern Stoicism, but it is also a rejection of the considered unseriousness Kierkegaard called the aesthetic stage. And the lone negative word is meant to prepare the way for the one-word religious affirmation at the hospital.

Binx's search might be said to be a search for realized selfhood. The most dreadful unreality of all is that of the ghostly self—being lost to oneself. For both Binx and Kate, this loss of self is the ultimate consequence of radical dislocation, and loss of self is Kierkegaard's definition of despair in the book from which Percy took his *Moviegoer* epigraph, *The Sickness unto Death*. For both writers, the only antidote to despair is to be oneself "transparently before God" (for example, *CWP* 110), a movement that faith enables. All the variations of alienation, fragmentation, and isolation that Binx notes have in one way or another to do with loss of transcendence, or, to use the term relevant to our O'Connor discussion, participation. World, society, and self sundered from God lose their coherence and meaningfulness. Nature becomes grist for the theoretical mill, with no inherent value beyond its yield of abstract generalizations, and the soli-

tary self of the observer, in principle excluded from the process of inves-
tigation, is also left unsatisfied by the knowledge so generated. Without
some trans-human mandate, human communities likewise teeter precip-
itously on the brink of autonomous anarchy. And finally, the human individual careens calamitously without purpose or direction. Despite the
fact that 98 percent of the American people say they believe in God, as
Binx records early in the novel, faith, in the sense of a real connection to
God, seems in short supply. But Binx, by novel's end, seems to have found
such faith, or perhaps more accurately, faith has finally been granted him.
And the means to that faith has been dialogue—a negative one with his
Aunt Emily showing him ultimately how her vision of the world is inadequate to him and his time, and a more positive one, where establishing sympathy and a common language with Kate provide him an analogue to faith that aids him in his final step into belief.

A Brief Excursus on Pride: Love in the Ruins

Binx Bolling's "search" might be described as a spiritual quest—one that
seems to have been completed by novel's end. His search begins with self-
discovery (for him the first revelation comes on a Korean battlefield), proceeds through trials and dead ends, and comes finally to a hopeful conclusion. This broad pattern obtains in some form for *Lancelot* and *The
Second Coming,* the two books we will use to explore the virtues of hope
and love. In each of these novels, the protagonist undergoes an existential
crisis that leads him to formulate an urgent question that he pursues in
the form of a search. And both characters ultimately are looking for God.
Lance, as we will see, undertakes a negative quest—a search for what he
calls the Unholy Grail. He believes that if he can discover true evil he will
have shown God's necessity. Will Barrett of *The Second Coming* tries to
force a direct word from God, descending into a cave from which he does
not intend to emerge unless God reveals himself. Neither character gets
exactly what he seeks, but each does receive a sign, which points him in
a hopeful direction. However, Percy does give us one protagonist who is
not a religious seeker but rather "a bad Catholic at a time near the end of
the world," as he is described in the subtitle of *Love in the Ruins* (1971).
    Tom More, descendant of the famous English Catholic saint, is already
fully convinced of God's existence and indeed of God's sacramental presence. Insofar as faith is rational assent to what cannot be proved, he is full
of faith. Yet More is a "lapsed" Catholic, one who no longer avails him-

self of the Eucharist, because, as he says, he loves his sins more than he loves God. Thus More is not a victim of unbelief, but of pride—*superbia*—that root of all sin, according to Augustine. And in this way, More might be said to be more theologically akin to O'Connor's protagonists than any of Percy's other characters. More must somehow be freed from the grip of sin and restored to the God in whom he already believes. And although he is prone to common indulgences—women, music, and alcohol—his primary temptation is one that plays no part in O'Connor's world: science. Dr. More's principal interest is not in saving his own soul, but in saving the world through a revolutionary scientific breakthrough. As events in the novel make clear, however, the world does not need a new savior, and the breakthrough that More does achieve is a personal one that follows from an act of humility.

Dr. Tom More has a degree of religious self-awareness unique among Percy's major characters. His self-assessment in the novel's opening pages is acute: "I . . . am a Roman Catholic, albeit a bad one. I believe in the Holy Catholic Apostolic and Roman Church, in God the Father, in the election of the Jews, in Jesus Christ His Son our Lord, who founded the Church on Peter his first vicar, which will last until the end of the world. Some years ago, however, I stopped eating Christ in Communion, stopped going to mass, and have since fallen into a disorderly life." He continues with a blunt summary of his current state: "I love women best, music and science next, and my fellowman hardly at all. . . . A man, wrote John, who says he believes in God and does not keep his commandments is a liar. If John is right, then I am a liar. Nevertheless, I still believe." As More makes these declarations, he stands watch over an abandoned Howard Johnson motel in which he has installed three women. He expects an imminent disaster. And yet his biggest worry is "that catastrophe will overtake us before my scientific article is published and so before my discovery can create a sensation in the scientific world" (*LR* 6).

The key to the article upon which More has pinned such high hopes is a set of metaphysical assumptions not shared by his scientific colleagues. He has constructed a "lapsometer," which in effect measures the state of the soul by taking electrical readings from the brain. Needless to say, resistance in the medical and scientific community has been stout. More is undeterred, but realistic: "Unfortunately, there still persists in the medical profession the quaint superstition that only that which is visible is real. Thus the soul is not real. Uncaused terror cannot exist. Then, friend, how come you are shaking?" (*LR* 28). Despite much doubt, More has persuaded coworkers to help him invent a diagnostic device, and using money left him by his wife he has had a number manufactured. And he is well on his way toward validating his theories through demonstration. Unfortunately, when the device is improved to the point of treating soul conditions by means of brain stimulation, multiple dangers lurk. First is the danger to individual patients, who can be stimulated into sexual overdrive or driven to a state of crippling abstraction, for example. In the wrong hands, the lapsometer can ruin a psyche rather than restore it to balance. Equally ominous is the potential effect of the lapsometer's discharges on the salt dome over which More's New Orleans environs sits. He fears a massive chemical reaction with widespread casualties. Yet the device does have potential for great good. More believes it can heal the riven soul of modern man, tormented as it is by such syndromes as "angelism/bestialism," which result from the Cartesian divorce of mind and body. By addressing this underlying illness, the lapsometer can help to head off impending social disaster. Political, racial, and religious bifurcation already threatens to destroy the United States.

The crucial factor in More's plans, however, is his ambition. Stymied in his attempts to perfect and distribute his invention through official channels, he is offered all he thinks he wants by a shadowy "liaison man" named Art Immelmann, whom the reader quickly spots as a satanic tempter and Tom's alter ego. As Desmond notes, Art is "a 'double' figure bent on helping More 'fulfill' his dreams of sexual and scientific conquest."[12] And Tom does seem to have sold his soul to this demonic con man. After a hilarious scene in the medical center where Tom uses his lapsometer to save a silent old man threatened with euthanasia, Art unleashes chaos by passing out duplicate devices as if they were water pistols. With catastrophe imminent, Art returns to claim his collaborating victim. Providentially, Tom's nurse, Ellen, highly ethical, extremely practical, and in love with her boss, steps in to do for him what he is unable to accomplish himself. In a final confrontation with Art, who seems to have accomplished his purposes in the United States once he has distributed Tom's chaos-creating instruments, Tom is about to be whisked away to Denmark, Art's home base. Once he is under Art's thumb and away from home, Tom's damnation will be complete. Tom seems paralyzed in this crisis—powerless to resist. At this point, Ellen in effect offers herself to the devil in Tom's place, "rescuing Tom by abandoning him," as Gary Ciu-

12. Desmond, *Percy's Search*, 133.

ba characterizes her action.[13] Stung by his own love for Ellen, and pro-voked to sexual jealousy by her agreement to serve as Art's "traveling sec-retary," Tom finally acts. Recoiling from Art's arms "outstretched like the Christ at Sacre Coeur in New Orleans," he prays: *"Sir Thomas More, kins-man, saint, best dearest merriest of Englishmen, pray for us and drive this son of a bitch hence"* (*LR* 355).

Tom's action is a prayer—a request for help that acknowledges his own powerlessness. In this novel, the key moment of dialogic revelation comes when the prideful would-be savior of the world turns in complete help-lessness to the communion of saints, begging for intercession with God. The power of the words themselves stuns the satanic interloper, as Ellen notes. When Art turns and disappears, it is clear that Tom's prayer has been answered. He has been saved through the loving ministrations of others—he could not save himself. His prayer to kinsman and saint might also be seen as an initial act of humility, one that comes to fruition when he is able finally to confess his sin and receive Communion.

In his final conversation with Father Smith, the faithful if troubled priest whom Tom befriends, Tom makes his confession. He lists his old foibles—lust, drink, loving himself better than God or man. Even worse, he must admit an inability to feel true contrition for his sin. In a sense, he hasn't changed. Yet now here he is, submitting to the Catholic Church's sacramental discipline. Rather than engage Tom in a lengthy discussion of his feelings, Father Smith simply asks him to pray for true contrition, and tells him to put on sackcloth and ashes, a newly revived penitential prac-tice. Tom follows these instructions, and afterwards, he records, "Father Smith says mass. I eat Christ, drink his blood" (*LR* 377). And not sur-prisingly, we next learn that Tom is likewise rejoined to the body politic (he will serve as a black friend's campaign manager) and that he has set-tled down to a contented Christmas with his good wife, Ellen.

Clearly, Tom More has survived the darkest temptations of pride by the grace of God. In theological terms, the true colors of pride are displayed in the attempt to play God. And as Desmond points out, Tom's self-idolatry is arrestingly portrayed midway through the novel in his vision of the "maculate Christ." Having fainted, the unwell doctor has been helped into his favorite bar by a black friend and a white friend, who normally would have little to do with each other. As he looks in the bar mirror, Tom thinks he sees a "sinful Christ" who draws together Victor and Leroy,

---

13. Gary M. Ciuba, *Walker Percy: Books of Revelations,* 161.

united now in their love for this savior they have helped out of a ditch
(*LR* 145). This new Christ is of course Tom More himself. Desmond sums
up his imagined role: "As the 'new Christ' More would presume to reconcile mankind to its fallen state, using the lapsometer. No more longing
for God or eternal life. No need for grace or repentance. Science replaces
Christ and the cross as the way of redemption."[14] This Christ image, mir-
rored in reference to Art Immelmann in the passage quoted earlier, shows
the extent of Tom's prideful self-delusion. The would-be savior is in effect an idolater who cuts himself off from the true source of salvation.

The best hope for Tom More and his broken world lies in the sacramental life to which he returns after the end of the world fails to arrive.
Tom was right—his troubles began when he drifted away from the Communion table, heartsick over the death of his daughter, Samantha, who, as
Ciuba notes, draws Tom to the church as fervently as Lonnie drew Binx.[15]
Even though Tom is never cured of the soul-sickness that drove him into
acedia and rendered him suicidal, he has at last turned to the true source
of spiritual nourishment in the sacramental practices of a faithful Christian community. The humility of sackcloth and the grace of the Eucharist,
not the scientific hubris of the lapsometer with its power to manipulate,
offer healing to the sin-sick soul.

In at least one respect, *Love in the Ruins* is Percy's most edifying novel,
for it shows the reader a deeply flawed sinner restored to a community of
the faithful and spiritually sustained by his return to sacramental practice.
But before abandoning this brief excursion into Percy's most directly
Catholic novel, we should make note of three troublesome items to be
found in the epilogue section, "Five Years Later." First, the religious community upon which Tom is spiritually dependent is a fragile one. Tom believes that the Roman Catholic Church will last until the end of the
world, yet it has already broken into three competing polities in the United States. Father Smith is pastor to a remnant flock that shares worship
space with Protestants and Jews. Second, Tom's own shakiness exceeds that
of the Catholic Church. One senses that he can backslide as easily as go
forward, and indeed, in Percy's final novel, Dr. More has again fallen on
hard times. In *Love in the Ruins,* however, the most ominous sign is More's
continued enthusiasm for the lapsometer. He tells us, "Despite the set-
backs of the past, . . . I still believe my lapsometer can save the world—

14. Desmond, *Percy's Search,* 134.
15. Ciuba, *Walker Percy,* 160.

if I can get it right" (*LR* 360). Though he no longer wants to be hailed as a savior, he still believes his device can overcome "the current hermaphroditism of the spirit" and restore humanity to the condition of sovereign wanderers and lordly exiles (*LR* 360–61). Thus while More has been saved from the worst effects of his pride, he has not forsaken his dream that science might overcome sin, or at least erase some of its more egregious expressions. Pride in the form of a triumphant science of the soul, based on theological principles but persuasive and effective outside the context of the church, remains a temptation for More, as indeed it seems to have been for Percy.

As Gerald Kennedy points out, Percy's attitude toward the lapsometer and the theories behind it is far from condemnatory: "More's contradictory attitude apparently mirrors Percy's own ambivalence toward scientific technology."[16] Indeed, More's analysis of the problem of the modern self is Percy's, as we know from *The Message in the Bottle*. Percy gives us no good reason for concluding that More's instrument might not work, as in fact it does, in the Pit for the elderly Mr. Ives. As I noted earlier in relation to Percy's attraction to Peirce, the lure of a rationally self-sufficient system of knowledge that in effect subsumed the Christian witness was strong for Percy.

Two of these difficulties—the fragility of communities necessary to foster intersubjectivity and the instability of selves fundamentally characterized by freedom—remain to be considered in our final assessment of Percy's work in relation to O'Connor's. But before proceeding to criticism—an activity perhaps appropriate to the subject of pride—we need to conclude our excursus and return to the more affirmative topic of the second and third theological virtues, hope and love.

16. J. Gerald Kennedy, "The Sundered Self and the Riven World: *Love in the Ruins*," 121.

7

Surviving Apocalypse through Hope and Love

W hile in the epilogue to *The Moviegoer* Binx seems to be at the beginning of a journey of faith, as *Lancelot* opens, Percy's protagonist is ruminating over an end produced by despair. As Gary Ciuba announces in his study of the apocalyptic nature of Percy's novels, "The end that has loomed over Percy's fiction from its very beginning finally explodes and implodes in *Lancelot*. Percy's most violent apocalypse explores the very limits of an already extreme genre." In *The Moviegoer* Binx had already expressed a secret desire for the end of the world, hoping that universal catastrophe would bring renewal, just as small mishaps such as car crashes can temporarily defeat malaise. And as we have seen, the novel immediately preceding *Lancelot, Love in the Ruins,* has as its subtitle *The Adventures of a Bad Catholic at a Time Near the End of the World.* But as Ciuba observes of *Lancelot*'s predecessor, no literal devastation occurs. Tom More's urgent predictions prove untrue. In *Lancelot,* however, we do witness a fiery end instigated by a "mad and murderous Antichrist," even though his initial strike does not extend beyond his own spacious home. Here, apocalypse is internalized and "becomes the self's reduction of the world and time to ashes as all history is consumed in Lancelot's self-referential story."[1]

Apocalypse in its biblical form always has hope as its aim. Whether the source be the Book of Daniel or John's Revelation, biblical apocalypse is meant to give hope to God's suffering people in a time of extremity, proclaiming in effect that God will dramatically intervene to save and restore those who cannot save themselves. As Percy's most intense apocalypse,

---

1. Ciuba, *Walker Percy,* 171.

Lancelot is the novel most directly addressed to the virtue of hope, although in the logic of this photographic-negative narrative, hope is elicited from the darkest despair. Dante says of himself in the passage from *The Divine Comedy* that Percy uses for his epigraph,

> He sank so low that all means
> for his salvation were gone,
> except showing him the lost people.

Lancelot represents Percy's attempt to draw a portrait of desperation so stark that it will point the reader toward his only salvific alternative.

Hope Deferred: Lancelot

Lancelot Andrewes Lamar is a dangerous man who as he begins his story is emerging from a long period of silence. Whereas Binx Bolling (and after him, Will Barrett in *The Last Gentleman*) are young men who have yet to stake out their direction in life, Lance is a middle-aged convict whose life has taken a wrong turn. The reader of *Lancelot* is listening in on what emerges as an unrepentant confession—a long, dramatic monologue uttered in a hospital for the criminally insane. Lance remembers what he did only as he tells his story to the psychiatrist priest who happens also to be an old friend. The friend, who was once called Percival, has taken the priestly name *John*. And although he is no criminal, he, like Lance, is in need of rehabilitation. Lance detects about him an air of failure and indecision. In the course of what may be Percy's most audaciously dialogical novel, these two characters will dramatically change each other, although one is given scarcely more than one-word utterances, with those coming only in the final pages.

Binx Bolling's search starts with the discovery that he himself is left over from the dyadic matrices explored by science, and it leads him to apparent faith and to that community in miniature, marriage. Lance Lamar's quest is an inversion of Binx's. It begins with the shock of betrayal and drives him to revenge and to a state approaching solipsism. At one point in *The Moviegoer* Binx implies that he is searching for God; Lance forthrightly declares that he is in quest of evil, which he hails as the Unholy Grail. Within the framework of Percy's thought, Binx has been able to glimpse true selfhood, which must be lived "transparently before God"; Lance follows the downward spiral marking the attempt to claim self-sufficiency. In Robert Brinkmeyer's words, "Lance, until the end of the novel, embodies what Percy sees as perhaps humanity's most destructive resistance to intersubjectivity—the myth of the autonomous self."[2] His negative search produces a hateful hope—a plan to purify the world by way of a social upheaval he calls the Third Revolution. Only the immanent sacramental witness of his priest friend at the novel's end offers the chance that this dark, reverse-image hope may be turned into its true form.

Lance's pursuit of autonomy begins with self-discovery. Like other existential heroes in and out of Percy's fiction, Lance "comes to himself." The occasion in his case is not battle, as it was for Binx in Korea or Prince André after the Battle of Borodino, but marital infidelity. While filling out an application for his younger daughter to go to camp, he notices that her blood type does not match his. A quick phone call to a doctor friend confirms that he could not possibly be Siobhan's biological father. After a slow descent into a somnambulant existence, Lance comes fully alert. When he discovers that his wife, Margot, has been unfaithful to him, he is led to a second great discovery: he had already lost himself. To Percival he confides, "Do you know what happened to me during the past twenty years? A gradual, ever so gradual, slipping away of my life into a kind of dream state in which finally I could not be sure that anything was happening at all" (*L* 57).

This sense of unreality takes poignant personal form when on the night after he has proved to himself that his younger daughter is not his biological child he alters his evening pattern and takes a different route out of his house on the way to the redecorated pigeonnier which serves as his private domain. "[A]s I crossed the room . . . something moved in the corner of my eye. It was a man at the far end of the room. There was something wary and poised about the way he stood, shoulders angled, knees slightly bent as if he were prepared for anything. He was mostly silhouette but white on black like a reversed negative. . . . Then I realized it was myself reflected in the dim pier mirror" (*L* 63–64). Unbeknownst to himself, Lance has lapsed into a kind of unreality that is exposed to him by his wife's dark deed. Her affair provides the contrast for him to see himself "like a reversed negative." Tellingly, when he later examines himself intentionally and closely in his bathroom mirror, he finds signs of dirt and neglect. He cleans himself up; he does push-ups; he prepares himself for action.

2. Robert H. Brinkmeyer Jr., "*Lancelot* and the Dynamics of Intersubjective Community," 161.

The action Lance pursues is what he later metaphorically describes to Percival as the quest for the Unholy Grail. On Belle Isle he lays his plans to videotape the sexual shenanigans of his wife and the movie-making crew to which she has opened their home, in part to prove to himself the depth of her betrayal. But at a deeper level his cinematic researches have a metaphysical aim: to give visual proof of real evil.

Just as Binx extrapolates from his own malaise to modernity's divorce from reality, so Lance believes his betrayal to be a sign of the times. Lance well knows that marital infidelity is commonplace, and in a sense his story is banal. Part of what makes it so has nothing to do with the fact that spouses have long cheated on each other, however. Lance observes that in our time, evil has disappeared. Crimes take place; perpetrators still create victims. But these wrongs are explained as the results of heredity, environment, or miscalculation. Lance considers objections to his thesis:

> But we have plenty of evil around you say. What about Hitler, the gas ovens and so forth? As everyone knows and says, Hitler was a madman. And it seems nobody else was responsible. Everyone was following orders. It is even possible that there was no such order, that it was all a bureaucratic mistake.
>
> Show me a single sin.
>
> One hundred and twenty thousand dead at Hiroshima? Where was the evil of that? Was Harry Truman evil? As for the pilot and bombardier, they were by all accounts wonderful fellows, good fathers and family men.
>
> "Evil" is surely the clue to this age, the only quest appropriate to the age. For everything and everyone's either wonderful or sick and nothing is evil. (*L* 138)

By Lance's lights, the sense of sin has evaporated from current culture. Yet he takes his own uncalculated outrage at the offense against him as a sign that perhaps evil can still be found. And if he can find it, if this Sir Lancelot, Knight of the Unholy Grail, achieves his quest, he can offer a boon to his priest friend: "Wouldn't that be a windfall for you? A new proof for God's existence! If there is such a thing as sin, evil, a living malignant force, there must be a God!" (*L* 52).

Lance's insane endeavor is wrong-headed for several illuminating reasons. First, it hangs upon what Augustine would immediately spot as a philosophical error: evil is the privation of good, not the other way around. Whereas evil may be understood as a defection from the goodness of God, God cannot be understood as a necessary answer to evil. An argument for the connection between God and evil works only in one direction, so to speak. One must begin with an idea of God in order to recognize evil. Further, Lance does not take into account that in his experiment, the outcome depends upon the state of the observer. Only the pure of heart could reach the Grail. Lance has no chance of finding even an Unholy Grail unless he has the spiritual eyes to see. His impure condition leads to the final reason he is doomed to failure. He is stepping into a madman's delusion, which has room only for one. The knights of the Round Table had a common quest; Lance, although he uses the labor of others, is on a solitary mission of false autonomy.

The Grail metaphor has significance beyond its neat fit with the names of Lancelot and Percival. The original Grail was the cup Christ used at his Last Supper, the meal in which, as the church believes, he instituted the Eucharist. The offense in which Lance expects to find his Unholy Grail is a sexual one, because sex, as Lance describes it, is the real sacrament. As John Desmond notes, Lance puts into practice the "transcendence-through-lewdness" theory of an earlier Percy character, Sutter Vaught of *The Last Gentleman,* by practicing what Desmond calls "inverted 'sacramentalism.'"[3] Speaking of his love for Margot, Lance tells his friend, "She was like a feast. She was a feast. I wanted to eat her. I ate her. That was my communion, Father—no offense intended, that sweet dark sanctuary, guarded by the heavy gold columns of her thighs, the ark of her covenant" (*L* 171). Lance asserts that in the moment of orgasm, human beings transcend themselves in the only way open to them. Within the framework of his quest, this transcendence leads him to believe that in the guilty sexual pleasure of others he will find the final proof of sin.

Not surprisingly, Lance's quest comes to naught. With the help of a brilliant African American college student whose family works on Belle Isle, Lance succeeds in filming his wife's liaisons with both Siobhan's biological father and the director of the film in progress. He also watches his older daughter's contortions with the male and female stars of the movie. But nowhere does he find "sin." Nor does he feel it when he creeps into the house, bowie knife and duct tape in hand, to divert natural gas into the rooms and seek his revenge. He manages to kill his wife's lovers and, without intending it, also kills Margot in an explosion that he engineers. Yet he reports that he felt and found nothing. He wonders, "Why

3. Desmond, "Walker Percy's Eucharistic Vision," 226.

did I discover nothing at the heart of evil? There was no 'secret' after all, no discovery, no flickering of interest, nothing at all, not even any evil. . . . As I held that wretched Jacoby by the throat, I felt nothing except the itch of fiberglass particles under my collar." What he does feel in the aftermath of this disaster is numbness. He tells Percival, "I feel nothing now except a certain coldness. I feel so cold, Percival" (*L* 253).

This numbness is Lance's most important symptom, for it speaks to the depth of his alienation from being. In gaining complete autonomy, Lance has sundered himself from God, humanity, and the natural world. Having taken his private quest in hand, he has managed to master his situation, but at the expense of destroying everyone on his "beautiful island" except himself. From the nadir of his catastrophe, having been literally blown out of his house by the force of exploding gas "like Lucifer blown out of hell" (*L* 246), Lance has regained his feet to launch a new plan. This project is as diabolical in its way as was the search for sin. Although he lacks proof of evil or God, he retains his moral outrage. He intends to project his sense of order on the world by leading what he calls the Third Revolution in America. Both the American Revolutionary War and the Civil War failed to produce a lasting, decent social order, so now a third effort is needed. Reviving Aunt Emily's Southern Stoicism in a new, virulent form that seeks to fight the descent into mediocrity and laxness rather than simply to regret it, Lance announces the beginning of new order. He will set up in the Shenandoah Valley of Virginia and await the self-destruction of the current society, after which he and like-minded warriors will establish an elite community based on a stern moral code.

Lancelot's plan is apocalyptic in the usual sense of envisioning a great devastation that only a remnant survive. But from the perspective of the theological virtue of hope, this apocalypse is as twisted from the biblical norm as is Lance's inverted sacramentalism. The Third Revolution represents another instance of the myth of autonomy, with brave men and their women living sternly by their own lights. Lance still lives in the "wintry kingdom of the self" that Percy named as the abode of the Southern Stoic. The Third Revolution thus establishes not a New Jerusalem, but rather an old mistake under a new name.

More truly hopeful is the fact that Lance admits his ominous symptom to his friend, calling him by name. Brinkmeyer deftly points out that "[w]ith this admission, Lance asks for—rather than offers—an explanation." By acknowledging in the presence of another the cold that has overtaken him, Lance opens the door to intersubjectivity. Brinkmeyer continues: "Though Lance immediately reasserts himself in an effort to maintain his monologic vision, he nonetheless has here initiated a true dialogue—an opening out to the other, both within to his own inner voice and without to Percival. His monologism is doomed."[4]

In fact, the most hopeful sign for Lance all along was his determination to tell his story to someone he could trust. His overture to his friend, along with his increasingly successful attempts to communicate with Anna, the rape victim in the adjoining room, provides the opportunity for dialogue. And Percival himself has been changed by what he has heard, slowly emerging as the priest who can speak a prophetic witness after the novel's final word. From an indecisive state when Lance first spies him, when he could be either priest or psychiatrist but is fully neither, Percival has reclaimed his priestly vocation. Early in his monologue Lance says that he has seen Percival in the cemetery on All Souls' Day, and from his shake of the head and brisk walk has concluded that he refused a woman's request for prayer. By the end, Percival is planning to take a parish in Alabama, where he will apply himself full time to the care of souls and the administration of sacraments. Lance's frequent insights into his friend's character and condition, as well as his frightening tale of twisted love and self-justifying revenge, have focused Percival's attention on what he now sees as the only antidote to the poison in Lance's soul. In place of the bitter draught from the Unholy Grail he will offer the cup of salvation, the blood of Christ.

Lance, of course, is not ready to accept this divine offer. To prepare the way for him, God must send the grace of dialogue, which is beginning in earnest only as the novel comes to an abrupt close. Lance, who has supplied all the answers, is ready to listen, and asks if his friend has anything to say. Percival, who now deserves to be called by his priestly name, Father John, stands ready to give witness to the church's truth. *Lancelot* ends with his one-word reply, "*Yes.*"

Although we never learn the content of Father John's rejoinder, we can be sure that it centers upon love, that theological virtue that gives substance to the hope of which the priest will speak. Hope born of righteous indignation hardly deserves the name. The coldness Lance feels warns us that hatred in whatever form is a dangerous motive. And it refers us to the subtext he has repeatedly invoked yet refused during his monologue: love

4. Robert H. Brinkmeyer Jr., "Walker Percy's *Lancelot:* Discovery through Dialogue," 41.

of God. Of course, Lance has been preoccupied with love throughout his monologue, especially the relationship between love and sex. In fact, it is the seeming disjunction between human love and sex that has driven him to search for evil, sex apparently having riven the human community rather than unified it. But the love Lance has occasionally considered only to reject is the love of God, and it is this love, as his friend knows, that must undergird all others. As O'Connor also knew, evil is a parasite on good; one cannot find evil and thus make one's way to goodness. Without the good, which has its source in God, there is no evil. Lance had it exactly backwards when he began his quest for the Unholy Grail. Sin is not the basis upon which the need for honor and morality can then be secured. Without transcendent good, there is no evil; and without God, the good disappears.

At several points, Lance's priest friend begins to speak of love of God as the root of human goodness, but he never manages to complete his affirmation. He almost breaks in when Lance denounces Christian love as being too soft: "You know the main difference between you and me? With you everything seems to get dissolved in a kind of sorrowful solution. Poor weak mankind! The trouble is that in your old tolerant Catholic world-weariness, you lose all distinctions. Love everything. Yes, but at midnight all cats are black, so what difference does anything make? It does make a difference? What? You opened your mouth and then thought better of it—" (*L* 130–31). Later, when Lance is proposing his new social order, he tells his friend, "Don't speak to me of Christian love" (*L* 158). American Christians have prostituted themselves to the wider society, Lance argues. In the new society, people will live by chivalry, duty, and honor. But the priest's question still weighs on him: how will you live if not with Christian love? Father John is on the verge of pressing the Christian case that without love of God, the human community can not sustain itself in the long run. Lance's late reference to Augustine's *City of God* reinforces this point, and gives the final clue to the content of the dialogue that continues after the reader turns the final page.

From the fact that Lance notes that his friend now speaks loud and clear, looking him directly in the eye, we can infer that Father John has gained certainty and is ready to speak without equivocation as one "having authority," in Kierkegaard's phrase. And although Percy abides by his principle of indirect communication, so that the message is withheld from us, it seems likely that it is a witness to that love alluded to by his very name: "John the Evangelist, who loved so much" (*L* 10). For Percy, there is no hope without love, and the only love ultimately capable of sustaining hope, as Augustine urged, is love of God.

Love's Language: The Second Coming

While *Lancelot* tellingly demonstrates hope's dependence upon love, it does not present a convincing case of wholesome love that might provide an analogue to divine love. Lance's communications with his fellow patient Anna, which by the end of his story have progressed from taps on the wall to conversation to a proposal on his part, constitute as yet no more than a hopeful sign. *The Moviegoer* comes closer to a presentation of fulfilling love, but Kate and Binx's commitment to each other comes late in the novel and as something of a surprise—to them as well as the reader. Not so in Percy's penultimate novel, *The Second Coming,* where the question of how Will Barrett's and Allie Huger's stories will intersect provides the central interest of the plot. In this novel, Percy explores to its fullest extent the sacramental potential of erotic love, a subject he had raised some fifteen years earlier in *The Last Gentleman,* when the character Will Barrett made his first appearance. In that novel, the cynical Sutter Vaught, a brilliant but alienated physician, abandons a set of casebooks, discovered by Barrett, that lay out a metaphysical analysis of sex similar in many respects to that of Lancelot Lamar. Sutter advances what Desmond calls the "transcendence-through-lewdness" theory, whereby sexual intercourse becomes the only means for joining flesh and spirit in a desacralized world. But of course, as Lance's story illustrates, turning to sex as a sacramental substitute is fraught with spiritual dangers. Not only is one's "altar" subject to violation, as Lance learned, but the druglike fix supplied by sex is both addicting and unreliable. When the gap between self and world yawns too wide, death lurks as the only dependable means for closing it. Thus Lance resorts to murder, and Sutter nearly commits suicide.

In *The Second Coming* Will Barrett confronts sex and death, allowing Percy to take up the relation of those universal themes so important to Freud. Ultimately for Percy, eros wins out over thanatos. And the key to this triumph is a recasting—indeed, a reversal—of the strategy whereby sex replaces sacrament. In *The Second Coming,* sex serves as an analogue or type of divine enfleshment in Eucharist and Incarnation. Thus its full and true meaning is not to be found in itself, and its significance, while great, is not final. And the same divine transcendence to which erotic love points provides the antidote to death, since the God of the Christian sacraments stands as the good creator and author of being, whose affirming Logos outweighs the pull of finitude and nothingness. Once again in this novel, language makes it possible for God's sacramental work to be done. Not only does the new language evolved by the lovers precipitate and form their love, language itself operates as a second sign of transcendence. As for all of Percy's characters, for Will and Allie, revelation is a language event enabled by dialogue.

Before they intersect, the parallel narratives of Will Barrett and Allison Huger disclose thematically complementary lives, despite sharp juxtapositions. Barrett lives in a luxurious prison of his own making, but in which he grows increasingly restless. Using the keen social radar he displayed in *The Last Gentleman,* Will has made of himself a huge professional and financial success by fulfilling the expectations of others. His recent years have been spent in semi-retirement, caring for his ailing, wealthy wife and helping her put her considerable fortune to charitable use. Yet this comfortable, commendable life lived in the beautiful North Carolina mountains leaves Barrett unfulfilled. Though his circumstances are different, he feels the grip of a living death as threatening as Binx's malaise or Lance's early middle-aged ennui. In fact, death is more than a metaphor for Will. The death of his wife both opens the door of his self-imposed prison and pushes him toward self-examination. Even more importantly, the remembered suicide of his father, in conjunction with the emptiness he feels, prompts him to regularly finger the German Luger he keeps in the glove compartment of his Mercedes. In the novel's second chapter he rehearses his own death: "He held the muzzle against his temple. Yes, that is possible, he thought smiling, that is one way to cure the great suck of self, but then I wouldn't find out, would I? Find out what? Find out why things have come to such a pass and a man so sucked down out of himself that it takes a gunshot to knock him out of the suck" (*SC* 14). Intensifying his flirtation with death is an undiagnosed brain disorder that begins to manifest itself in physical and psychological symptoms. During the course of the novel, Will will require medical intervention to save his life.

As her story begins, Allie is emerging from a similarly troubled state. She escapes from a mental hospital, where she was placed after descending to a state of isolation and withdrawal so severe that she had to be pulled out of the closet where she sat starving, having folded into herself like a star going down to white dwarf, as she says. One might go so far as to call her an "ex-suicide," a term that Percy uses elsewhere to describe the spiritual condition of the modern writer and that Desmond assigns to Will's condition at the end of the novel.[5] This crucial similarity with Barrett is balanced by a number of contrasts. While he has made a career out of meeting the expectations of others, she has failed miserably at "fulfilling her potential," as her mother, particularly, would see it. The relationship that eventually develops between Will and Allie will be greatly complicated by the coincidence that her mother had nearly married Will herself, and still harbors romantic designs upon him. Perhaps the most important difference between Allie and Will lies in the fact that she is recovering as he is slipping toward crisis. She carries out a clever plan to evade the dangerous ministrations of Dr. Duk, the psychiatrist who insists on electric-shock treatments, and secretly sets up for herself in the abandoned greenhouse of a favorite aunt who has died and left the property to her. Thus she is starting over in what amounts to a potential Eden, where she lives as though she is the first human being.

Essential to her recovery is the medium she will come to share with Will: a new language. In many ways, Allie represents the artistic apogee of Percy's concern with language, as well as his most fully realized female character. Loss of language is her most severe symptom, and her unique reappropriation of speech in the course of her relationship with Will is the means by which she recovers herself. Remembering Percy's favorite example of language acquisition, we might say that she is a twenty-something Helen Keller who can see and hear, but who must, like Helen, recover the symbolic connection between language and the world that is so natural as to be invisible to most of us.

While Allie's difficulties come in at a higher level of sophistication than Helen's, there are marked similarities. For Helen before the "Delta Factor" breakthrough of the running water, words were mere indicators of things, rather than symbols in a universe of discourse. Allie has trouble connecting words to the world of human social interaction:

> She took words seriously to mean more or less what they said, but other people seemed to use words as signals in another code they had agreed upon. For example, the woman's questions and commands were evidently not to be considered as questions and com-

---

5. Desmond, "Language, Suicide, and the Writer: Walker Percy's Advancement of William Faulkner," 132.

mands, then answered accordingly with a yes, no, or maybe, but were rather to be considered like the many signboards in the street, such as Try Good Gulf for Better Mileage, then either ignored or acted upon, but even if acted upon, not as an immediate consequence of what the words commanded one to do. (*SC* 34)

These reflections, which follow an exchange with a proselytizing evangelical who has asked her if she feels lonely and invited her to "a little get-together we're having," reveal Allie's acute awareness of the social dimension of language. Syntax and vocabulary are not sufficient to understand how it works. Taking words seriously to mean more or less what they say has its limitations. "Words surely have meanings, she thought, and there is my trouble. Something happens to words coming to me from other people. Something happens to my words. . . . People don't mean what they say. Words often mean their opposites" (*SC* 82).

This lack of confidence in language to serve as bridge to others bends back reflexively on Allie's sense of self. The gap between the self she knows herself to be as speaker and the self she hears herself becoming for her audience is too wide, and she can't seem to close it. She thus avoids talking altogether: "She had trouble talking. It was like walking out on a stage. She could answer questions, . . . even ask questions. But to make a statement on your own, surely you had to know what you were talking about" (*SC* 88). This anxiety over self is expressed in a query to her doctor: "I feel bad? Which I? It was the lilt at the end of a question that let her say it, freed her up. She did not want to go down just yet the way a statement goes down flat and hard, ends. Isn't there a difference between the outside-I, the me you see, the meow-I and the inside deep-I-defy?" (*SC* 89). It takes Allie's claiming of her verbal freedom for her to begin to unite the "me you see" and the "deep-I-defy." Only when she acts truly on her own for the first time by escaping both her doctor and her parents, and setting up for herself, does she find that she can begin to make assertions and to fashion her place in the linguistic world. She is aided in this endeavor by an opportunity to create her world in a physical way in the old greenhouse, which she sets out to rehabilitate on her own, thus becoming another of Percy's Robinson Crusoes. One kind of making reinforces the other, words and work together forming a human world.

Coming into this new world aborning for Allie, and completing it, is Will Barrett, a man in desperate need of such an oasis. He, for his own part, has been parched for a life-restoring word, and in time such words will arise between them. When he crashes into her greenhouse, Will is at the nearly tragic conclusion of a quest to wrest that word from God.

By fits and starts, through a series of brilliantly presented associations, recollections, and deductions, Will has concluded that what came to be referred to as "the hunting accident" was in fact his father's attempt to kill them both, an intention he avoided only by swerving at the last instant. Thus Will comes to believe that his father came to love death as the ultimate thrill, the final, orgasmic assertion of one's will over one's destiny. This discovery nudges Will toward taking his own turn at the family game, a suicidal disposition Percy was familiar with from his own family history. The one serious argument Barrett can make to himself for not putting a Luger to his temple or a Greener in his mouth requires God's existence. If God is there, then perhaps history makes sense and life has a purpose after all. In his nuttiness and despair, Will concocts what he believes to be a foolproof test of God's existence, as definitive as the Michelson-Morley experiment on the nature of space (*SC* 192). He resolves to descend into a cave and stay there until God shows him a sign or he dies. If God does not exist, Will has no reason to live; if God is there, so he seems to believe, God will show himself in order to save this honest seeker.

Predictably, the experiment fails. But two things about the manner of its misfiring are noteworthy. First, Will abandons his test when he is struck by a throbbing toothache, which restores him to full awareness of his bodily and creaturely nature. The toothache leaves him no leisure for abstract pursuits. Second, his botched exit from the cave lands him nearly in Allie's lap. Perhaps Will has his sign after all. For what he most needs is someone to love—someone who can elicit his deep desire and return it in kind, and thus mirror his God-hunger while feeding it with the feast of grace that Will has demanded. And this is what he soon finds in Allie.

From their first encounter, Allie has found that Will can follow her elliptical speech, so that real conversations are possible between them. He seems to be in tune with her intentions in ways that put her words in the proper context, in part because he has gone through similar struggles. Nursing Will after his fall from the upper reaches of the cavern, Allie feels a sexual attraction for him that answers two of her most pressing questions. In building her new life, she has wondered if she needs people at all, given her difficulty with them. She also wonders what love is, and whether it is for her, much as Will has earlier questioned his old friend Sutter in a letter declaring that the word signifies nothing to him beyond a kind of protectiveness toward his daughter, Leslie. Allie's lone sexual escapade had left her unimpressed. But when she becomes sexually attracted to Will, she finds that not only does she recognize and need love, but that this love provides the definitive connection between words and world.

As Will talks, it seems to her that the words have a meaning beyond themselves, but this meaning, rather than being puzzling and foreign, is intended only for her: "When he began to talk she found that she could not hear his words for listening to the way he said them. She cast about for his drift. Was he saying the words for the words themselves, or for what they could do to her? There was something about the way he talked that reminded her of her own rehearsed sentences. . . . Though he hardly touched her, his words seemed to flow across all parts of her body. Were they meant to? A pleasure she had never known before bloomed deep in her body" (*SC* 262). When Will places his hand on the small of her back, another wave of pleasure passes over her. She tells him, "Now I understand how the two work together." "What two?" he wonders. "The it and the doing," she answers, "the noun and the verb, sweet sweet love and a putting it to you, loving and hating, you and I." The linguistic process Allie describes is one that establishes the bridge she previously could not cross, one that makes a connection between self and world, self and other. With Will, nouns and verbs match things and actions, establishing a universe of meanings held in common. And though of course this microcosm is dependent upon the larger universe of social discourse and practices, access to it is opened and validated for Allie by love for this particular man. In her rhyming summary phrase, "One plus one equals one and oh boy almond joy" (*SC* 263).

Allie is not alone in finding in this linguistic-sexual connection a vital joining together that supplies the missing link between spiritual longing and finite existence. According to Desmond, Percy has signaled a Eucharistic context for the assertion that "the it and the doing, the noun and the verb" have been united, and it is this link that supplies what Will needs even more desperately than does Allie. Just before the crucial utterance about love, Allie has told Will about a visit from her "sister Val," a nun whom Will had met in the earlier novel as Kitty's sister. Allie says Val now teaches in a school in Pass Christian run by the Little Eucharistic Sisters of St. Dominic. The two muse over the "outrageous" name, thus underscoring its significance. Desmond observes of Allie that she "intuits the union of word and act at the core of love as the 'secret' of human fulfillment of the self, and analogue of divine love." And he concludes:

> Allie discovers the *relation* between being and doing, matter and spir-
> it. In effect, she discovers the mystery of love that is the heart of the
> Incarnation, the triad of being-doing-saying made flesh through the
> mysterious action of the "coupler," the Holy Spirit. Will and Allie's
> human love is a sign of enfleshed divine love. Hence Percy could le-
> gitimately claim that the novel overcame alienation *through* a recov-
> ery of Christianity, through the sign. For his part, Will confirms the
> new direction of his life—he will "do what is expected of me. Take
> care of people who need taking care of."[6]

Thus does their sexual love serve as an analogue to the sacramental presence of Christ in the Eucharist, which itself reenacts God's presence in
Christ through the Incarnation. Percy's constant iteration of the "real
presence" of God in language finds here its most direct expression in his
fiction.

Desmond's point to the effect that this revelatory moment is followed
by an opening out to others underscores one way that what we might call
sacramental eros reverses Sutter's lewdness-as-transcendence. Rather than
turning lovers into private consumers of spiritual stimulation, this love
directs them outward in charity toward community. Another urgent difference concerns the origin of love. Sutter and Lance describe a passion
that springs from sexual heat, the hand on the warm, naked thigh. For
Sutter's kind of transcendence, love needs go no further than coupling.
But the love of Allie and Will, though it grows fully erotic, starts as neighbor love, each seeking simply to help the other. Allie literally cares for
Will after his ordeal in the cave, "hoisting" him with skills she has learned
installing a massive woodstove. Will, who had helped her earlier, when he
first stumbled into her from the golf course, continues to come to her aid
once he regains his feet. This erotic love walks hand in hand with charity, moving naturally into larger community. Yet as the final episodes of
the novel unfold, it becomes clear that this sacramental analogy will not
be fully recognized by either Will or Allie.

Again Desmond makes the telling point, to which we will return in
the next chapter: "In this novel Percy chose to bypass the traditional
Catholic sacramental signs, largely devalued in the culture, and instead
create an intricate web of fresh and open-ended signs to suggest the real
possibility of divine presence and agency within the natural, human
world." Thus while the sacramental eros of this couple draws its true

6. Desmond, *Percy's Search,* 203–4.

meaning and power from the Christian sacramental reality to which it points, the church itself is not present, except as what we might call a necessary assumption and hope. When Will looks to the visible church for help, he finds signs, but no certainty, as when he requests the sacrament of marriage. As Allen Pridgen notes in his fine study of sacramental presences in Percy's work, "[Will] goes to Father Weatherbee at the end of the novel in search for clues to the mysterious source of the love he has recently witnessed."[7] But what he finds in the aging, "timid" Episcopal priest is a man who has yielded his authority to teach and who will not offer the sacramental blessing Will seeks.

Will himself falters yet again before embracing his new life. But after dealing with a final crisis that shows he has been suffering from a chemical imbalance in his brain that has aggravated his more metaphysical speculations, Will seems about to extricate himself from the rest home where his daughter has tried to place him, and to join Allie in a new life. His love for her is in all ways a match for her love of him, and neither of them has any remaining quibbles about the meaning of the word or the reality of the bond it creates. He affirms to her that what they are saying is "part and parcel" of what they are doing. And yet there is one more piece to this comedy of hope fulfilled.

Will approaches the retired missionary who is serving as supply chaplain at the nursing home that his deceased wife built. Wanting to know whether Father Weatherbee will perform the wedding he and Allie are planning, Will also asks, "Do you believe that Christ will come again and that there are in fact certain unmistakable signs of his coming in these very times?" (*SC* 360). Though Will maintains that he is not a believer, he insists that some kind of divine culmination is necessary in order for history to make sense, and so he turns to this frail and hesitant old man as a priestly believer, one who can speak with authority. Will gets no answer, but his own final declaration completes the circle of love's theology:

> For some reason the old man did not move but looked at him with a new odd expression. Will Barrett thought about Allie in her greenhouse. . . . His heart leapt with secret joy. What is it I want from her and him, he wondered, not only want but must have? Is she a gift and therefore a sign of the giver? Could it be that the Lord is here, masquerading behind this simple silly holy face? Am I crazy to want

7. Ibid., 183; Allen Pridgen, *Walker Percy's Sacramental Landscapes: The Search in the Desert,* 138.

both, her and Him? No, not want, must have. And will have. (*SC* 360)

Will is following a hunch that Percy might explain if this were not a novel, where communication must be indirect. Human love, however rapturous, is incomplete without love of God. God is both the source of love and the end to which love is directed. Cut off from God, love becomes fractured and fractious, radically in need of redemption. Will's spiritual radar senses that such a redemption on the other side of late modern fragmentation is yet possible, but only through the work of the loving God whom he can't prove, but whom he still "must have. And will have." In this way, Percy points beyond the erotics of sexuality to a more fundamental eros: desire for God. Barrett's train of thought moves precisely in this Augustinian direction. The human self is indeed driven by love, first and foremost. And in the disordered state sin has engendered, it is inevitable that human desire manifest itself as a hunger for earthly things. By means of sexual love we find temporary fulfillment of both our bodily natures and our need for communion. But these satisfactions are always fleeting and preliminary.

As Augustine famously says in his *Confessions,* the soul is restless till it rests in God. The gift is indeed a sign of the giver; without God at the other side of the beloved, so to speak, love will ultimately fail. It is only as love of another is seen as a channel connecting us to the Source and End of desire that it becomes a means of grace rather than a site for demonic irruption. Lance Lamar has felt the chill hand of love cut off from its source and turned to hate. Sexual love is true only as it points beyond itself to a deeper eros.

8

Southern Strangers and the Sacramental Community

ʚᎧɞ

From Aristotle to MacIntyre, thinkers have insisted that no set of virtues can be sustained without a community to nourish them. The same might be said for the sacramental vision Percy shared with O'Connor, and indeed for the entire aesthetic of revelation they pursued. The assertion that God is concretely present in the world is, for the Catholic Christian, an extrapolation from Eucharistic worship. Likewise, faith, hope, and love are not mere abstract goals, but rather names of qualities necessary to follow Christ, qualities which the church fosters and affirms in specific ways. Although one can certainly have faith in something other than the Christian God, and although hope and love have meaning outside the Christian sphere, these three form the unity by which they deserve to be called the theological virtues only when they share the specific telos carried forward through the centuries by Christian communities.

Walker Percy's exploration of love in *The Second Coming* points toward community as our final, inevitable topic. Just as for the Christian theological tradition love is the highest virtue, so for Percy it represents the answer to the questions of faith and hope raised in *The Moviegoer* and *Lancelot*. Marriage is an aid to establishing the identity that faith requires if one grants with Percy's mentor Gabriel Marcel that selfhood is ultimately intersubjective. We find ourselves only through a process of triangulation requiring the presence of others. And we know ourselves most deeply when the bonds connecting us are bonds of love. Love, we might say, provides the element of communion that unites us to reality beyond ourselves and frees us from Cartesian detachment, just as, in Percy's Peircean semiotics, symbol is the means whereby, in concert with a linguistic community, we come to inhabit a world. Thus, both love and symbol push us to recognize community. Symbol function can never be a private transaction, or even an exchange between two. While of course it is possible to develop a unique vocabulary and a derivative syntax (as do Allie and Will), these are always dependent upon a prior language and an inherited set of social practices, as Wittgenstein showed. Less obvious in our individualized culture, but nonetheless true, is the fact that love, too, requires community. Although there is certainly in *The Second Coming* a strong element of starting over by building a new community, just as there is a new beginning hinted at in the more drastic and apocalyptic *Lancelot,* in both cases as also in *The Moviegoer* erotic love finds its home in marriage, and marriage takes its place among larger social connections.

Within the theological orbit, love leads to community in two very specific ways, one having to do with love's origin, and the second with its return. As O'Connor's and Percy's favorite theologian, St. Thomas Aquinas, knew well, the ontological origin of love lies within the Godhead itself. God as Trinity is, so to speak, already a community bound by love. Creation issues from an overflow of this divine, self-giving love. The individual human being, supported by this love without which there is nothing, is meant for free and full participation in the divine dynamic. And the name for the creature's love of the Creator is worship. But just as love originates in a community (the Trinity), so it is best returned by means of the worshipping community (the church). Christ's foundation of the church is confirmation of man's social nature, even as it also recognizes that the restoration of humanity in the wake of sin through the right worship of God is the joint responsibility of all God's people. As James Smith argues, Christian desire is "always an embodied desiring for the Creator that, as in the Trinity, involves a third: the Other." For humanity, this Other is the church, which Graham Ward has tellingly termed an "erotic community."[1]

Both Percy and O'Connor would certainly give assent to this theological outline of how love inescapably involves us in communities, as they both affirmed the Roman Catholic insistence on social embodiment and connection in the midst of modern abstraction and isolation. But when it comes to dealing with the two communities with which they are most closely associated, difficulties arise for each in ways we need to explore

---

1. James K. A. Smith, *Introducing Radical Orthodoxy: Mapping a Post-secular Theology,* 246–47; Graham Ward, *Cities of God,* 152–81.

briefly. While theoretically the church might be the universal community rightly directing our worship to God, in fact we live in competing and conflicting communities. As southerners who made no secret of their religious allegiance, O'Connor and Percy were forced by circumstance if not by inclination to address the relation between church and regional culture.

Beyond Memory

One of the relevant circumstances is that of American literature in the 1950s and 1960s. As we have seen, O'Connor and Percy wrote in the wake of the Southern Renaissance, the outpouring of remarkable work that followed H. L. Mencken's dismissive declaration in 1917 that the South was "the Sahara of the Bozart."[2] Dominated by the influence of Faulkner, and including the work of such writers as Eudora Welty, Robert Penn Warren, and Allen Tate, the mode of the renaissance was what Lewis Simpson called "the aesthetic of memory," and the characteristic mood has been dubbed by Richard King as "despairing monumentalism." One might characterize the fiction and poetry of these writers as the attempt of white southerners who identified with the planter class to come to terms with the social paralysis engendered by the loss of the Civil War and the reactionary mind-set fostered by that loss. One could describe the literary attitude toward the South as ambivalent. This approach to the past was anti-romantic and critical, but at the same time admiring. Often feeling stifled by the region they were making famous, these writers sometimes lived in self-chosen exile. On the other hand, they resented the condescension evident in Mencken's remark and made prevalent in other parts of the country, especially the Northeast.

A significant number of these intellectuals, though by no means all, took part in the short-lived Agrarian movement, which in 1930 issued the manifesto called *I'll Take My Stand*. Although it is difficult to imagine either O'Connor or Percy having contributed to this volume had they been old enough to do so, one significant member of the group later became important to both of them: Allen Tate. Tate's essay "Remarks on the Southern Religion" throws the two younger writers' views into relief.

Tate's essay is allusive and his argument sometimes elusive, but his thesis is clear: the one missing ingredient that prevented the South from becoming a fully coherent agrarian society was Roman Catholicism.

2. H. L. Mencken, *Prejudices: A Selection*, 74.

Protestantism was too disjointed, individualistic, and predisposed toward capitalism to underwrite a stable, non–industrial culture. The Catholic Church, with its claims to universality, its sacramental attitude toward nature, and its respect for hierarchy was much better suited to provide resistance to the corrosions that the Agrarians saw at work in the mechanized and anonymous North. Although the southerner was by habit disposed to the concrete, the practical, and the personal, he lacked a coherent vision (what Tate calls a myth) to anchor these inclinations, and so had nearly lost them.

One can certainly hear in Tate's remarks the footsteps that would carry him over the threshold of the Roman Catholic Church in the next decade, but more pertinent to our purpose is the contrast between his positions and the later views of O'Connor and Percy. Despite his obvious sympathies with Catholicism, Tate's view toward religion was instrumentalist. The value he found in religion lay in its contribution to the general culture. The right kind of religion helps produce and sustain the right kind of society. At this early point in his career, Tate was more interested in cultural and artistic goals than he was in God. Further, Tate's approval of what he took to be the prime values of the old South was unequivocal. Although he could discern the seeds of destruction from the beginning—Jamestown was established as a commercial enterprise, and Thomas Jefferson mistakenly believed that "the ends of man are sufficiently contained in his political destiny"[3]—Tate still believed that, insofar as the old South represented the last outpost of "feudal" Europe, it was good.

On both of these fronts O'Connor and Percy were at odds with Tate's 1930 views. For them, the church offered access to transcendent truth, which is in turn the means by which society can be judged. The terms of cultural engagement derive from the church rather than from a prior cultural criticism, so to speak, and this is one important reason why *aesthetic of revelation* is an apt term for their approach. By the same token, Percy and O'Connor were critical not simply of the South's internal philosophical tensions but also of what Tate considered to be its best traditions. Two examples will indicate Percy and O'Connor's divergence. In an essay he wrote for *Commonweal* in 1956, Percy describes what he calls "Stoicism in the South."[4] The fact that he published in a Catholic journal is

3. Allen Tate, "Remarks on the Southern Religion," in Twelve Southerners, *I'll Take My Stand*, 173.
4. Percy, "Stoicism in the South," in *SSL*, 83–88.

significant in itself, but even more revealing is the sharp distinction he draws between what might now be called the ideology of the southern planter over against the Christian point of view:

> The greatness of the South, like the greatness of the English squire-archy, had always a stronger Greek flavor that it ever had a Christian. . . . How immediately we recognize the best of the South in the words of the Emperor [Marcus Aurelius]: "Every moment think steadily, as a Roman and a man, to do what thou hast in hand with perfect and simple dignity, and a feeling of affection, freedom, and justice." And how curiously foreign to the South sound the Decalogue, the Beatitudes, the doctrine of the Mystical Body. (*SLL* 84)

Clearly for Percy, the code by which planters actually lived was at odds with the spirit of humility and reconciliation one finds in Christianity. It was equally plain to Percy that the social structure that supported Southern Stoicism was gone for good, the recent sign being the 1954 Supreme Court decision ending school segregation by race. Percy believed that southerners could no longer live as Stoics while paying lip service to the church, but instead faced a clear choice: the church's witness over against the traditional values of the old South at its best.

Flannery O'Connor's rejection of the standards of the old South is perhaps best approached indirectly through her story "A Late Encounter with the Enemy," written in 1952. General Flintrock Sash, the protagonist, is 104 years old. He had never been a general, but more likely a foot soldier, although he does not remember the war at all. Until his death vision at the story's denouement, he is a comic character, serving as an emblem for a war that has been romanticized, its reality as remote from those who memorialize it as it is from the senile old veteran. The highlight of his life has been his participation in a movie premiere obviously modeled on that of *Gone with the Wind*. When the vain centenarian does confront memories that he has successfully repressed, they are nightmares of war's terrors and of his personal failures in regard to his family and his fellow man. He dies on the stage during his granddaughter's college graduation ceremony, a failed monument to a dead past. The loutish boy who wheels him out doesn't even notice that he is dead, and we last see Sash's corpse seated in the wheelchair, holding the boy's place in line for the Coca-Cola machine.

We might say that O'Connor distances herself from the old South more decisively than does Percy. In this story and in others—"Everything

That Rises Must Converge," for example—echoes of the old South always include an element of pretense. O'Connor does not even concede the nobility of the old order, which Percy mentions, and to which he was indeed direct heir by being born into an established, distinguished, and wealthy family. She indicates in essays and letters that being Catholic—not being aristocratic—often set her apart from her Bible Belt neighbors. And moments of illumination in her fiction regularly require estrangement from social norms, which often act as blinders. The grandmother must surrender the notion that she is a "lady" and "not a bit common" before she can have her moment of grace in "A Good Man Is Hard to Find." Lancelot must likewise come to the end of his bitter Southern Stoic monologue and prepare himself for the answering, alternative word of his priestly friend before there is any hope for him in Percy's novel. Simpson is justified in finding in the fiction of these two Catholic writers a break with the typical mode of renaissance literature. Thus in the terms we have borrowed from him, the aesthetic of memory has been replaced by the aesthetic of revelation, as he sets forth in the aptly titled chapter "What Survivors Do" in *The Brazen Face of History.*

Yet as he develops it in his essay, Simpson's distinction, helpful as it is for locating O'Connor and Percy within the development of what he calls "literary consciousness" in the South, is limited in what it can disclose about the relation between the revelation itself and the communities to whom it is directed. Robert Brinkmeyer takes up this issue in his study of Tate, Gordon, and Percy, *Three Catholic Writers of the Modern South,* by arguing that for all three figures the South represented a means of "resistance" to modern society and that Catholicism provided a means to "transcend" it. Brinkmeyer focuses upon the writers' attitudes to their various audiences, showing how allegiances amongst communities came to be played off against one another in the writers' work. Yet as Farrell O'Gorman has recently demonstrated in *Peculiar Crossroads,* this scheme is overly simple.[5] Percy and O'Connor were much more detached from the old South than were the older writers, and they never held up its values as a serious alternative to the modern wasteland, as we have seen. Percy's Lancelot is meant to frighten us, but he is also an anachronism on the border of sanity; his Third Revolution does not have Percy's endorsement, but rather is meant to elicit from the reader a sane alternative to it. But

5. O'Gorman, *Peculiar Crossroads,* 52n.

the question of whether the church provided a means to transcend contemporary dilemmas is more complicated and problematic.

Transcend can mean either to overcome or to escape. O'Gorman insists that in the cases of Percy and O'Connor, "transcendence" included engagement with contemporary culture, and thus that these artists are innocent of the charge sometimes leveled at literary modernists that they are caught up in a kind of apolitical formalism. But while it is true that both Catholic writers found resources within the church to take moral stands on pressing social issues, it is also the case that for them there was no clear sense of how the church might actually reform the larger society. Thus while church rather than South became the community of primary allegiance for O'Connor and Percy, neither found a satisfactory way to bring church and South (or more generally, modern society) into fruitful relationship. O'Connor famously declared the South to be "Christ-haunted," and took both amusement and inspiration from her Protestant fundamentalist neighbors, in whose worship and belief she spied elements of proto-Catholicism. But her work is so firmly fixed on the drama of the individual soul that she offers no positive vision of life together to counter her scathing satire of consumer society. She seems to have enjoyed the whiff of oddity that being Catholic gave her in the Bible Belt, but felt no inclination to change the cultural balance, so to speak. Percy, who was more politically attuned, was capable of chastising both southerners and Catholics on the matter of race, as is evident from the *Commonweal* article on Southern Stoicism. And Percy did serve on boards and committees aimed at fostering cooperation amongst the races. But Percy, too, had difficulties bridging the gap between private and public when it came to religious matters, as will appear more clearly when we look at existential themes in his work.

Catholic Existentialists

Catholic existentialists is the term O'Gorman uses to distinguish O'Connor and Percy from their renaissance predecessors. In his admirable study, what unites these writers, sets them apart from the Southern Renaissance, and allows them to serve as influential forerunners of a postmodern southern fiction is the orientation they take from Maritain, Marcel, Guardini, and other Catholic thinkers who combined a form of neo-Thomism with insights from Kierkegaard, Heidegger, and Sartre. O'Gorman draws upon an essay in which Thomas Merton praised the sort of Christian existentialism he found in current writers such as O'Connor. For such writers, "the authentic person is not born in stoic isolation but in [an] openness and dialogue of love" where "true communication is possible." The existentialist knows that "he cannot evade the present and fly from it into a safe and static past, preserved for him in a realm of ideal essences to which he can withdraw in silent recollection." O'Gorman concludes that this aesthetic is "antithetical to the Southern Renascence aesthetic—it is not historical and tragic, but rather ahistorical and comic"; O'Connor and Percy "possessed a vision that was essentially planted in the spiritual drama of the here and now." Theologically, O'Gorman finds the roots for this emphasis on the concrete to lie in Catholic sacramentalism. He approvingly quotes Ross Labrie's book, *The Catholic Imagination in American Literature:* "In adhering to the world as sacrament, Catholic writers have, whether deliberately or not, committed themselves to reality in whatever unwelcome and inconsistent form it might appear, in the expectation that God, the epitome and ultimate author of all reality, will thereby somehow be present."[6]

The difficulty in this account in relation to O'Connor and Percy is that it effectively removes sacramental understanding from the sacramental life of the church, and thus exacerbates what one might call the "existentialist" problem, which is precisely the ahistoricism that O'Gorman points out. When he calls the Catholic existentialism of Percy and O'Connor ahistorical, O'Gorman has in mind a feature of post-renaissance southern fiction that many have noted: it is no longer laden with a sense of the past still alive in the present; it is "reflexive," to use Michael Kreyling's term. As O'Connor remarked in 1960, echoing Percy, the Civil War carries no more weight with the new generation of southerners than does the Boer War.[7] That the iron grip of the monumentalized past has been broken may be a good thing, but to cut off all connection to the past is to render history meaningless. The new South of strip malls, golf courses, Jeff Foxworthy, and *The Dukes of Hazzard* sees its past as just another item to be marketed or ignored in the eternal present of American consumer society. It is true that Percy, and to a lesser extent O'Connor, made use of an existentialist analysis that showed how modern alienation includes estrangement from the past. Aunt Emily is correct when she says that for Binx there is no longer "a set of meanings held in common," and that he

---

6. Ibid., 101, 105.
7. Rosemary Magee, ed., *Conversations with Flannery O'Connor,* 75.

has slipped the grip of his patrician heritage. O'Connor's General Flint-rock Sash can't remember even the allegedly glorious past he personally experienced.

As Kreyling has explained, the southern sense of community has grown increasingly reflexive, constructed, and self-conscious. According to Scott Romine's account, Percy was the first southern writer of note "to confront reflexivity as a given." Romine observes, "Where Quentin Compson and Jack Burden find they can no longer sustain the tacit dimension of a traditional culture, Binx Bolling appears on the first page of *The Moviegoer* without having that dimension available."[8] What was once a burden to be shouldered or shirked is now simply a distant memory. But it is for this very reason that the existentialist element in O'Connor and Percy makes the possibility of community even more remote. Intense scrutiny of the fact of alienation may show the need for communion, but it does not supply the lack. And while the comic quality that O'Gorman lists as the second distinction that sets these two writers apart from their renaissance predecessors does presume a theological alternative to nihilism, that alternative is at best merely anticipatory concerning community.

To be more specific, one looks in vain in the fiction of O'Connor and Percy for examples of a realized community that might take the place of the more organic southern society they both know to be disintegrating. Perhaps the most telling O'Connor story in this regard is "The Displaced Person," where the micro-community of the farm is utterly disrupted by murderous complicity against the Polish refugee newcomer. The best outcome that O'Connor can envision for Mrs. McIntyre is her potentially being received into the church under the care of the old priest as she spirals toward death. In a certain sense the church stands as the new community to replace the old one destroyed by sin, but it is only dimly on Mrs. McIntyre's horizon. In general, O'Connor's moments of grace are solitary, private, and usually silent, Hazel Motes's illumination serving as the first of many.

Percy's novels, which show the South at yet a further remove from its agrarian and cohering past, are also sparing in their glimpses of more wholesome communal alternatives. As we saw, in *The Moviegoer* Binx has brief but significant discussions with his devout half brother, Lonnie, whose Eucharistic offering for his brother's faith may be instrumental in

8. Scott Romine, *The Narrative Forms of Southern Community,* 199.

the new direction Binx has taken in the Epilogue. In *The Last Gentleman* Will Barrett stops at the orphanage run by his employer's older daughter, now a nun, and finds much to admire there, but Val's camp in the pine barrens of Alabama is a much-needed charity, not the first installment of a new order. More promising are congregations we occasionally hear of— perhaps that of Tom More in *Love in the Ruins* chief among them. In the midst of a badly polarized United States, in which the Roman Catholic Church has split into factions along with most other institutions, Tom belongs to the small group that remains faithful to Rome and walks a middle way between political extremes. This remnant has reclaimed old penitential practices such as sackcloth and ashes, of which Tom avails himself at the end of a nearly disastrous pact with the devil. But despite these and other salutary encounters with the church and its representatives, the primary thrust of Percy's thought on community lies in an apocalyptic direction. The faithful remnant in *Love in the Ruins* might indeed be said to fit in this category, since the novel is set in the future and is subtitled *The Adventures of a Bad Catholic at a Time Near the End of the World*. Percy's parody of self-help manuals, *Lost in the Cosmos,* contains a "space odyssey" reminiscent of one of his favorite contemporary novels, *A Canticle for Leibowitz*. It features astronauts who return to an earth devastated by nuclear warfare and set up a commune with the help of a Benedictine abbot, who is but one of a handful of human survivors.

Perhaps the best explanation for this tendency is to be found in *The Second Coming*. The community that Will Barrett hopes to help build at the end of the novel is set over against the wily scheme of the ambitious Rev. Jack Curl, who wants to use Will's money to build "a true faith-and-love community lived according to the rhythm of God's own liturgical year" (*SC* 127). The ambitious, trend-conscious Episcopal priest is one of many Christians in the novel whose notions of community are too debased to be credible. John Desmond puts the point sharply: "The 'world' Percy depicts in the novel is largely a decadent 'Christian' community in which the traditional signs and language of belief and religious commitment have been, at best, emptied of meaning, and at worst, appropriated and manipulated by the purveyors of a bland, desacralized simulacrum of genuine faith."[9] Barrett seems to have no reasonable choice in his pursuit of community except to step outside the circle of American Christianity.

For Percy, communities of hope seem to lie only on the other side of

9. Desmond, *Percy's Search*, 181.

the end of the world. For O'Connor, although the present church seems to be a place of refuge, it is nearly always out of sight, its doctrine and witness necessary to make sense of things, but failing to bind people to each other in "the here and now" of which O'Gorman speaks. To borrow a term from anthropologist Victor Turner, no present community has *communitas*—that spontaneous unity that holds up the individual without diminishing her freedom.

There are, as one might expect, a number of reasons why O'Connor and Percy give us only glimpses of church life. One is a refusal to write "church" fiction, with its associations of sentimentalism and unctuousness. Another is the desire to have an impact on a wider audience than could be expected to share what might appear to be a sectarian point of view. In the case of Percy, all of whose novels except one were published after O'Connor's death, reluctance to portray the inside of church life grew as post–Vatican II Catholicism began to spin off in experimental directions he found to be misguided, as his sharp reaction to the Berrigan brothers' attack on draft-board records indicates.[10] Kieran Quinlan claims that by the late 1960s, "[t]he relatively stable and seemingly unified Church to which Percy was converted in the 1940s has begun to disintegrate."[11] Although *disintegrate* seems an exaggeration, certainly Percy had reason to be concerned about the Roman Church's faithfulness and coherence. But the reasons for the paucity of depictions of church life run deeper than these concerns, and indeed are rooted in the very thinkers O'Connor and Percy drew upon.

Existentialism is a notoriously vague term, about which Percy often complained in interviews. For the sake of clarity, we might break down its common associations into three themes: the necessity to root knowledge in the concrete world ("existence over essence"), emphasis on the plight of the individual and the role of the will in achieving authenticity, and the spiritual bankruptcy of modernity. To some degree, each of these themes is important to O'Connor and Percy, and there is no inherent reason why any one of them need push a writer outside the bounds of Christian conviction. O'Gorman is right to point out that the first theme is common to neo-Thomists, as Catholic philosophers James Collins and Frederick Copleston—both of whose work was owned and annotated by Percy and O'Connor—recognized. Likewise the third

10. Tolson, *Pilgrim in the Ruins,* 353.
11. Quinlan, *Walker Percy,* 118.

theme is indubitably present throughout the corpus of both writers, and it serves what we might go so far as to call an evangelistic purpose, preparing the way for the Good News of unexpected transcendent affirmation. Even though some critics have been disturbed by what they see in O'Connor as a Manichean tendency to disparage physical reality, most concede that after *Wise Blood* this temptation is subsumed into an orthodox sacramentalism. The chief theological difficulty comes with the second theme, the quest of the alienated self for authenticity.

The problem is more pronounced in Percy than in O'Connor. As I argued in the chapter on language, Percy's understanding of the self, despite qualifications, remains atomistic. Despite his theoretical commitment to Peirce, he never escaped his penchant for the role of the detached observer, for what he termed the "Martian" perspective. In more directly theological matters, Percy's attachment to Kierkegaard seems to have inclined him to a notion of grace that is private and decisionistic, as I have argued more thoroughly elsewhere.[12] Of course, there is a tension in Percy between this Protestant tendency and his Catholic commitments, as evidenced by the dueling epigraphs from Kierkegaard and Aquinas at the beginning of "The Message in the Bottle." But the very rhetorical strategy Percy adopted in his novels, that of indirect communication, pushes him in Kierkegaard's direction. Percy, like Kierkegaard, is hoping to lead the reader to the point where he will decide to change the orientation of his life. But an orientation dependent upon one's private decision is always reversible. As Augustine forcefully insisted against Pelagius, the human will is too leaky a vessel to serve as the ship of salvation. And the selfhood of Percy's characters seems especially volatile. From Binx Bolling to Tom More, they carom through life with varying degrees of distractedness, dislocation, and outright mental pathology. Any decision they make seems temporary, which in turn makes their relationships to the church tenuous and secondary. Of course, this shakiness is increased by the fluidity of the communities surrounding Percy's characters. Where the Roman Catholic Church itself is concerned, this danger is directly portrayed in *Love in the Ruins,* wherein American Catholics have split into three factions, only one of which accepts Rome's authority.

A related difficulty concerns authenticity. While for Percy it is clear that this existential goal is achieved only through Christian faith, the priority of this goal skews his presentation of the Christian life in the direction of

12. John D. Sykes, Jr., "The Imperious Castaway: Walker Percy on Guilt and the Self."

a certain kind of "selfishness" that Binx describes in *The Moviegoer*. When he stops at the ticket window of one of his favorite cinemas, he lingers to talk to the cashier. But the visit is not for her sake, he explains: "Show me a nice Jose cheering up an old lady and I'll show you two people existing in despair. My mother often told me to be unselfish, but I have become suspicious of her advice. No, I do it for my own selfish reasons. If I did not talk to the theater owner or the ticket seller, I should be lost, cut loose metaphysically speaking" (*MG* 75). This wry twist on selfishness does not rule out helping others; it does not even deny that one has an obligation to do good. Binx's point has more to do with the nature of the self. But there does seem to be an underlying assumption to the effect that one's first duty is to oneself, an assumption also to be found in Uncle Will's Southern Stoicism.

As we have seen, the novels typically begin with self-discovery, from which the quest for self-fulfillment or authenticity proceeds. Even though the measure of this self-fulfillment is always some outward movement toward serving others, the telos of the process itself is the healing of the protagonist's soul. There is more than a little truth in Ralph Wood's stark claim that "[h]owever communal the self must eventually become, Percy's most notable characters remain essentially isolated and self-obsessed."[13] In short, there is a strong disposition in Percy's work toward understanding the self as the center of value, even though ultimately, for Percy, the self finds completion only through faith in God, and God, in turn, can only be known through community.

The same cannot be said of O'Connor. In her work, the theme of authenticity is overshadowed by that of humiliation and suffering as pathways to God. This is not to say that Percy's protagonists don't suffer—in fact their quests are typically triggered by an ordeal that leads to inner turmoil and often physical danger. But none of Percy's protagonists embrace the direct bodily violence figured first in Hazel Motes's mortification and death in *Wise Blood*. Physical suffering as *imitatio Christi*—the image so prominent and final in O'Connor—is lacking amongst the protagonists in Percy's intentionally open-ended fiction. With the exception of Tom More, Percy's protagonists are more beset by a spiritual emptiness—despair—than they are by pride. In O'Connor's work, pride is the principal form of human sin. Her protagonists typically begin in a state of hubris

13. Ralph C. Wood, "The Alienated Self and the Absent Community in the Work of Walker Percy," 364.

that blinds them to their neediness until they are humbled by some un-expected blow, often a physical one. But what one does find in her work in common with the existentialists is what Frederick Asals calls "the lan-guage of extremity, an insistence on duality, dissociation, splits, paradox, the tension of opposites."[14] The effect of these tensions on the individ-ual is to launch her characters into a state of dread.

Anxiety is another staple of the existentialist lexicon, and like authen-ticity, it is both a product and a cause of alienation. In O'Connor's world, this estrangement is ultimately due to separation from God, but in a mod-ern world, it takes modern forms. The reluctant prophets of O'Connor's two novels find themselves in rebellion against father figures who are no longer present. Cities and strangers wait to trap them—and do. But most significantly, the calling they deeply dread, once it does overpower their resistance, proves to be their salvation. Anxiety drives the landowner of "Circle in the Fire," as indeed it does all of O'Connor's women of prop-erty. It even lurks behind the bluff of such apparently confident paragons as Mr. Head in "The Artificial Nigger." And though this dread turns out always to be an anticipation of a divine irruption filling an unacknowl-edged need, as with Percy, these are private encounters that shape only the individual life. The one exception to this general rule is young Tar-water in *The Violent Bear It Away:* at the end of the novel, he is headed to the city to deliver the word of the Lord. But despite his determination to find an audience, he is hardly part of a community, his calling and his training having been handed him by means of a single old man and his own peculiar prophetic visions. In O'Connor, God isolates as one of his many ways of painfully eviscerating our deluded sense of self-sufficiency, but seldom do we receive the hospitality of the household of faith after the surgery.

Thus insofar as Percy and O'Connor are Christian existentialists, their existentialism threatens their Christianity, especially when the theme of the alienated self rises to the fore. With the exception of "The Artificial Nigger," O'Connor's moments of grace do not include reconciliation with sister or brother even when they include reconciliation to God. And the church as a community of healing, instruction, prayer, and witness is present only at the periphery of her preferred spiritual country, the eter-nity "where the silence is never broken except to shout the truth" (*CW* 478). Percy's protagonists, though they may have found connection to a

14. Asals, *Flannery O'Connor,* 35.

lover and the prospect of larger social connection, have made only a tentative step toward God, which they are liable to retract should their quest for full selfhood lead them in a different direction. In neither writer does the church appear to be either the ark of salvation, as Cyprian termed it, or Augustine's hospital for souls. However, there is one sense in which the church remains decisively present and absolutely necessary in the cure of souls that these two writers describe: the church is the source of the sacraments.

Sacramental Community

The fiction of both writers has been called "sacramental," almost as long as their work has drawn serious critical commentary. Two worthy books of recent years have included the word in their titles: Susan Srigley's *Flannery O'Connor's Sacramental Art* and Allen Pridgen's *Walker Percy's Sacramental Landscapes*. Theologically minded readers rightly employ the term to describe both a conviction about material reality and an attitude toward nature. The first conviction might be summarized as the belief that God is present in the created world as it is, or as even more succinctly put by Rowan Williams, sacramentalism "identifies the real finally with the good."[15] This is the notion used by Labrie to identify a distinctive feature of Catholic fiction in America, namely, a willingness to employ realism no matter how seemingly sordid, on the assumption that God's good purposes must be at work everywhere. The second, more specific attitude is borne out both by the occasional epiphanies that strike Percy's characters in the nonhuman world and by O'Connor's portentous skies and woods. Percy and O'Connor have a sometimes Hopkinsesque openness to nature as the field of God's grandeur. But while both these senses of sacramental are valid and illuminating, the pertinent fact about sacraments in forming community is that they are at home, so to speak, only in the church. There is no sacrament without ritual, and it is as a communal rite that sacraments have their greatest relevance to O'Connor and Percy as Catholic writers.

This is the major insight of Ralph Wood's review of O'Gorman's *Peculiar Crossroads: Flannery O'Connor, Walker Percy, and Catholic Vision in Postwar Southern Fiction*. The sacramental vision can only be sustained through its connection to the practices of the church. While the church is only

15. Rowan Williams, "Lecture 3: Flannery O'Connor: Proper Names," 2.

peripherally present in the fiction of O'Connor and Percy, it casts a very long shadow. Or, to change the metaphor, the church is always there as a kind of photographic negative of other signs and practices, and chief among these are intimations of sacramental rites. O'Connor's stories are rife with examples.

Baptism is the real subject of "The River" and *The Violent Bear It Away,* where, as Williams explains, it is the crucial act in properly naming the things of God for the rebellious young prophet, Francis Marion Tarwater. While neither Tarwater nor Bevel Summers, the young evangelist of "The River," are priests or even Catholics, it is clear that their baptism "counts"; it is a valid reflection of that sacrament preserved in its most complete form in the Catholic Church. Further, in each case this action is literally the crux of at least one character's life, both in the sense of serving as a turning point and in the sense of marking him with the cross. For Tarwater, the baptism/drowning of his nephew marks his unwitting acceptance of the mantle of prophet, and for the retarded boy he drowns, the act imprints him as a child of God despite the desperate efforts of his atheist father. Bevel likewise drowns, though not at the hands of the faithful preacher who previously baptized him. He innocently drowns himself, and so "finds the final kingdom not by repeating his once-and-for-all sacramental baptism, but by seeking—in a watery and literal-minded way—precisely what baptism at once enables and demands: total burial with Christ."[16] Not only does the church stand as the earthly source of the rite in "The River," but the church in its eternal, triumphant form also serves as the ultimate destination of the baptized.

Though less prominent in Percy's novels, a similar treatment of baptism may be found in *The Last Gentleman,* when Will Barrett secures a priest for the dying Jamie Vaught, who, like O'Connor's baptismal candidates, is not fully aware of what is happening to him as he undergoes the rite. And although in Percy's treatment there is considerable uncertainty about what is happening, and in keeping with his method of indirect communication, we receive no elucidating word from the author, the implications are strong. The baptism comes at the climax of the novel, underscoring the significance of the event. When the priest seeks permission, the cynical doctor whose spiritual diagnoses Barrett trusts gives tacit approval, indicating to Barrett that here, in the mystery of this sacred action, lies the cure that Barrett craves for himself.

16. Wood, *Christ-Haunted South,* 173.

The Eucharist is the heart of Catholic worship and the central rite for understanding the sacramental vision. I have already argued its importance for O'Connor, whose very technique is shaped by it. Although the consecrated elements figure prominently in only one story ("A Temple of the Holy Ghost") in undisguised form, the Eucharist is figured forth repeatedly as the prime medium of God's continuing presence. It may appear as a blood-red sun representative of the wine-drenched Host or be suggested by gnawing hunger that food cannot sate, but it is never far from O'Connor's consciousness. And even when the epiphany of a story is not about the Eucharist, the form of its reception partakes of what a worshipper experiences at Mass, again as I have previously demonstrated. Indeed, the function of suffering in O'Connor, which is to serve as an *imitatio Christi,* might also be said to reenact the sacrifice of the Mass.

While the Eucharist is not so centrally located in Percy's fiction, with his alternative emphasis on language and dialogue as the key difference between him and O'Connor, it still has an important place. In fact, one could argue that in Percy's account of language, the linguistic symbol is the site of a kind of transubstantiation, where the sensible meets the supersensible. And in *Love in the Ruins,* the churchly rite itself plays an important role. Tom More is Percy's only Catholic protagonist, and the chief sign of his spiritual ill health is his inability to feel contrition and thus his unfitness to receive Communion. He has lapsed from both confession and Mass. The resulting weakness of soul renders him susceptible to the tempter who soon appears. By contrast, his restored health is signaled by the midnight Mass he attends on Christmas Eve and the sackcloth he is wearing in the final chapter.

If Percy gives a smaller place to the Eucharist in the world of his fiction than does O'Connor in hers, he gives a greater one to the sacrament of marriage. Three of the novels end either with marriage or its prospect, and *Lancelot* ends with the possibility of betrothal. *The Thanatos Syndrome,* Percy's final book, concludes with an older Tom More's shaky marriage having been restored. Weddings have supplied the happy endings to comic plots from time out of mind, and there is nothing inherently Christian about such a conclusion. But in Percy's fiction there does seem to be a sacramental connection. Marriage signals a coming to terms with the split between mind and body, or in the language he adapted from Maritain, between angelism and bestialism. For in Christian marriage, unlike in extramarital sexual liaisons, there is an attempt to subsume an aspect of one's bodily life into the life of the body of Christ. This double metaphor refers both to the church and to the sacramental principle that Christ remains in our midst. It is no accident, then, that the marriages in Percy's books are part of religious renewal: Binx Bolling makes his religious affirmation in the wake of his marriage, Tom More's marriage heralds his return to religious practice, Will Barrett's choice of priests for his wedding reflects his desire for religious instruction, and Ellen More's final return to sanity and the embrace of her husband coincide with a "born again" experience. Even Lance's delusory decision to leave the hospital and go in search of the rape victim he hopes to homestead with is immediately followed by his sitting down to hear his priest-friend's Christian alternative to the Third Revolution. In fact, Percy's entire analysis of modernity's preoccupation with sex might be said to be a prolegomenon to a sacramental understanding of marriage.

The logic of Percy's position is most plainly laid out in *Lost in the Cosmos*. The modern self, for reasons we have already touched on, is sundered from world, others, and God, the victim of Cartesian dualism and inflated notions of autonomy. Without these connections, the self is neither complete nor coherent, and it thus adopts various desperate strategies of transcendence and reentry. Science and art represent attempts to transcend the world and the self, but since human nature is also bodily, the self needs a means to "reenter" the physical world, and the chief modern means to do so are sex and violence. As Percy sees it, the contemporary situation has become ominous, as sexual behavior has become increasingly demonic and the human capacity for unleashing violence has reached the level of annihilation. Despite his tendency toward the overly noetic, it is clear that in the scenario Percy describes, the sacraments take on a life-and-death importance. For ultimately, it is only through them that the basic spiritual needs of the self can be met. The sacraments restore us to the world by affirming the connection between the spiritual and physical. For example, the elements of Communion become the body and blood of Christ, as Percy affirmed with O'Connor. Secondly, the sacraments reconcile us to God, satisfying our need for transcendence. Percy insists with Kierkegaard that the self can only gain coherence—can only "be itself"—before God. And finally, the sacraments are performed within a community that is itself preserved and nourished by the sacraments.

These elements are memorably and succinctly rendered in the scene Percy stages near the end of *Lost in the Cosmos*. The abbot Liebowitz is explaining to two astronauts and their children why they should join him in what amounts to a Christian commune from which the earth might eventually be repopulated. First, he proposes to marry the captain and Dr. Jane Smith, the mother of the captain's children. Then he will baptize the children. And finally, he and his two monks will travel with the astronauts to Lost Cove, Tennessee, to start a new society. He feels compelled to make this request "because the Church will survive until the end of earth time and until Christ himself comes" (*LC* 250). Why should the captain and Dr. Smith help him? "The only reason from your [agnostic] point of view, is that you have no choice. You know now that if what I say is not true, you are like the gentiles Paul spoke of: a stranger to every covenant, with no promise to hope for, with the world about you and no God. You are stuck with yourselves, ghost selves, which will never become selves. You are stuck with each other and you will never know how to love each other" (*LC* 250–51).

Without the Christian sacramental community, you will remain ghosts to yourselves and never know how to love each other, says the abbot. This might serve as a final benediction on the work of O'Connor and Percy. While their work stops short of disclosing a vital Christian community in action as a place of healing, reconciliation, and witness, it powerfully exposes our utter dependence on the church to cure our peculiar modern (and postmodern) maladies. Without the continuing presence of the Crucifixion made real in the Eucharist, there is no redeeming of human suffering, as O'Connor painfully knew in her life and work. Without baptism, the people of God lack their proper names. Without marriage, the sharpest form of bodily eros has no home or habitation. And without the sacraments as a whole, God remains afar, and we are left to carom distractedly about the cosmos, propelled futilely by eros in its most potent form, *amor Dei*. From the midst of our broken lives, O'Connor seizes the crucifix we can not see and holds it up for our grateful contemplation. Percy, for his part, confronts us with the dialogic challenge of one who has read the message in the bottle: I've found news from across the seas, he says. Listen. I think we'd both better pay attention to this—

Bibliography

ᕲᑫᕲ

Asals, Frederick. *Flannery O'Connor: The Imagination of Extremity.* Athens: University of Georgia Press, 1982.

Baumgaertner, Jill Peláez. *Flannery O'Connor: A Proper Scaring.* Chicago: Cornerstone Press, 1999.

Beebe, Maurice. "The Artist as Hero." Introduction to *Ivory Towers and Sacred Founts.* New York: New York University Press, 1964.

Brinkmeyer, Robert H., Jr. *The Art and Vision of Flannery O'Connor.* Baton Rouge: Louisiana State University Press, 1989.

———. "'Jesus, Stab Me in the Heart!': *Wise Blood,* Wounding, and Sacramental Aesthetics." In *New Essays on "Wise Blood,"* ed. Michael Kreyling, 71–89. Cambridge: Cambridge University Press, 1995.

———. "*Lancelot* and the Dynamics of Intersubjective Community." In *Walker Percy: Novelist and Philosopher,* ed. Jan Nordby Gretlund and Karl-Heinz Westarp, 155–66. Jackson: University Press of Mississippi, 1991.

———. *Three Catholic Writers of the Modern South: Allen Tate, Caroline Gordon, Walker Percy.* Jackson: University Press of Mississippi, 1985.

———. "Walker Percy's *Lancelot:* Discovery through Dialogue." *Renascence* 40, no. 1 (1987): 30–42.

Brooks, Cleanth. *The Well Wrought Urn.* New York: Harcourt, Brace, and World, 1947.

Brooks, Cleanth, and Robert Penn Warren. *Understanding Fiction.* 2nd ed. New York: Appleton-Century-Crofts, 1959.

Broughton, Panthea Reid, ed. *The Art of Walker Percy: Stratagems for Being.* Baton Rouge: Louisiana State University Press, 1979.

Carrithers, Gale H., Jr. "Colonel Tate, in Attack and Defense." In *Southern Literature and Literary Theory,* ed. Jefferson Humphries, 48–65. Athens: University of Georgia Press, 1990.

Cash, Jean. *Flannery O'Connor: A Life.* Knoxville: University of Tennessee Press, 2002.

Ciuba, Gary M. *Walker Percy: Books of Revelations.* Athens: University of Georgia Press, 1991.

Desmond, John F. "Language, Suicide, and the Writer: Walker Percy's Advancement of William Faulkner." In *Walker Percy: Novelist and Philosopher,* ed. Jan Nordby Gretlund and Karl-Heinz Westarp, 131–40. Jackson: University Press of Mississippi, 1991.

———. *Risen Sons: Flannery O'Connor's Vision of History.* Athens: University of Georgia Press, 1987.

———. "Walker Percy's Eucharistic Vision." *Renascence* 52, no. 3 (Spring 2000): 219–31.

———. *Walker Percy's Search for Community.* Athens: University of Georgia Press, 2004.

Di Renzo, Anthony. *American Gargoyles: Flannery O'Connor and the Medieval Grotesque.* Carbondale: Southern Illinois University Press, 1993.

Eagleton, Terry. *Literary Theory: An Introduction.* Minneapolis: University of Minnesota Press, 1983.

Elie, Paul. *The Life You Save May Be Your Own.* New York: Farrar, Straus and Giroux, 2003.

Faulkner, William. *As I Lay Dying.* New York: Random House, 1964.

———. Introduction to *The Sound and the Fury.* In *A Faulkner Miscellany,* ed. James B. Meriwether, 156–61. Jackson: University Press of Mississippi, 1974.

Felch, Susan M., and Paul Contino, eds. *Bakhtin and Religion: A Feeling for Faith.* Evanston: Northwestern University Press, 2001.

Fitzgerald, Sally. "A Master Class: From the Correspondence of Caroline Gordon and Flannery O'Connor." *Georgia Review* 33 (Winter 1979): 827–46.

Fodor, Sarah. "Proust, 'Home of the Brave,' and *Understanding Fiction:* O'Connor's Development as a Writer." *The Flannery O'Connor Bulletin* 25 (1996–97): 62–80.

Fouts, Roger. *Next of Kin: What Chimpanzees Have Taught Me about Who We Are.* New York: William Morrow, 1997.

Frei, Hans. *The Identity of Jesus Christ.* Philadelphia: Fortress, 1975.

Giannone, Richard. *Flannery O'Connor and the Mystery of Love.* New York: Fordham University Press, 1999.

Gordon, Caroline, and Allen Tate. *The House of Fiction: An Anthology of the Short Story with Commentary.* 2nd ed. New York: Scribner's, 1960.

Gordon, Sarah. *Flannery O'Connor: The Obedient Imagination.* Athens: University of Georgia Press, 2000.

Harpham, Geoffrey Galt. *The Ascetic Imperative in Culture and Criticism.* Chicago: University of Chicago Press, 1987.

Hartt, Julian. *The Lost Image of Man.* Baton Rouge: Louisiana State University Press, 1963.

Hawkes, John. "Flannery O'Connor's Devil." In *Flannery O'Connor,* ed. Robert Reiter, 25–37. St. Louis: Herder, 1968.

Hobbs, Janet. "Binx Bolling and the Stages on Life's Way." In *The Art of Walker Percy: Stratagems for Being,* ed. Panthea Reid Broughton, 37–49. Baton Rouge: Louisiana State University Press, 1979.

Joyce, James. *Dubliners.* New York: Penguin, 1976.

———. *A Portrait of the Artist as a Young Man.* New York: Penguin, 1993.

———. *Stephen Hero.* New York: New Directions, 1963.

Kennedy, J. Gerald. "The Sundered Self and the Riven World: *Love in the Ruins.*" In *The Art of Walker Percy: Stratagems for Being,* ed. Panthea Reid Broughton, 115–36. Baton Rouge: Louisiana State University Press, 1979.

Kierkegaard, Søren. *Concluding Unscientific Postscript to Philosophical Fragments.* Vol. 12 of *Kierkegaard's Writings,* ed. and trans. Howard V. Hong and Edna H. Hong. Princeton: Princeton University Press, 1992.

———. *The Essential Kierkegaard.* Ed. and trans. Howard V. Hong and Edna H. Hong. Princeton: Princeton University Press, 2000.

———. *Philosophical Fragments, or a Fragment of Philosophy.* Vol. 7 of *Kierkegaard's Writings,* ed. and trans. Edna H. Hong and Howard V. Hong. Princeton: Princeton University Press, 1985.

———. *The Point of View for My Work as an Author.* In *The Point of View,* vol. 22 of *Kierkegaard's Writings,* ed. and trans. Howard V. Hong and Edna H. Hong. Princeton: Princeton University Press, 1998.

King, Richard H. *A Southern Renaissance: The Cultural Awakening of the American South, 1930–1955.* New York: Oxford University Press, 1980.

Kobre, Michael. *Walker Percy's Voices.* Athens: University of Georgia Press, 2000.

Kreyling, Michael. *Inventing Southern Literature.* Jackson: University Press of Mississippi, 1998.

Labrie, Ross. *The Catholic Imagination in American Literature.* Columbia: University of Missouri Press, 1997.

Lawson, Lewis A. *Following Percy.* Troy, NY: Whitson Publishing, 1988.

———. *Still Following Percy.* Jackson: University Press of Mississippi, 1993.

Lawson, Lewis A., and Victor A. Kramer, eds. *Conversations with Walker Percy.* Jackson: University Press of Mississippi, 1985.

Lentricchia, Frank. *After the New Criticism.* Chicago: University of Chicago Press, 1980.

Lubbock, Percy. *The Craft of Fiction.* 1921. Reprint, New York: Viking, 1957.

MacIntyre, Alasdair. *After Virtue.* 2nd ed. Notre Dame: University of Notre Dame Press, 1984.

Magee, Rosemary, ed. *Conversations with Flannery O'Connor.* Oxford: University Press of Mississippi, 1987.

Maritain, Jacques. *Art and Scholasticism and Other Essays.* Trans. J. F. Scanlan. New York: Scribners, 1937.

———. *Creative Intuition in Art and Poetry.* Princeton: Princeton University Press, 1953.

Mencken, H. L. *Prejudices: A Selection.* Ed. James T. Farrell. New York: Random House, 1958.

Michaels, Walter Benn. Review of *The Message in the Bottle,* by Walker Percy. *The Georgia Review* 29 (Winter 1975): 972–75.

Milbank, John. *Being Reconciled: Ontology and Pardon.* London: Routledge, 2003.

Nagle, Thomas. "Sin and Significance." Review of *The Message in the Bottle,* by Walker Percy. *New York Review of Books,* September 18, 1975.

O'Connor, Flannery. *The Complete Stories.* New York: Farrar, Straus and Giroux, 1972.

———. *Flannery O'Connor: Collected Works.* New York: Library of America, 1988.

———. *The Habit of Being.* New York: Farrar, Straus and Giroux, 1979.

———. *Mystery and Manners.* Ed. Sally Fitzgerald and Robert Fitzgerald. New York: Farrar, Straus and Giroux, 1969.

O'Gorman, Farrell. *Peculiar Crossroads: Flannery O'Connor, Walker Percy, and Catholic Vision in Postwar Southern Fiction.* Baton Rouge: Louisiana State University Press, 2004.

Percy, Walker. *Lancelot*. New York: Farrar, Straus and Giroux, 1977.

———. *The Last Gentleman*. New York: Farrar, Straus and Giroux, 1966.

———. *Lost in the Cosmos: The Last Self-Help Book*. New York: Farrar, Straus and Giroux, 1983.

———. *Love in the Ruins: The Adventures of a Bad Catholic at a Time Near the End of the World*. New York: Farrar, Straus and Giroux, 1971.

———. *The Message in the Bottle*. New York: Farrar, Straus and Giroux, 1975.

———. *The Moviegoer*. New York: Knopf, 1961.

———. *The Second Coming*. New York: Farrar, Straus and Giroux, 1980.

———. *Signposts in a Strange Land*. Ed. Patrick Samway. New York: Farrar, Straus and Giroux, 1991.

———. *The Thanatos Syndrome*. New York: Farrar, Straus and Giroux, 1987.

Percy, Walker, and Shelby Foote. *The Correspondence of Shelby Foote and Walker Percy*. Ed. Jay Tolson. New York: Norton, 1997.

Percy, Walker, and Kenneth Laine Ketner. *A Thief of Peirce: The Letters of Kenneth Laine Ketner and Walker Percy*. Ed. Patrick Samway. Jackson: University Press of Mississippi, 1995.

Percy, William Alexander. *Lanterns on the Levee: Recollections of a Planter's Son*. Baton Rouge: Louisiana State University Press, 1973.

Pridgen, Allen. *Walker Percy's Sacramental Landscapes: The Search in the Desert*. Selinsgrove: Susquehanna University Press, 2000.

Prown, Katherine Hemple. *Revising Flannery O'Connor*. Charlottesville: University Press of Virginia, 2001.

Quinlan, Kieran. *Walker Percy: The Last Catholic Novelist*. Baton Rouge: Louisiana State University Press, 1996.

Ransom, John Crowe. *God without Thunder: An Unorthodox Defense of Orthodoxy*. 1930. Reprint, Hamden, CT: Archon Books, 1965.

Richter, David. *The Critical Tradition: Classic Texts and Contemporary Trends*. 2nd ed. Boston: Bedford, 1998.

Romine, Scott. *The Narrative Forms of Southern Community*. Baton Rouge: Louisiana State University Press, 1999.

Samway, Patrick. *Walker Percy: A Life*. New York: Farrar, Straus and Giroux, 1997.

Scarry, Elaine. *The Body in Pain*. New York: Oxford University Press, 1985.

Shloss, Carol. *Flannery O'Connor's Dark Comedies*. Baton Rouge: Louisiana State University Press, 1980.

Simpson, Lewis P. *The Brazen Face of History: Studies in the Literary Con-

sciousness in America. Baton Rouge: Louisiana State University Press, 1980.

Singal, Daniel J. *William Faulkner: The Making of a Modernist.* Chapel Hill: University of North Carolina Press, 1997.

Smith, James K. A. *Introducing Radical Orthodoxy: Mapping a Post-secular Theology.* Grand Rapids: Baker Academic, 2004.

Srigley, Susan. *Flannery O'Connor's Sacramental Art.* Notre Dame: University of Notre Dame Press, 2005.

Stewart, John L. *The Burden of Time: The Fugitives and Agrarians.* Princeton: Princeton University Press, 1965.

Sykes, John D., Jr. "Christian Apologetic Uses of the Grotesque in John Irving and Flannery O'Connor." *Literature & Theology* 10, no. 1 (March 1996): 58–67.

———. "The Imperious Castaway: Walker Percy on Guilt and the Self." *Religion and Literature* 27, no. 3 (Autumn 1995): 53–71.

———. Review of *Walker Percy: The Last Catholic Novelist,* by Kieran Quinlan. *Literature & Theology* 12, no. 1 (March 1998): 114–15.

Tate, Allen. *Essays of Four Decades.* Chicago: Swallow Press, 1968.

———, ed. *The Language of Poetry.* New York: Russell and Russell, 1960.

Thornton, Weldon. "Homo Loquens, Homo Symbolificus, Homo Sapiens: Walker Percy on Language." In *The Art of Walker Percy: Stratagems for Being,* ed. Panthea Reid Broughton, 169–91. Baton Rouge: Louisiana State University Press, 1979.

Tolson, Jay. *Pilgrim in the Ruins.* Chapel Hill: University of North Carolina Press, 1992.

Tracy, David. "Form and Fragment: The Recovery of the Hidden and Incomprehensible God." *Reflections* 3 (1999): 62–89, http://www.ctinquiry.org/publications/tracy.htm (accessed December 20, 2005).

Twelve Southerners. *I'll Take My Stand.* 1930. Reprint, Baton Rouge: Louisiana State University Press, 1977.

Ward, Graham. *Cities of God.* London: Routledge, 2000.

West, Nathanael. *"Miss Lonelyhearts" and "The Day of the Locust."* New York: New Directions, 1969.

Westling, Louise. *Sacred Groves and Ravaged Gardens.* Athens: University of Georgia Press, 1985.

Williams, Rowan. "Lecture 3: Flannery O'Connor: Proper Names." Clark Lectures, Trinity College, Cambridge, 2005. http://www.archbishopofcanterbury.org/sermons_speeches/050210.htm.

———. *On Christian Theology.* Oxford: Blackwell, 2000.

Wimsatt, W. K., Jr. *The Verbal Icon*. Lexington: University of Kentucky Press, 1954.

Wood, Ralph C. "The Alienated Self and the Absent Community in the Work of Walker Percy." In *Morphologies of Faith: Essays in Religion and Culture in Honor of Nathan A. Scott, Jr.*, ed. Mary Gerhart and Anthony Yu, 359–76. Atlanta: Scholars Press, 1990.

———. *Flannery O'Connor and the Christ-Haunted South*. Grand Rapids: Eerdmans, 2004.

———. Review of *Peculiar Crossroads: Flannery O'Connor, Walker Percy, and Catholic Vision in Postwar Southern Fiction*, by Farrell O'Gorman. *Mississippi Quarterly* 57, no. 4 (Fall 2004): 661–65.

Wyatt-Brown, Bertram. *The House of Percy: Honor, Melancholy, and Imagination in a Southern Family*. New York: Oxford University Press, 1994.

Index

ॐ

Aeschylus, 27

Aestheticism: definition of, 3; and Maritain's *Art and Scholasticism,* 4, 29–32; of Wilde, 31

Aesthetic of memory: and Foote's advice to Percy, 117; and New Criticism, 11–17; Simpson on, 1, 11, 155, 158; in southern literature generally, 1–2; and Southern Renaissance, 9

Aesthetic of revelation: and O'Connor generally, 1–8, 38, 158; and Percy generally, 1–8, 86, 104, 158; Simpson on, 1, 9, 158

Affective fallacy, 12

African Americans. *See* Blacks

Agrarianism, 9–10, 13, 20, 155–56

Alienation, 94, 98–101, 141, 166

American Sign Language (ASL), 106, 107

Anagogical: Dante on, 39; definition of, 39; and O'Connor, 39–41, 44

Analogy of being, 39

Anthony, St., 47

Anxiety, 166

Apocalypse, 136–37, 141, 162

Aquinas, Thomas. *See* Thomas Aquinas, St.

"Araby" (Joyce), 71–72

Aristotle, 16, 29, 153

"Ars Poetica" (MacLeish), 26

Art and Scholasticism (Maritain), 4, 29–32

"Artificial Nigger, The" (O'Connor), 5, 20, 54–58, 61–62, 85, 166

Asals, Frederick, 23–24, 42, 45–46, 48–50, 73n4, 166

Asceticism, 46–50

ASL (American Sign Language), 106, 107

Atonement, 45, 54–61, 70

Auden, W. H., 28

Augustine, St.: on evil, 62, 63, 139–40; on human will, 164; on love of God, 144, 152; and Percy's *Lancelot,* 143; on sin, 65, 67, 98, 131; on symbol, 89

Austen, Jane, 17

Authenticity, 164–65

Ayer, A. J., 28

Bakhtin, Mikhail, 4, 77–78, 78n8, 79, 84, 117

Baptism: in O'Connor's "The River," 6, 36, 85, 101, 168; in O'Connor's *The Violent Bear It Away,* 68, 168; in Percy's *The Last Gentleman,* 6, 101, 168

Barth, Karl, 62

Beebe, Maurice, 6

Berrigan brothers, 163

Biographia Literaria (Coleridge), 26

Blacks: in O'Connor's "The Artificial Nigger," 54–58; in O'Connor's "The Displaced Person," 60; in O'Connor's "Revelation," 80, 81; in Percy's *Lancelot,* 140; in Percy's *Love in the Ruins,* 133–34; in Percy's *The Moviegoer,* 122; suffering of, 54–58

Body: Eucharist as body of Christ, 42;
    Mary Ann's face distorted by cancer,
    40–41; in O'Connor's "The Artificial
    Nigger," 54–58; in O'Connor's "The
    Displaced Person," 58–61; in O'Con-
    nor's "Parker's Back," 50–54; in O'Con-
    nor's *The Violent Bear It Away,* 61–69;
    in O'Connor's *Wise Blood,* 45–50, 165;
    in O'Connor's works, 5, 25, 39–70; res-
    urrection of, 40; role of, in salvation,
    45–54; tattoo on, 50–54
Brazen Face of History, The (Simpson), 1,
    158
Brinkmeyer, Robert, 22–24, 42, 46, 78,
    137–38, 141–42, 158
Brooks, Cleanth, 11–13, 16, 18, 19, 27
Brothers Karamozov, The (Dostoevsky), 127

Caldwell, Erskine, 43
Canticle for Leibowitz, A, 102, 162
Carnival, 117
Cassirer, Ernst, 27
*Catholic Imagination in American Literature,
    The* (Labrie), 160
Catholicism: and Atonement, 45, 54–61,
    70; and church as community, 154–55,
    159, 166–67; and Creation, 45, 61–69,
    70; and existentialism, 159–67; and
    faith and knowledge, 95–103; and
    Gordon, 10, 28; and Index of Pro-
    scribed Books, 31; and Joyce, 117; Mar-
    itain and Catholic Revival, 4, 28–32;
    and Mass said in Latin, 71, 71n1, 84, 87;
    and O'Connor, 5, 7–8, 28–32, 71, 84,
    87, 156, 158, 159, 163; in O'Connor's
    "A Temple of the Holy Ghost," 72–77;
    and Percy, 5–8, 28, 86, 102–3, 108,
    115, 156–57, 163, 164; in Percy's *Love
    in the Ruins,* 130–35, 162, 164, 169;
    post–Vatican II Catholicism, 163; and
    Tate, 10, 13, 14, 28, 155–56; and view
    of artist by O'Connor and Percy, 7–8;
    view of death by, 39–41; and virtues,
    118, 153. *See also* Baptism; Eucharist;
    Religion

"Catholic Novelists and Their Readers"
    (O'Connor), 7–8
Catholic Revival, 4, 28–32
Catonism, 123
Chekhov, Anton, 20, 44
Chimpanzees, 106, 107
Chomsky, Noam, 104
Christ: cross of, 24, 25, 41, 45, 47, 58, 61,
    77, 171; Eucharist as body of, 42, 70–
    85, 140; and Incarnation, 45–54, 57,
    61, 70, 76, 103, 109, 144, 150; Kierke-
    gaard on, 114; at Last Supper, 140; in
    O'Connor's "The Artificial Nigger,"
    54–58; in O'Connor's "The Displaced
    Person," 58–61, 72; in O'Connor's
    "Parker's Back," 50, 51–54; participa-
    tion in suffering of (*imitatio Christi*), 42,
    45, 56–57, 165, 169; in Percy's *Lost in
    the Cosmos,* 102–3; in Percy's *Love in
    the Ruins,* 133–34; redemptive suffer-
    ing of, 42; Resurrection of, 40, 58; as
    scapegoat, 58. *See also* Eucharist
Christ-Haunted South, The (Wood), 57
Christianity. *See* Catholicism; Christ;
    Protestantism; Religion
Church. *See* Catholicism; Protestantism
"Circle in the Fire" (O'Connor), 166
City of God (Augustine), 143
Ciuba, Gary, 132–33, 134, 136
Civil War: and Lost Cause myth, 2;
    O'Connor on, 160
Coleridge, Samuel Taylor, 14, 26
Collins, James, 163
Commonweal, 156–57, 159
Communion. *See* Eucharist
Community: church as, 154–55, 159,
    166–67; and love, 153–54; and love
    of Trinity, 154; in O'Connor's "The
    Displaced Person," 161; in Percy's *The
    Last Gentleman,* 162; in Percy's *Lost in
    the Cosmos,* 170–71; in Percy's *Love in
    the Ruins,* 162; in Percy's *The Movie-
    goer,* 161–62; in Percy's *The Second
    Coming,* 150, 153, 154, 162; sacramen-
    tal community in works by Percy and

O'Connor, 167–71; southern sense of, 161; and symbol, 153–54; Turner on, 163

Concluding Unscientific Postscript to Philosophical Fragment (Kierkegaard), 114

Confessions (Augustine), 152

Conrad, Joseph, 17

Copleston, Frederick, 163

Craft of Fiction, The (James), 16

Creation, 45, 61–69, 70

Creative Intuition in Art and Poetry (Maritain), 32

Cross of Christ, 24, 25, 41, 45, 47, 58, 61, 77, 171

Crucifixion. *See* Cross of Christ

Dante, 39, 68, 77, 137

Darwin, Charles, 106

Davidson, David, 13

Dawson, Christopher, 28

"Dead, The" (Joyce), 37–38

Death: Christian view of, 39–41; Faulkner on, 40; in O'Connor's "The Displaced Person," 58–61; in O'Connor's "A Good Man Is Hard to Find," 85; in O'Connor's "The Lame Shall Enter First," 85; in O'Connor's *The Violent Bear It Away*, 63, 67, 168; in O'Connor's *Wise Blood*, 165; in Percy's *Lancelot*, 140–41, 144; in Percy's *The Last Gentleman*, 144; in Percy's *The Second Coming*, 144, 145, 148; violent death in O'Connor's works generally, 42, 45. *See also* Suffering; Suicide; Violence

"Delta Factor, The" (Percy), 90–91

Descartes, René, 27, 120, 121, 153, 170

Desmond, John: on Eucharist as central to Percy's work, 101, 108; on Peirce's influence on Percy, 90, 108–10; on Percy's *The Last Gentleman,* 140; on Percy's *Love in the Ruins,* 132, 133; on Percy's *The Moviegoer,* 120, 127–28; on Percy's *The Second Coming,* 146, 149, 150, 162

Devil: in O'Connor's *The Violent Bear It*

Away, 62, 67–69; in Percy's *Lancelot,* 141; in Percy's *Love in the Ruins,* 132–33, 162

Dewey, Bradley, 113

Dewey, John, 28

"Difference between a Genius and an Apostle, The" (Kierkegaard), 113

Di Renzo, Anthony, 76

"Displaced Person, The" (O'Connor), 5, 54, 58–62, 72, 85, 161

Divine Comedy, The (Dante), 77, 137

Donne, John, 14–16

Dostoevsky, Fyodor, 5, 57, 59, 84, 127

Eagleton, Terry, 13, 16

Elie, Paul, 29, 50

Eliot, T. S., 12, 16, 20, 31

"Enduring Chill, The" (O'Connor), 112

Engle, Paul, 11, 17

Epiphany, 36–38, 44, 72n2, 167, 169

Eucharist: as body of Christ, 5, 42, 70–85; and broken bodies in O'Connor's writings, 70; consecration of, during Mass, 71, 84; hymn on, 74, 75, 77; in Joyce's "Araby," 71–72; McCarthy on, 70, 71; mystery of, 70, 84; O'Connor on, 70; in O'Connor's "The Displaced Person," 61; in O'Connor's "Revelation," 77–85; in O'Connor's "A Temple of the Holy Ghost," 72–77, 83, 85, 169; in O'Connor's writings generally, 5, 101, 169; Percy on, 108, 170; in Percy's *Lancelot,* 140, 142; in Percy's *Love in the Ruins,* 131, 133, 134, 169; in Percy's *The Moviegoer,* 127–28, 161–62; in Percy's *The Second Coming,* 144–45, 149–50; in Percy's works generally, 101–2, 169; and privileging of sight over hearing, 70–71, 77–85

"Everything That Rises Must Converge" (O'Connor), 111–12, 157–58

Evil: Augustine on, 62, 63, 139–40; Barth on, 62; connection between God and, 139–40, 143; and deficiency of diminished will, 63–67; and devil, 62, 67–69;

O'Connor on, 143; in O'Connor's *The Violent Bear It Away,* 61–69; in Percy's *Lancelot,* 130, 137–43, 152; as privation of good, 45, 61–69; radical evil, 62. *See also* Sin

Existentialism, 20, 81, 103, 108, 159–67

Faith: and authenticity, 164–65; Hegel on, 109; Kierkegaard on, 108, 113–17; and knowledge, 95–103; in Percy's "The Message in the Bottle," 95–97, 109; in Percy's *The Moviegoer,* 126–30, 134, 136, 153, 161–62; Percy's quest for, 111–35; and reason, 34, 109–10; rhetoric of, 113–19; Thomas Aquinas on, 97, 113; and virtues, 118, 153

Fallacies, 12

Faulkner, William: and aesthetics of memory, 1, 2, 155, 161; Christ figure in, 59; on death, 40; and Southern Renaissance, 129, 155

—works: *Light in August,* 22; *The Sound and the Fury,* 3

Feeling and Form (Langer), 32–33, 88

"Fiction Writer and His Country, The" (O'Connor), 3

Fitzgerald, Sally and Robert, 29

Flannery O'Connor: The Imagination of Extremity (Asals), 23–24

Flannery O'Connor's Dark Comedies (Shloss), 72

Flannery O'Connor's Sacramental Art (Srigley), 167

Flaubert, Gustave: compared with Gordon, 20; compared with O'Connor generally, 26, 43; and epiphany, 44; Foote on, 6; and Percy, 3; and realism, 43; and symbol, 17, 35

Foote, Shelby, 3, 6–7, 104, 117

Fouts, Roger, 107

Frei, Hans, 59

Frye, Northrop, 27

"Geranium, The" (O'Connor), 17–23, 34–35

German Idealism, 26, 88, 91

Giannone, Richard, 73, 76n6

Gilson, Etienne, 28, 32, 34

Giroux, Robert, 48

God without Thunder (Ransom), 13, 28

Goodall, Jane, 107

"Good Country People" (O'Connor), 85

"Good Man Is Hard to Find, A" (O'Connor), 85, 158

Gordon, Caroline: Brinkmeyer on, 158; and Catholicism, 10, 28; as editor of O'Connor's writings, 17–18; as mentor to O'Connor, 3–4, 10, 17, 22, 43; as mentor to Percy, 3–4; and New Criticism, 10; on O'Connor's *Wise Blood,* 23, 30; point of view in writings by, 22

—works: *The House of Fiction,* 10, 17, 35; *The Malefactors,* 22; "Old Red," 17–22

Gordon, Sarah, 19, 20, 26, 50, 75, 76, 78

Grail metaphor, 130, 137–41

Greene, Helen, 25

"Greenleaf" (O'Connor), theological emphasis of, 5

Grotesque, 41–44, 73–76

Guardini, 159

Habit of Being, The (O'Connor), 17–18

Harpham, Geoffrey Galt, 47

Hartt, Julian, 117

Hawkes, John, 38, 41

Hawthorne, Nathaniel, 17, 43, 50

Hegel, G. W. F., 92, 97, 109, 120

Heidegger, Martin, 91, 92, 120, 159

Hemingway, Ernest, 17

Heresy of paraphrase, 12

Hermaphrodite, 73–76

Hester, Betty, 17, 22, 41, 75

Hill, Lyn, 115–16

Holocaust, 62

Hope: and faith, 118; and love, 144; and Percy's *Lancelot,* 130, 137–44, 153

House of Fiction, The (Tate and Gordon), 10, 17, 35

House of Percy, The (Wyatt-Brown), 121

Icon, 12–13

Identity of Jesus Christ, The (Frei), 59

I'll Take My Stand, 13, 155–56
Image, 12
Incarnation, 45–54, 57, 61, 76, 103, 109, 144, 150
Indirect communication, 113–15, 143, 164
Intentional fallacy, 12
Intersubjectivity, 94–95, 103, 105–6, 108, 135, 141–42, 153
Inventing Southern Literature (Kreyling), 9
Iowa Writers' Workshop, 4, 10, 11, 17, 22, 29, 37, 71
Irony: Brooks on, 16; and Joyce, 117; and New Criticism, 16, 21, 34; in O'Connor's "The Geranium," 21; in O'Connor's "Revelation," 81; O'Connor's use of generally, 117; in O'Connor's *Wise Blood,* 22, 22–23, 25; in West's *Miss Lonelyhearts,* 24, 25
Ivory Towers and Sacred Founts (Beebe), 6

James, Henry: compared with O'Connor generally, 26, 36, 43; and epiphanies, 44; on fiction, 16–17; and point of view, 17, 20, 22, 25; and symbols, 17, 18, 35
Johnson, Samuel, 45
Joyce, James: and Catholicism, 117; compared with Gordon's "Old Red," 20; epiphanies of, 4, 44; and irony, 117; Percy on, 3; and symbol, 36–38
—works: "Araby," 71–72; "The Dead," 37–38; *A Portrait of the Artist as a Young Man,* 72n2, 119; *Stephen Hero,* 36–37

Kafka, Franz, 94
Kazin, Alfred, 28
Keller, Helen, 86, 90–91, 92, 146–47
Kennedy, Gerald, 135
Kermode, Frank, 14
Ketner, Kenneth Laine, 90, 109
Kierkegaard, Søren: on Christianity, 97; on despair, 125, 129; and existentialism, 159; on faith, 95, 108, 113–17; on having authority, 143; on Hegel, 92, 120; on indirect communication, 113–15, 143, 164; as influence on Percy gener-

ally, 3, 4, 5, 92, 164; Percy on, 116–17; pseudonymous works by, 114–15, 116; on scientism, 108; on self, 100, 103, 170; *Sickness unto Death* by, 97–98, 100, 129
King, Barbara, 87–88
King, Richard H., 1, 2, 123, 155
Knowledge: and faith, 95–103; Hegel on, 97; from science, 96; trustworthiness of, 96; types of, 95–96
Kobre, Michael, 117, 128
Kreyling, Michael, 9, 160, 161

Labrie, Ross, 160, 167
"Lame Shall Enter First, The," 85
Lancelot (Percy): Anna in, 142, 144, 169; apocalyptic nature of, 136–37, 141, 154; blacks in, 140; death and violence in, 140–41; devil in, 141; as dialogical novel, 137, 141–42; epigraph of, 137; Eucharist in, 140, 142; Grail metaphor in, 130, 137–41; and hope, 130, 137–44, 153; language in, 95; love in, 142–44; marital infidelity in, 138–40; myth of autonomous self in, 137–38, 141–42; Percival/John in, 137, 138, 141–44; and quest for Unholy Grail, 130, 137–43, 152; sexuality in, 138–40, 143, 144, 150, 152; Southern Stoicism in, 158; theological questions in, 118, 130; Third Revolution in, 138, 141, 158–59, 170; transcendence through lewdness in, 140; uncertainty and unreality in, 138
Langer, Susanne, 32–33, 87–91, 104
Language: behaviorist approach to, 33, 104, 106; of chimpanzee Washoe, 106, 107; critique of Percy's language theory, 103–10; dialogical versus monological language in O'Connor's works, 77–78; and indirect communication, 113–15, 143, 164; and intersubjectivity, 94–95, 105–6; and Keller, 86, 90–91, 92, 146–47; Langer on, 87–90; O'Connor and fallenness of, 77; O'Connor's use of, 77–78; Percy on, 4, 86–111; in Per-

cy's *Lancelot,* 95; in Percy's *The Moviegoer,* 94, 125, 130; in Percy's *The Second
Coming,* 94–95, 144–49, 154; scientific
approach to, 105, 109–10; symbolic
language use as unique and exclusive to
humans, 106–7; Thomas Aquinas on, 4;
Wittgenstein on, 104–5, 154
Language of Poetry, The (Tate), 27
Lanterns on the Levee (Will Percy), 121
Last Gentleman, The (Percy): baptism in, 6,
101, 168; community in, 162; com-
pared with *Lancelot,* 137; compared
with *The Second Coming,* 145; psy-
chotherapy in, 93; sexuality in, 140,
144, 150; and spiritual poverty of
South, 2; suffering in, 101–2; suicide in,
144; unreality and uncertainty in, 112–
13
"Late Encounter with the Enemy, A"
(O'Connor), 2, 85, 157, 161
Lawrence, D. H., 3
Lawson, Lewis A., 121, 125
Lentricchia, Frank, 14
Life You Save May Be Your Own, The (Elie),
29
Light in August (Faulkner), 22
Literary Theory (Eagleton), 13
"Loss of the Creature, The" (Percy), 93–
94, 120
Lost Cause myth, 2
Lost Image of Man, The (Hartt), 117
Lost in the Cosmos (Percy), 92, 98–103,
162, 170–71
Love: and community, 153–54; and faith,
118; of God, 143–44, 151–52, 154; and
hope, 144; in Percy's *Lancelot,* 142–44;
in Percy's *The Moviegoer,* 94, 125–29,
137, 144; in Percy's *The Second Coming,*
94–95, 119, 130, 144–53; of Trinity,
154
Love in the Ruins (Percy): apocalyptic nature of, 136, 162; black character in,
133–34; Catholicism in, 130–35, 162,
164, 169; Christ in, 133–34; community in, 162; devil in, 132–33, 162; Ellen's
love for Tom More in, 132–33; epi-

logue section of, 134–35; Eucharist in,
131, 133, 134, 169; Father Smith in,
133, 134; prayer by Tom More in, 133;
pride in, 130–35; science and lapsometer in, 131–32, 134–35; subtitle of,
130, 136, 162; suffering in, 101–2; unraveling social fabric in, 113
Lowell, Robert, 28
Lubbock, Percy, 16
Lytle, Andrew, 11

MacFarlane, James, 37
MacIntyre, Alasdair, 153
MacLeish, Archibald, 26, 32
Malefactors, The (Gordon), 22
"Man on the Train, The" (Percy), 94
Mansfield, Katherine, 20
Marcel, Gabriel-Honoré, 92, 153, 159
Maritain, Jacques, 4, 14, 25, 28–34, 104,
120, 159
Marriage: betrothal in Percy's *Lancelot,*
144, 169, 170; courtship and marriage
in Percy's *The Moviegoer,* 94, 125–29,
137, 144, 154, 170; love and marriage
in Percy's *The Second Coming,* 94–95,
119, 130, 148–53, 170; marital infideli-
ty in Percy's *Lancelot,* 138–40; in Per-
cy's *Thanatos Syndrome,* 169; as religious
renewal in Percy's fiction, 169–70
McCarthy, Mary, 70, 71
Meaning in New Criticism, 12
Memoir for Mary Ann, A, 31, 40
Memory. *See* Aesthetic of memory
Mencken, H. L., 155
Merton, Thomas, 28, 48, 159–60
Message in the Bottle, The (Percy), 92, 103,
104–7, 135
"Message in the Bottle, The" (Percy), 95–
98, 109, 164
Michaels, Walter Benn, 104–6
Milbank, John, 41, 62, 64
Miss Lonelyhearts (West), 24–25, 29, 87
Modernism: and Foote, 117; MacFarlane
on, 37
Moviegoer, The (Percy): apocalyptic nature
of, 136; Aunt Emily in, 121–23, 128–

30, 141, 160–61; award for, 111; black butler in, 122; community in, 161–62; compared with O'Connor's protagonists, 111–12; courtship and marriage of Binx and Kate in, 94, 125–29, 137, 144, 154, 170; despair and depression in, 94, 125–26; dialogue with reader in, 5; Eucharist in, 127–28, 161–62; faith in, 126–30, 134, 136, 153, 161–62; fragility of social world in, 119, 122–24; friendship in, 123–24; Kobre's analysis of, based on Bakhtin, 117; language in, 94, 125, 130; Lonnie in, 127–28, 134, 161–62; love affairs in, 124–25; movies and references to movie stars in, 112, 124–25, 129, 165; narrator of, 5; scientism and cult of expert in, 113, 119–21, 137; search for God in, 137; self in, 119, 125–26, 129–30, 137, 165; selfishness in, 165; significant new features of, 111; Southern Stoicism in, 121–23, 127, 129, 141; suffering in, 101–2; suicide considered in, 126; theological questions in, 6, 118, 137; unreality and uncertainty in, 112, 118, 119, 120–21

Mozart, Wolfgang Amadeus, 6–7

Myth: Lost Cause myth, 2; and New Criticism, 26–28; Promethean myth of the artist, 6–7

Nagle, Thomas, 104–5, 107

Narrative voice: in O'Connor's "The Geranium," 21–22, 23; O'Connor's narrators generally, 4, 26, 33, 42; in O'Connor's *Wise Blood,* 22–24, 25; in West's *Miss Lonelyhearts,* 24

"Nature and Aim of Fiction, The" (O'Connor), 34, 35, 36

Nausea (Sartre), 112

New Criticism: and aesthetic of memory, 11–17; characteristics of, 12, 16; and fiction, 16–17; and Gordon, 10, 17–22; and Iowa Writers' Workshop, 4, 10, 11, 17; and irony, 16, 21, 34; and models of excellent literature, 16; and myth, 26–

28; and O'Connor, 10–26, 71; and O'Connor's "The Geranium," 17–22; and O'Connor's *Wise Blood,* 22–25; and Percy, 10; and poetry, 12–17; and point of view, 17, 20–21, 25; and religion, 12–16; and Scholastic view of art, 31–32; and symbol, 12, 14, 16–20, 26, 34; and Tate, 10, 13–16; on verbal icon, 4

New Yorker, 86

New York Review of Books, 104

Next of Kin (Fouts), 107

Niebuhr, Reinhold, 28

Nietzsche, Friedrich, 57

O'Connor, Flannery: and aesthetic of revelation generally, 1–9, 38, 158; and ambiguity, 19; and anagogical, 39–41, 44; and analogy of being, 39; and artist as God's witness, 6, 7–8; book reviews by, 31; and Catholicism, 5, 7–8, 28–32, 71, 84, 87, 156, 158, 159, 163; characters of generally, 111–12, 118, 165–66; childhood of, 30, 86; on Civil War, 160; dialogical versus monological language in works by, 77–78; dramatic versus didactic in works by, 17; drawing and painting by, 30, 86–87; Eucharist as revelation in works by, 70–85; and existentialism, 160, 161, 163–67; feminist critics on, 75, 78; Giroux as editor of, 48; and goal of Mystery, 39; Gordon as editor of writings by, 17–18; Gordon as mentor to, 3–4, 10, 17, 22, 43; and grotesque, 41–44; health problems of, 29, 31; human body in works by, 5, 25, 39–70; at Iowa Writers' Workshop, 4, 10, 11, 17, 22, 29, 37, 71; later stories of, 50, 84; narrators of, 4, 26, 33, 42, 117; and New Criticism, 10–26, 71; and Old South, 157–58; Percy on, 100, 101, 116; photograph of, 87; and Protestantism, 158, 159; rhetorical strategy of, 4; sacramental community in works by, 167–71; and search for theophany, 2–3, 4, 101; and southern litera-

ture, 9–10; and strategy of dispossession, 84; theological message of generally, 5, 6, 39–41, 101, 153, 159, 164, 167, 171; violence in works by generally, 41–54, 101; on writing experience, 44. *See also* titles of specific works
O'Gorman, Farrell, 158–61, 163, 167
"Old Red" (Gordon), 17–22
Other: as church, 154; in O'Connor's "The Artificial Nigger," 55–56; and Trinity, 154

"Parker's Back" (O'Connor), 50–54, 85
Partisan Review, 28
Pascal, Blaise, 3
Peculiar Crossroads (O'Gorman), 158, 159, 167
Peirce, Charles, 89–90, 92, 104, 108–10, 135, 153, 164
Pelagius, 164
Percy, Ann, 87
Percy, Walker: and aesthetic of revelation generally, 1–9, 86, 104, 158; apocalyptic nature of novels by, 136–37; and apologetics, 103–4; and artist as God's witness, 6, 7, 8; and Catholicism, 5–8, 28, 86, 87, 102–3, 108, 115, 156–57, 163, 164; characters of generally, 112, 118, 164–67; daughter of, 87; and dialogue with reader, 4–5, 115–16; on Eucharist, 108, 170; and existentialism, 160–61, 163–67; on faith and knowledge, 95–103; family background of, 121; Gordon as mentor to, 3–4; health problems of, 90; on hope, 130, 137–44; Langer as influence on, 32–33, 87–90; on language, 4, 86–111, 125, 130, 144–49; on love, 94–95, 119, 130, 144–53; narrators of, 5; National Endowment for the Arts Jefferson Lecture by, 92, 106–7; and New Criticism, 10; on O'Connor, 100, 101, 116; and Old South, 156–57, 158; painting of, 115–16; Peirce's influence on, 89–90, 92, 104; and quest for faith, 111–35; and

race relations, 159; rhetorical strategy of, 4–5, 164; sacramental community in works by, 167–71; satire by, 93; and search for theophany, 2–3, 101–2; on self, 92–95, 164, 170; self-description of, 115–16; and southern literature, 9–10; on Southern Stoicism, 156–57, 159; and symbol, 32–33, 87–92, 108; teleological method of, 115, 117; themes in works by, 91, 112–13, 118–19; theological emphasis of generally, 5–6, 86, 87, 100–101, 108, 153, 167, 171. *See also* titles of specific works
Percy, William Alexander, 121
Philosophical Fragments, or a Fragment of Philosophy (Kierkegaard), 114
Philosophy in a New Key (Langer), 87–90
Pilgrim in the Ruins (Tolson), 119
Poe, Edgar Allan, 17, 43
Poetry: Coleridge on, 26; irony in, 16; MacLeish on, 26; Maritain on, 32; and New Criticism, 12–17; Tate on, 27; Wheelwright on, 27
"Point of Dying: Donne's 'Virtuous Men, The'" (Tate), 14–16
Point of view: in Gordon's "Old Red," 20; and James, 17, 20, 22, 25; and New Criticism, 17, 20–21, 25; O'Connor on difficulties of, 22; in O'Connor's "The Geranium," 20–22; in O'Connor's *Wise Blood,* 49–50
Point of View for My Work as an Author, The (Kierkegaard), 114
Portrait of a Lady (James), 17
Portrait of the Artist as a Young Man, A (Joyce), 72n2, 119
Pride: in O'Connor's "The Artificial Nigger," 54–58; in O'Connor's "A Good Man Is Hard to Find," 85; in O'Connor's works, 165–66; in Percy's *Love in the Ruins,* 130–35
Pridgen, Allen, 151, 167
Promethean myth of the artist, 6–7, 8
Protestantism: dialogue with, in O'Connor's works, 74, 76–77, 78; and O'Con-

nor, 158, 159; in O'Connor's "A Tem-
ple of the Holy Ghost," 74, 76–77; and
Percy, 164; Tate on, 156
Proust, Marcel, 7, 117
Prown, Katherine Hemple, 10

"Questions They Never Asked Me" (Percy), 115–16
Quinlan, Kieran, 28, 108, 163

Racism: in O'Connor's "The Artificial
Nigger," 54–58; in O'Connor's "Reve-
lation," 80–81
Ransom, John Crowe, 11–14, 27, 28
Rape: in O'Connor's *The Violent Bear It
Away,* 68; in Percy's *Lancelot,* 142, 144
Reason: Hegel on, 109; Peirce on, 109;
Thomas Aquinas on, 34
Redemption. *See* Christ; Death; Suffering
Redemptive violence, 41, 42, 54–62
Religion: indirect communication on,
113–15; and myth, 26–28; and New
Criticism, 12–16; and Promethean
myth of the artist, 6–7, 8; Ransom on
God without thunder, 13, 27, 28; and
Scholastic view of art, 4, 7–8; and sci-
ence, 88; Tate on southern religion,
155–56; in West's *Miss Lonelyhearts,* 24.
See also Catholicism; Protestantism
Resurrection: of body, 40; of Christ, 40,
58
Revelation. *See* Aesthetic of revelation
"Revelation" (O'Connor), 77–85, 111
Revelatory violence, 41
Revising Flannery O'Connor (Prown), 10
Richards, I. A., 27
Ricoeur, Paul, 89
"River, The" (O'Connor), 6, 35–36, 85,
101, 168
Romance, 43, 50
Romantic Image (Kermode), 14
Romine, Scott, 161

Sacramentalism, 167–71. *See also* Baptism;
Eucharist; Marriage

Samway, Patrick, 108
Sartre, Jean-Paul, 112, 159
Scapegoat, 56, 58, 85
Scarry, Elaine, 47
Scholastic view of art, 4, 7–8, 29–31, 88–
89
Science: and displacement of self, 93–94;
Kierkegaard on scientism, 108; knowledge from, 96; and language, 105, 109–
10; in Percy's *Love in the Ruins,* 131–
32, 134–35; in Percy's *The Moviegoer,*
113, 119–21, 137; in Percy's works, 91;
and religion, 88; and self, 99, 103
Scientism, 108, 113, 119–21
Second Coming, The (Percy): Allie in, 149–
50; community in, 150, 153, 154, 162;
death in, 144, 145, 148; Eucharist in,
144–45, 149–50; Father Weatherbee
in, 151; language in, 94–95, 144–49,
154; love story in, 94–95, 119, 130,
148–53, 170; parallel narratives of Will
Barnett and Allison Huger in, 145–48;
psychiatrist in, 146; self in, 147; sexuality in, 144–45, 148–50, 152; suicide in,
145–46, 148; test of God's existence in,
148; theological questions in, 119, 130;
uncertainty and unreality in, 112
Self: alienation of, 94; autonomous self,
99–100, 138, 141–42; characteristics
of, 92–94; completion of, in God, 97–
98, 100, 129–30; dis-ease in, 93–94;
elusiveness of, 92–93; and faith, 97–98;
identification of, with other selves or
things, 99; and I-it relationship, 92; incompleteness of, 97; and I-Thou relationship, 92; Kierkegaard on, 100, 103,
170; Marcel on, 153; and naming function, 92; Percy on, 92–95, 164, 170; in
Percy's *Lancelot,* 137–38, 141–42; in
Percy's *The Moviegoer,* 119, 125–26,
129–30, 137, 165; in Percy's *The Second
Coming,* 147; and science, 99, 103; and
selfishness, 164–65; semiotic fall of,
98–100; and symbol, 97–98; and therapy culture, 93

"Semiotic Primer on the Self, A" (Percy), 92

Semiotics, 89–90, 92–93, 104, 153–54

Seven Storey Mountain, The (Merton), 48

Sexuality: in O'Connor's "A Temple of the Holy Ghost," 72–77; in Percy's *Lancelot,* 138–40, 143, 144, 150, 152; in Percy's *The Last Gentleman,* 140, 144, 150; in Percy's *The Second Coming,* 144–45, 148–50, 152

Shakespeare, William, 6–7, 27

Shloss, Carol, 72n2

Sickness unto Death (Kierkegaard), 97–98, 100, 129

"Simple Heart, A" (Flaubert), 35, 36

Simpson, Lewis, 1, 9, 11, 13, 155

Sin: Augustine on, 65, 67, 98, 131; Christ's defeat of, 58; grotesque and original sin, 43; in O'Connor's "The Artificial Nigger," 54–58; in O'Connor's "A Good Man Is Hard to Find," 85; in O'Connor's "Revelation," 78–81; in O'Connor's *The Violent Bear It Away,* 61–69; in O'Connor's works generally, 62, 165–66; Percy on, 98–99, 100; in Percy's *Lancelot,* 130, 137–43; in Percy's *Love in the Ruins,* 130–35; violence of, 41

Skinner, B. F., 104

Smith, James, 154

"Some Aspects of the Grotesque in Southern Fiction" (O'Connor), 43, 44

Sound and the Fury, The (Faulkner), 3

Southern literature, 9–10, 43, 155. *See also* Southern Renaissance; and specific authors and titles of works

Southern Renaissance, 9, 11, 129, 155, 159, 160

Southern Renaissance, A (King), 1

Southern Stoicism, 121–23, 127, 129, 141, 156–59, 165

Srigley, Susan, 167

Stafford, Jean, 28

Stendhal, 17

Stephen Hero (Joyce), 36–37

Stevens, Wallace, 27

Stewart, John, 13

Strategy of dispossession, 84

Stream of consciousness, 22

Suffering: of blacks, 54–58; of Christ, 42; and conviction of sin, 56; Foote on, 7; in O'Connor's "The Artificial Nigger," 54–58, 61–62; in O'Connor's "The Displaced Person," 54, 58–62; in O'Connor's *The Violent Bear It Away,* 61–69; and participation in Christ's suffering, 42, 56–57; in Percy's works generally, 101, 165; of scapegoat, 56, 58; shared/vicarious suffering, 56–57; value of, as *imitatio Christi,* 42, 45, 56–57, 165, 169. *See also* Death; Violence

Suicide: in Percy's *The Last Gentleman,* 144; in Percy's *The Moviegoer,* 126; in Percy's *The Second Coming,* 145–46, 148. *See also* Death

Symbol: Augustine on, 89; and community, 153–54; and Flaubert, 17, 35; functions of, 14; in Gordon's "Old Red," 18–19; and James, 17, 18, 35; and Joyce, 36–38; Langer on, 32–33, 88–89, 91; Maritain on, 34; in New Criticism, 12, 16, 26, 34; O'Connor on, 33–34; in O'Connor's "The Geranium," 18–20, 34–35; in O'Connor's "The River," 35–36; in O'Connor's "The Turkey," 34–35; and Percy, 32–33, 87–92, 106–8; Ricoeur on, 89; Romantic concept of, 26–28, 33; and self, 97–98; symbolic language use as unique and exclusive to humans, 106–7; Thomas Aquinas on, 32, 32–34, 88–90, 95; in West's *Miss Lonelyhearts,* 25

"Symbol as Need" (Percy), 32–33

Tate, Allen: and aesthetics of memory, 1; and Agrarianism, 13; Brinkmeyer on, 158; and Catholicism, 10, 13, 14, 28, 156; on Donne's "A Valediction," 14–16; and Iowa Writers' Workshop, 11; and Maritain, 4; and New Criticism, 10, 13–16; and O'Connor's writings, 17; on poetry, 27; and Southern Re-

naissance, 155; on stating and render-
ing, 17
—works: *The House of Fiction,* 10, 17, 35;
I'll Take My Stand, 13, 155–56; *The
Language of Poetry,* 27; "The Point of
Dying: Donne's 'Virtuous Men'"
(Tate), 14–16
Tattoos, 50–54
Teilhard de Chardin, Pere, 40
"Temple of the Holy Ghost, A" (O'Con-
nor), 5, 72–77, 83, 85, 169
Terrace, Herbert, 106, 107
Thanatos Syndrome (Percy), 112, 169
Thomas Aquinas, St.: Eucharistic hymn
by, 74, 76; on faith, 97, 113; on lan-
guage, 4; on love of God, 154; and
Maritain, 4, 30–33; and O'Connor, 74,
76, 113; and Percy, 32–33, 88–90, 95,
97, 104, 108, 113; on revelation and
reason, 34; on symbol, 32–34, 88–90,
95; on Trinity, 154; and universals, 32
Thornton, Weldon, 110
Three Catholic Writers of the Modern South
(Brinkmeyer), 158
Tillich, Paul, 28
Tolson, Jay, 87, 119
Totemism, 99
Tracy, David, 5
"Tradition and the Individual Talent"
(Eliot), 16
"Turkey, The" (O'Connor), 34–35, 36
Turner, Victor, 163
Twain, Mark, 74

Understanding Fiction (Brooks and Warren),
11, 16, 18, 19, 35, 71

"Valediction: Forbidding Mourning, A"
(Donne), 14–16
Verbal Icon, The (Wimsatt), 12–13
"View of the Woods, A" (O'Connor), 85
Violence: and body's role in salvation,
45–54; and cross of Christ, 24, 25, 41,
45, 47, 58, 77; and death in O'Connor's
works, 42, 45; and grotesque, 40–44;
O'Connor on, 45; in O'Connor's "The

Artificial Nigger," 54–58; in O'Connor's "The Displaced Person," 54, 58–
61; in O'Connor's "A Good Man Is
Hard to Find," 85; in O'Connor's
"Parker's Back," 50–54; in O'Connor's
The Violent Bear It Away, 61–69, 168; in
O'Connor's *Wise Blood,* 45–50, 165; in
O'Connor's works generally, 41–54,
101; in Percy's *Lancelot,* 140–41, 144;
redemptive violence, 41, 42, 54–62;
revelatory violence, 41; as sacramental,
42; of sin, 41; and value of human suffering, 42, 45. *See also* Death; Suffering
Violent Bear It Away, The (O'Connor):
alienation in, 166; baptism in, 68, 168;
devil in, 67–69; evil as privation of
good in, 61–69; homosexual rape in,
68; problem of freedom in, 63–67; title
of, 41
Virtues. *See* Faith; Hope; Love

Walker Percy's Sacramental Landscapes (Prid-
gen), 167
Walker Percy's Voices (Kobre), 117
Ward, Graham, 154
Warren, Austin, 29
Warren, Robert Penn, 1, 11, 18, 19, 155
Washoe (chimpanzee), 106, 107
Wasteland, The (Eliot), 20, 50
Well Wrought Urn, The (Brooks), 12
Welty, Eudora, 1, 155
West, Nathanael, 24–25, 29, 87
Westling, Louise, 75
Wheelwright, Philip, 27
Wilde, Oscar, 31
Williams, Rowan, 84, 167, 168
Wimsatt, W. K., Jr., 12–13
Wise Blood (O'Connor): alienation in,
166; Asals on, as Manichean, 42, 45–46,
48–50; asceticism in, 46–50; body in,
45–50, 165; compared with "Revela-
tion," 83; death in, 165; editing of, by
Gordon, 17–18; Gordon on, 23, 30;
and Gordon's influence generally, 4, 10;
irony in, 22–23, 25, 117; narrative voice
in, 22–24, 25; and New Criticism, 22–

25; point of view in, 49–50; publication date of, 14; redemption as theme
of, 25; repentance in, 48–49; theology
underlying, 48–49
Wittgenstein, Ludwig, 104–5, 154

Wood, Ralph, 57, 76*n*7, 78, 165, 167
Woolf, Virginia, 17, 72*n*2
Wordsworth, William, 16
Wyatt-Brown, Bertram, 121
Wylder, Jean, 11